THE FUTURE OF EUROPE

Also by Valerie Symes

UNEMPLOYMENT IN EUROPE

Also by Carl Levy

ITALIAN REGIONALISM – HISTORY, IDENTITY, POLITICS (*editor*)
SOCIALISM AND THE INTELLIGENTSIA (*editor*)

Also by Jane Littlewood

ASPECTS OF GRIEF

The Future of Europe

Problems and Issues for the Twenty-First Century

Edited by

Valerie Symes
Lecturer in Economics
Goldsmiths College
University of London

Carl Levy
Lecturer in European Politics
Goldsmiths College
University of London

and

Jane Littlewood
Senior Lecturer in Social Policy
Goldsmiths College
University of London

First published in Great Britain 1997 by
MACMILLAN PRESS LTD
Houndmills, Basingstoke, Hampshire RG21 6XS
and London
Companies and representatives
throughout the world

A catalogue record for this book is available
from the British Library.

ISBN 0–333–66600–3

First published in the United States of America 1997 by
ST. MARTIN'S PRESS, INC.,
Scholarly and Reference Division,
175 Fifth Avenue,
New York, N.Y. 10010

ISBN 0–312–16423–8

Library of Congress Cataloging-in-Publication Data
The future of Europe : problems and issues for the twenty-first
century / edited by Valerie Symes, Carl Levy, and Jane Littlewood.
p. cm.
Includes bibliographical references and index.
ISBN 0–312–16423–8
1. Economic forecasting—European Union countries. 2. European
Union countries—Forecasting. 3. European Union countries—Politics
and government. 4. Twenty-first century—Forecasts. I. Symes,
Valerie, 1941– . II. Levy, Carl, 1951– . III. Littlewood,
Jane, 1955– .
HC241.2.F856   1996
330.94'001'12—dc20   96–27831
                                                              CIP

10   9   8   7   6   5   4   3   2   1
05   04   03   02   01   00   99   98   97   97

Printed in Great Britain by
The Ipswich Book Company Ltd
Ipswich, Suffolk

Contents

List of Figures

List of Tables

Notes on the Contributors

Tony Butcher, Senior Lecturer in Government, Goldsmiths College, University of London.

Wayne David, Member of the European Parliament, Leader of the EPLP and Vice-President of the Socialist Group, European Parliament.

David Edye, Senior Lecturer in Politics, University of North London.

Jussi Hanhimäki, Lecturer in International History, London School of Economics and Political Science.

Frances Heidensohn, Professor of Social Policy, Goldsmiths College University of London.

Klaus Heidensohn, Principal Lecturer in Economics, Middlesex University.

Carl Levy, Lecturer in European Politics, Goldsmiths College, University of London.

Jane Littlewood, Senior Lecturer in Social Policy, Goldsmiths College, University of London.

Valerio Lintner, Principal Lecturer in Economics at Guildhall University, London.

Juliet Lodge, Professor of European Politics, Jean Monnet Professor of European Integration, University of Leeds.

Michael Newman, Professor of Politics, University of North London.

Ed Randall, Lecturer in Social Policy, Goldsmiths College, University of London.

Valerie Symes, Lecturer in Economics, Goldsmiths College, University of London.

List of Abbreviations

ACP	African, Caribbean and Pacific Ocean Countries
ACT	Advanced Communications, Services and Technologies
ADSL	Asynchronous Digital Subscriber Loop
API	Application Programming Interface
ATM	Asynchronous Transfer Mode
CAP	Common Agricultural Policy
CATV	Cable Television
CDMA	Code Division Multiple Access
CEC	Commission of the European Communities
CEE	Central and Eastern Europe
CEEC	Central and Eastern European Countries
CELAD	European Committee to Combat Drugs
CENELEC	Comité Européen de Normalisation Électrotechnique = European Committee for Electrotechnical Standardisation
CFSP	Common Foreign and Security Policy
CIA	Common Information Area
CMEA	Council for Mutual Economic Assistance
CSCE	Conference on Security Cooperation in Europe
CSF	Community Structural Funds
DCS	Digital Cellular Standard
DECT	Digital, European Cordless, Telecommunications
DGII	Directorate General for Economic and Financial Affairs
DGV	Directorate General for Employment, Industrial Relations and Social Affairs
EAEC	European Atomic Energy Community
ECB	European Central Bank
ECJ	European Court of Justice
ECSC	European Coal and Steel Community
EDC	European Defence Community
EDI	Electronic Data Interchange
EEC	European Economic Community
EFTA	European Free Trade Area
EHMA	European Healthcare Management Association

EIB	European Investment Bank
EIS	European Information System
EMCDDA	European Monitoring Centre for Drugs and Drug Addiction
EMI	European Monetary Institute
EMS	European Monetary System
EMU	European Monetary Union
EP	European Parliament
EPC	European Political Cooperation
ERM	Exchange Rate Mechanism
ESC	Economic and Social Committee
ESCB	European System of Central Banks
ESPRIT	European Strategic Programme for Research and Development in Information Technology
ETSI	European Telecommunications Standards Institute
EUREKA	European Research Coordination Agency
EUROPOL	European Police
EVUA	European Virtual Network Users Association
FCC	Federal Communications Commission
GATT	General Agreements on Tariffs and Trade
GSM	General Standard for Mobile Communications
GSP	General System of Preference (CSFR)
HD-MAC	High Definition-Multiplexed Analogue Components
HDTV	High Definition Television
HoC	Health Committee
IBN	Integrated Broadband Network
ICPO	International Police Organisation
IGC	Inter-Governmental Conference
ISDN	Integrated Services Digital Network
ITU	International Telecommunications Union
JESSI	Joint European Silicon Structures Initiative
JHA	Justice and Home Affairs
LAN	Large Area Networks
LEO	Low-Earth-Orbiting Satellite
LFR	Less Favoured Region
MEP	Member of the European Parliament
MFN	Most Favoured Nation
MISSOC	Mutual Information System on Social Policy in the Community

MNE	Multi-National Enterprises
MS-DOS	Microsoft-Disk Operating System
NAFTA	North American Free Trade Area
OECD	Organisation for Economic Co-operation and Development
Oftel	Office of Telecommunications
PCN	Personal Communication Network
PfP	Partnership for Peace
PSTN	Public Switched Telecommunications Network
PTT	Post, Telegraph and Telecommunications Organisation
PTO	Public Telecommunications Organisation
QMV	Qualified Majority Voting
RACE	Research and Development in Advanced Communication
RBOC	Regional Bell Operating Company
SEA	Single European Act
SEM	Single European Market
SIS	Schengen Information System
STAR	Special Telecommunications Action for Regional Development
TCP/IP	Transmission Control/Internet Protocol
TEN	Trans-European Network
TEU	Treaty of European Union
TFR	Total Fertility Rate
TREVI	Terrorism, Radicalism, Extremism and Political Violence International
TO	Telecommunications Organisation
UMTS	Universal Mobile Telecommunications System
UNCTAD	United Nations Conference on Trade and Development
UNI	User Network Interface
VANS	Value-Added-Network Services
VSAT	Very Small Aperture Terminal
WEU	Western European Union

Introduction

The twentieth century in Europe has been a time of conflict and change unprecedented in its history, the first half dominated by national self-interests and political ideologies culminating in two world wars; the second half seeking a process through which co-operation and integration were to link countries that, over the centuries, had experienced only fleeting and uneasy alliances of political and economic interest. The process has not been an easy one and is not yet complete. It has brought about changes within Europe which could not have been anticipated 50 years ago. The changes have not been without conflict, but this conflict is of a very different scale. Positive outcomes are expected with the intention, if not always the reality, that everyone will emerge a winner.

Economic co-operation began in 1951 with the Treaty of Paris and the setting up of the European Coal and Steel Community (ECSC) between six countries – Germany, France, Italy, the Netherlands, Belgium and Luxembourg. In 1957 came the Treaty of Rome, which had the general objectives of establishing a Common Market that would progressively integrate the economic policies of its Member States, bringing an increase in stability, raised living standards and closer relations between states. There was a clear political purpose even at this stage, with the stated objective in the Preamble for 'an even closer union among the European peoples', and also provisions for commitment to the co-ordination of social welfare goals in the fields of employment and living and working conditions. The European Court of Justice was set up to interpret the provisions of the Rome Treaty and future European Economic Community (EEC) decisions, and has the power to override national laws in its areas of competence.

The EEC came into being in 1958 with the six members of the ECSC. Britain's successive applications for membership in 1961 and in 1967 were vetoed by the French president, General de Gaulle, as were applications from Ireland

and Denmark. These three countries finally became Member States in 1973, by which time one of the major economic policies of the Community, the Common Agricultural Policy (CAP), had already been implemented. By the mid-1980s the European Community had grown to 12 members with the accession of Greece in 1981, and Spain and Portugal in 1986. These last members had very different kinds of economies and had only recent experience of democratic government. Spain and Portugal had had long-standing dictatorships, and Greece had been ruled for many years by a military junta. It was considered that EC membership would strengthen and maintain these new (less than a decade-old) and potentially fragile democracies. Economically, the advantages to existing members were minimal, the prospect of greater European stability dominating the agreement to accession. Economic and social convergence became more of a problem at this point.

The last decade has seen the pace of change in Europe accelerating. The Single European Act of 1987 came into being, but not without conflict. The original aims to increase the powers of the European Parliament and the setting-up of a Charter of Fundamental Social Rights were modified largely at the insistence of the UK government, but the date for a Single European Market (SEM) was set for 1992, and came into being in January 1993 when the EC became the European Union (EU). The Intergovernmental Conferences (IGCs) that began at the end of 1990 had on the agenda European Monetary Union (EMU), political union and a social dimension. Political union involved strengthening the European Parliament (EP), introducing a common foreign and security policy, and establishing a European citizenship and structure of civil rights. There was to be intergovernmental co-operation on judicial and police matters, and an extension of competence in several social areas such as health, education, the environment and consumer protection. The eventual outcome, in the form of the Maastricht Treaty, agreed a date for monetary union (1999), together with stages for implementation, and included social measures with the new Social Chapter (with Britain opting out). References to federalism were deleted at Britain's request, and proposals to give the EP substantial additional powers were vetoed. In

1995 three new members – Sweden, Finland and Austria – joined the EU. Integration of Europe, economically, politically and socially, was greatly advanced in the 1990s, and the changes brought about not only by the SEM and the provisions of the Maastricht Treaty, but also by recession, the growth of a global economy and the democratisation of Eastern Europe, entail problems for the future of Europe.

This work reflects the concerns of the late twentieth century in Europe, the fears inherent in rapid change within nation-states and the different effects of EU policy on Member States and their citizens: the difficulties of improving social welfare and, in the context of a free market economy, the effects of a single currency and monetary union, the desire (or otherwise) for a more federal Europe and a more democratic Europe; the effects of an ageing population; issues of health care and crime; the outcome of the communications revolution. How will and should Europe be in the future? Will further integration result in more or less conflict? What needs to be done to address people's needs and concerns?

Wayne David (chapter 1) addresses these questions from a politician's viewpoint. In his opinion the great achievements of the EU are the maintenance of peace and the creation of the SEM. The issues he is concerned with and that should be addressed at the 1996 IGC are related to making Europe more relevant to people's lives. Unemployment is seen as, perhaps, the major problem, which is worsening as deflation policies are imposed on Member States in the struggle to meet the nominal convergence criteria of Maastricht for European Monetary Union (EMU). The need for intergovernmental co-operation in this area at the macroeconomic level and greater skills training, education, R&D expenditure and the importance of information technology to cope with this problem are dealt with by Symes (Chapters 10 and 11) and Levy (Chapter 8). As a Member of the European Parliament David is concerned to see greater democratic control. The European Parliament should have a greater role in budgetary matters and use its powers to give greater infrastructural support for regions and provide an anti-cyclical recovery fund for the economy. It should also have the power to make the Commission more accountable and have influence on legislation and the nomination of candidates for the presidency. There is a need also for making the Council of Ministers' meetings more transparent (for further discussion see Newman in Chapter 2). The issue which towers above all others though is that of the fragile peace in Europe and the important role that the EU can play to encourage the emerging democracies in Central and Eastern Europe with practical support (see Heidensohn, Chapter 7) and the development of a common foreign and security policy (see Hanhimäki, Chapter 6).

Several of the chapters address three interrelated problems: subsidiarity, the democratic deficit and the relationship between the EU and Member State citizenship. Newman (Chapter 2) presents a model of liberal democracy suitable for the governance of the EU. He emphasises the shifting definition of liberal democracy in a post-Keynesian, globalised economy. The 'new democratic politics' stress the deconcentration and decentralisation of power. This seems to fit quite closely with the concept of subsidiarity. But, Newman argues, there are limits to its usefulness. Histories and accounts of the institutions of the EU have stressed the intergovernmental, state-centred nature of European integration. However, if the pace of integration has been driven by the mutual and individual needs of the Member States, the cumulative effect has been the surrender of certain prerogatives of national sovereignty. On the one hand, the European and global economy is no longer controllable at national level; on the other, the evolution of EU law has caused the Member States to bow to the judgments of the European Court of Justice (ECJ). Much of this European case law has been driven by the logic of the SEM. At the same time, however, parliamentary control of this process is still weak. The use of qualified majority voting (QMV) in the Council of Ministers may have weakened the absolute power invested in the national veto; however, the secrecy which surrounds the proceedings of the Council of Ministers and the European Council means that the parliaments of the Member States have seen their powers eroded. In this respect, Newman believes that certain forms of Europeanisation will be undemocratic if they do not address this inherent weakness. EMU will be undemocratic if there are no democratically accountable bodies overseeing the activities of the European Central Bank (ECB), as Lintner (Chapter 8) also points out. The relationship between Member State parliaments and the European Parliament must be clarified; subsidiarity will not be enough of a safeguard. Indeed, subsidiarity might even lead to fragmentation of Europe. Like David, Newman considers unemployment the greatest danger to the future of European integration. He suggests that there could be scope for a European and democratically controlled, Keynesian full employment policy.

Butcher (Chapter 3) addresses the issue of subsidiarity by analysing the transformation of local government throughout Europe. What are the common causes of this 'reinvention of local government'? He argues they are the effects of economic recession, the demands for efficiency by sophisticated consumers expecting new services, the argument that slimmed down local government helps businesses to compete in the global marketplace and the harmonisation induced by the SEM. The UK model is discussed, because it has been seen as the 'market leader'. However, if the drive for efficiency is shared in the United Kingdom and other Member States, the drive for the decentralisation of power has not been embraced by the British. Therefore, the concept of subsidiarity may not really link the British example with those Member States that now have regional or federal government.

Edye (Chapter 4) examines EU citizenship. If subsidiarity was meant to prevent an over-centralised Europe, EU citizenship seems to press for a shared set of values at the supranational level. Edye argues that EU citizenship implies a shared political culture, but he believes that in so far as the EU is not a nation-state, it is hard to discern its boundaries. Lack of interest in European parliamentary elections means that the voting rights given to EU citizens have had little impact. Edye also emphasises the limitations of the new rights conferred with EU citizenship. Freedom of movement is limited in some cases and the problem of non-citizen residents has still not been properly addressed.

Frances Heidensohn (Chapter 5) introduces her chapter by noting that the Maastricht Treaty introduced the 'third pillar' of justice and home affairs (JHA) to the EU. She goes on to discuss contemporary debates concerning the

different types of modern policing systems, together with
the nature and role of the state in relation to policing today. The chapter continues with a brief history of organisations dealing with policing matters between European nations,
and identifies current trends, future strategies and relevant
issues. The chapter also includes a review of the state of
crime in Europe and considers what responses this may eventually evoke at the European level. The distinctive features
of the relevant policies are clearly documented, together
with the various views concerning the directions taken in
the past and a consideration of where the directions of the
future might lie. The chapter concludes by identifying the
sheer complexity of the issues involved.

   Hanhimäki (Chapter 6) discusses common foreign and
security policy (CFSP). Like European citizenship and JHA
(see Heidensohn, Chapter 5), CFSP is an innovation of the
Maastricht Treaty (TEU). The limitations of CFSP are similar to those of European citizenship. Hanhimäki believes
that effective joint security and foreign policy will only occur when the European electorates share a sense of common destiny. His major concern is to locate where CFSP
might be made. In this chapter he reviews the historical
background from the Cold War to post-1989 Europe, a period that witnessed the transformation of the weaker EPC
(European Political Co-operation) to the potentially more
robust CFSP. But the reconfiguration of policy-making institutions after 1989 demonstrates that both the Conference
on Security and Co-operation in Europe (CSCE) and the
Western European Union (WEU) were unable to meet the
challenges posed in the Maghreb, the Middle East, Eastern
Europe and the CIS. CFSP is still limited by the unanimity
principle, which prevails in the Council of Ministers. Even
if QMV were to function once key policy areas are defined,
it is precisely this first hurdle which Member States have
found so difficult to surmount. Whereas France has expressed
a great interest in the Magreb and the Middle East, the
Germans have been the patron of the East European lobby.
This also leaves the issue of expansion to the East (see
Heidensohn, Chapter 7) unresolved. The Yugoslav tragedy
has demonstrated the relative ineffectiveness of CFSP and
the continuing relevance of NATO.

Klaus Heidensohn (Chapter 7) examines the changing trade relations of East and West Europe from the major contributions made by countries such as Hungary and Czechoslovakia to world exports before the Second World War, through the decline in trading contact during the Cold War, to the current situation and the prospect of eastern enlargement of the EU. The EU has supported the CEECs' transition to market economies by liberalising trade, albeit in a limited way, but tariffs, quantitative restrictions and non-tariff barriers are still in place. He discusses the Europe Agreements designed to establish bilateral free trade for industrial goods by the end of the century, but feels that the EU is still maintaining too many rights to protectionism in the agreements by viewing eastern trade as a potential threat, which case studies demonstrate are negligible, while benefits to the East are great. Full membership could, however, result in the need for a vast expansion in the agricultural and regional budget, and is unlikely to take place within the next two decades.

Monetary union and the issue of a single currency have dominated national political agendas in the 1990s and have important consequences on national governments' economic sovereignty. Lintner (Chapter 8) points out that monetary policy set at EU level is unlikely to be able to accommodate every country's policy preferences, but argues that there are already limits to the extent of real national sovereignty in this area. Both the costs of meeting convergence criteria and the costs of structural change, after implementation of EMU, are likely to fall disproportionately on weaker Member States. He is concerned at the use of criteria based on financial rather than real variables as preconditions for full membership of EMU and also about the prospect of lack of democratic control with the provision of an independent European Central Bank (ECB), questioning the wisdom of freezing current views on economic priorities into the constitution of a new ECB. The backlash against the EMU in the United Kingdom and France makes it unlikely that widescale monetary union will be achieved within the next decade.

Levy (Chapter 9) analyses the role of the EU (particularly the Commission) in shaping the European Information Superhighway. The control of new technology and the position of Europe within the global information technology (IT) market are directly related to future economic prosperity. But this telecommunications revolution may also affect the nature by which the citizens of the EU express their political opinions and communicate with their political representatives.

Levy assesses the impact of previous technological policy at the European level. Since the mid-1980s the Commission has adopted a liberal approach towards the future restructuring of digital telecommunications. The Commission has become the liberaliser of Member States' telecommunications markets. At the same time, it has tried to establish standards for the new technical digital gateways. The Information Superhighway will come about through the interlinking of various technologies and networks. A *dirigiste* model fostering European champions has been replaced by the support for European participation in Global champions.

Levy concludes by discussing the future roles of the Commission and the Court of Justice as regulators of a liberalised digital multi-media industry. What future is there for univeral service in a deregultaed telecommunications market? How will the Less Favoured Regions fare? How can the EU regulate powerful Global champions? These key questions impact on the future of accountable democratic government, but the very process of Commission networking and lobbying, which underlies the Information Superhighway policy, raises issues of democratic accountability addressed by Newman, in Chapter 2.

The desirability of economic and social convergence and the likelihood of significant change in disparities between regions is discussed by Symes (Chapter 10). The SEM has brought most of the benefits of growth to the core regions, and tends to widen the gap between rich and poor. Similarly, adjustments needed to meet the Maastricht convergence criteria have had greatest negative impacts on weaker national economies, which, on the whole, suffer higher rates of inflation and larger budget deficits. The narrowing of income gaps in the 1980s has been reversed. Inadequacy of current criteria for CSF aid, and estimates of the scale of budgetary transfers needed within the EU to bring about any significant convergence of income and social welfare provision, make it unlikely under current conditions that there will be much improvement in the next decade. Enlargement of the EU into Eastern Europe could exacerbate the problem. The political will of the majority of wealthy members to bring about a large-scale transfer of funds for long-term development is necessary if conflicts are not to be generated through continuing inequalities.

The IGC in March 1996 identified unemployment as the most serious problem facing Europe in the next decade. In Chapter 11 the scale of the problem and the trend of increasing unemployment in Europe over the past two decades are examined, together with an analysis of the reasons why Europe has experienced higher rates than both Japan and the United States. The most disturbing features of unemployment are the high rates of youth unemployment in nearly all Member States, and the 9 million unemployed who have been without work for over a year. The causes and cures for unemployment are discussed within the framework of the current wisdom of new neoclassical thought (followed in essence by the policy stance of the European Commission), and suggestions by post-Keynesian analysts of how growth in employment could be achieved through changes in monetary and fiscal policy while avoiding inflationary pressure. Symes concludes that the supply-side strategies recommended by the Commission are, in themselves, very worthwhile, especially in upgrading skill levels, but they will not help create new jobs, and the macroeconomic strategy of the EU has contributed to loss of employment. Without an agreement on policy change in this area at the IGC there will be little prospect of a change in the level of unemployment for many years to come.

Jane Littlewood (Chapter 12) introduces her chapter by identifying the major demographic changes which have taken place in the EU. However, she indicates clearly that as a predictive 'science' demography is somewhat imprecise. The second part of the chapter is concerned with trends in social expenditure in the EU. Whilst a general trend towards an increased expenditure in percentage of GDP being spent on social expenditure is identified, Littlewood argues that the share of social expenditure being spent on elderly EU citizens has, in general terms, remained fairly constant. Littlewood further identifies a trend towards increasing rates of social contributions. The third and final part of the chapter considers relevant policy issues and alternatives for the future. Littlewood suggests that to date the implications of an ageing population have been addressed in part only by the EU, that the political impetus for change would appear to be lacking, and that the EU also lacks the structural prerequisites to ensure that social protection becomes anything other than secondary to the social and economic imperatives of securing an 'economic market'.

Ed Randall (Chapter 13) commences his chapter by presenting an argument which suggests that the EU is well placed to establish and influence co-operation concerning common health problems. He identifies the common health problems faced by the EU and suggests that a community approach may be essential and that the EU already plays an important role in the provision of information in this area. Randall then discusses the evolution of health policy in the EU and identifies health and safety at work, mutual recognition of professional qualifications and the establishment of a European Medicines Evaluation Agency as important initiatives. The chapter then documents EU involvement in health campaigns against cancers, AIDS and drug dependency, together with other relevant EU public health initiatives. Randall concludes by suggesting that the EU may, in the future, play a key role in enabling and assisting the health care systems of Member States to promote effectively health, prevent disease and improve resource management.

Lodge (Chapter 14) concludes the book by considering many of these issues for the future of the EU in the light of the November 1996 IGC. She suggests that the future of CFSP and JHA are interrelated. Although JHA has been neglected until now, this will receive more serious consideration during the IGC. However, the key issues on the agenda have to do with improving the accountability and efficiency the EU through institutional and budgetary reform.

Valerie Symes
Carl Levy
Jane Littlewood
Goldsmiths College, University of London
July 1996

1 1996 – An Opportunity to Make Europe Relevant
Wayne David

Today, the European Union (EU) is at a crossroads. Many of the assumptions of only a few years ago are being openly questioned. Movement towards the 'ever closer union', so firmly proclaimed in the Maastricht Treaty, is no longer taken for granted, even by the staunchest advocates of a federal Europe. Across the political spectrum and from the highest levels of government to the ordinary man and woman in the street, there are doubts and reservations about the nature, and even the desirability, of European co-operation. Such misgivings are to be heard throughout the EU, but nowhere are they more prevalent than in the United Kingdom.

There are many reasons for the rise of Euroscepticism in Britain. In part, the reasons are linked to, and arise from, the internecine conflict within the Conservative Party. But it is very clear that many people have serious concerns about the European project, and these cannot be dismissed as mere reflections of nationalist prejudice. All too often, the EU is seen as remote, bureaucratic and unresponsive to the needs of Europe's citizens, and leading towards the creation of a European 'superstate'.

The reality, of course, is very different from the caricature. The EU, despite its shortcomings, has achieved much over the past few decades. The maintenance of peace in Western Europe and the creation of the Single European Market are two achievements which should not be underestimated. At a time of increasing uncertainty, the necessity for collective arrangements to maintain and extend political stability is greater than ever. This is just as true for Britain as it is for any mainland European country. Equally, the development of the Single Market means that nearly 60 per cent of British exports are sold in other EU countries. As this trade will surely grow, any suggestion that it would be in Britain's interest to withdraw from the EU is sheer folly.

1

It is important to emphasise, however, that the EU is in need of fundamental reform. A whole range of changes are required if the challenges of the future are to be met and public support secured. One of the most consistent critics of the EU over the past 17 years has been the British government. But despite constant whingeing, the British government, under both Margaret Thatcher and John Major, has been either unwilling or unable to initiate a programme of real change in the EU. The crucial question for the United Kingdom and Europe as a whole is how the EU can be changed for the better.

The 1996 Intergovernmental Conference (IGC) provides a vitally important opportunity – perhaps even a last chance – for the European project to be invested with the credibility it so urgently requires. For Europe's heads of government, the key objective at the IGC must be to reconstruct the EU to make it 'relevant' to Europe's peoples. This means that the Treaty of European Union has to be amended in a number of key areas, to ensure that the priorities of Europe's citizens are reflected and addressed.

There are nearly 17.5 million people unemployed in the EU, 5 million of whom are under the age of 25. There can, therefore, be no issue of greater social importance. Unemployment is not only an appalling burden on the individuals and families directly affected by it, but, it is also an enormous loss of human potential to each Member State and a threat to the very fabric of our societies. Achieving full employment in Europe will be an enormous task, but it is a challenge from which we must not flinch.

Since the late 1970s, we have seen the national economies of Europe becoming increasingly interdependent. While it would be a huge exaggeration to suggest that the scope for national economic intervention is insignificant, it is the case that individual Member States can no longer pursue one-nation Keynesian policies, irrespective of the economic strategies being followed by their neighbours. The increasing internationalisation of economic activity makes it vitally important for joint growth policies to be developed on the basis of intergovernmental co-operation, through the institutions of the EU.

In 1993, the then President of the European Commission, Jacques Delors, produced a White Paper on 'Growth, Competitiveness and Employment'. One of the central proposals of the Paper was the creation of 15 million new jobs before the end of the decade. This was to be achieved through a range of measures at national and European levels. Unfortunately, despite rhetorical statements from the Council of Ministers, little has been done.

This lamentable inactivity has been strongly criticised by the Swedish government, which, in 1995, put forward its own proposals for job-creation by making a proposal to amend the European Treaty. Central to the Swedish suggestion was the introduction of a new Chapter on employment policy to make the attainment of a high level of employment a common European objective. To secure the stated goal of full employment, Member States would commit themselves to an unprecedented degree of economic co-operation.

Firm proposals about how such commitments could be acted upon are not difficult to find. The British Labour Party, for instance, has called for a re-orientation of the EU budget away from agricultural expenditure, in favour of increased investment in training and research and development. It has also called for the development of Trans-European Networks (TENs) in transport, energy and telecommunications, in order to provide a stronger base for industrial regeneration. In the same vein, the Labour Party has argued for the establishment of an anti-cyclical European Recovery Fund. It is envisaged that such a fund would be able to harness the creditworthiness of EU institutions to raise finance for Europe-wide investment. During periods of recession it would operate in deficit, and in periods of growth it would be in surplus.

A not dissimilar proposal has come from the European Parliament. Here, the Temporary Committee on Employment has proposed a massive expansion of the already established European Investment Fund in order to provide soft loans for, in particular, TENs and small and medium-sized businesses. As the Fund would operate on a transnational basis, it has been convincingly argued that the European borrowing would not be measured against national borrowing requirements. This is an important point, because a number of Member States are currently struggling to reduce their national deficits and public debts to qualify for membership of Economic and Monetary Union (EMU). The result of Member States' efforts to meet the 'nominal' convergence criteria of the Maastricht Treaty is that there is significant deflationary pressure on the European economy. Although the European Commission has confidently predicted that EMU will create 13 million new jobs, many economic commentators see the forecast as wildly optimistic, dependent, as it is, on a range of factors not related directly to a single currency. It is more likely that as the EMU deadline of 1999 draws closer, unemployment will rise, unless there are effective countervailing measures introduced at European level. This was precisely the point that was made by the European Parliament's Temporary Employment Committee.

EMU, as such, is unlikely to be considered formally at the IGC. It will, nevertheless, form part of the backdrop to all the discussions on Treaty reform. For the United Kingdom, EMU could bring a number of clear benefits, not least the removal of currency transaction costs for business and an end to European currency speculation. But, on the other hand, if the Maastricht convergence criteria were rigidly adhered to, any national efforts to encourage growth and reduce unemployment would be severely constrained.

There are other problems with EMU. In so far as a single European currency would obviously deprive Member States of the ability to devalue their currencies, it is essential that any government is quite certain that its industries will be able to compete effectively before it commits itself to EMU. This is particularly important for the United Kingdom because of the effect which 17 years of regressive economic policies have had on the competitiveness of the British economy.

Under the terms of the Maastricht Treaty, the single currency will be administered by a European Central Bank. This bank will be broadly based on the model of the Bundesbank and will be run independently of real democratic influence. Neither the European Parliament nor the Council of Economic and Finance Ministers will have any real control over the Bank's long-term objectives or its day-to-day priorities. The concern of many is that the Bank's preoccupations will be price stability and monetary stringency, and little else besides. This is why the issue of democratic accountability needs to be reintroduced into the EMU debate.

Furthermore, as there are no new proposals to transfer resources from the richer to the poorer regions of Europe, EMU is likely to exacerbate the EU's growing economic disparities. Already the single market is tending to concentrate wealth-creation in the most prosperous regions. Without a far more redistributive and pro-active regional policy, the likelihood is that EMU will reinforce the existing trends and make the goal of economic and social cohesion extremely difficult to achieve.

For EMU to be a success, there has to be a convergence of real economic performance between the national economies of the EU. Before Britain joins EMU, levels of employment, growth and productivity have to be given careful consideration and, in any evaluation, the acid test will be the overall impact which membership will have on job creation.

An additional prerequisite for joining EMU is, of course, the consent of the British electorate. Signing up for a single currency would be the biggest step towards European integration since Britain joined the EC in 1973. It is a decision that will require popular support.

If Europe is to be made 'relevant', the concept of a Social Europe is a theme which must be developed at the 1996 Intergovernmental Conference (IGC). The EU has virtually completed its legislative programme for the internal market; most of the impediments to the free movement of goods, capital and services, have been, or are in the process of being, removed. What is lacking is a commensurate European social dimension. If business is to compete on equal terms, there must be agreed minimum standards for all employees.

Co-operation on workers' rights is important because if the Single European Market is to achieve its full potential, it has to be based on the principle of 'partnership' – partnership, that is, not only between the EU, government and industry, but also between employers and employees. Instead of accepting the inevitability of industrial conflict, concerted efforts ought to be made to achieve acceptance of new models of industrial co-operation.

Minimum standards for employees are also vital if a downward spiral of social devaluation is to be avoided. Without

agreed minimum standards, there will always be the danger
that Member States will seek to attract inward investment
through deregulation and attempts to drive down wages and
conditions. Indeed, it was John Major's belief that he could
gain a competitive advantage for the United Kingdom, which
led to his insistence on Britain's opt-out from the Social
Chapter, or social protocol, of the Maastricht Treaty.

There is, however, abundant evidence to indicate that the
best way to create a prosperous society is to invest in skills
training, education and research and development, rather
than attempt to encourage a low-skill, low-wage, low-motiva-
tion, assembly-line economy. This is being recognised not
only by other European countries, but also by countries in
the Far East, most notably Taiwan. Taiwan recognises that
it cannot hope to compete with mainland China, with its
huge labour force, by trying to offer lower wages. Therefore it is attempting to build a high-tech, value-added
economy. It is surely about time that the United Kingdom
learned at least some lessons from the Taiwanese experience.

In Britain, at long last, there are signs of real changes of
attitude in industry. Despite the Conservative government's
claim that the Social Chapter will impose excessive burdens
on companies, dozens of British-based multinationals have
decided voluntarily to implement the provisions of the European Works Council Directive, even though Britain has
formally opted out of the social protocol. Increasingly, it is
being recognised that the Social Chapter is not a checklist
of unrealistic demands, but a set of principles, which provide a common-sense base for sensible partnership. This is
why Britain's opt-out from the Social Chapter should be
brought to an end.

There is more, of course, to the social dimension than
the Maastricht Social Chapter. In fact, most of the employment legislation which has been introduced in recent years
has been brought forward on the basis of the Single European Act. What is required now is a fresh impetus to address those social issues that are still outstanding. Further
measures are needed to favour disabled people, to promote
equal opportunities for women and to establish new rights
to information and consultation for workers in medium-sized
companies.

At the same time, racism in the workplace has to be addressed at the European level. There is already an anti-sex discrimination clause in the first 'pillar' of the Treaty; a clause should be added to enable anti-race discrimination measures to be introduced. Legislation brought forward on this basis should then be subject to qualified majority voting (QMV) at the Council of Ministers. To ensure that the fight against racism is placed high on the European agenda, a Commissioner responsible for anti-racism should be appointed.

There is a further issue which needs to be considered in this context. An obvious and important area of international co-operation is the environment. It is a truism that pollution does not recognise international boundaries. The pollution of the environment in one country increasingly affects the environment of other countries. The Chernobyl disaster is a stark reminder of this. And yet, much of the impetus in favour of EU measures to protect and enhance the environment has been lost in recent years. One of the main reasons is the use of the term 'subsidiarity' to justify the 'repatriation' of European competencies to Member State governments. Even when there has been a clear rationale and a strong legal base for European involvement, national governments have sought to thwart European legislation by invoking this principle.

Rather than providing a crude excuse for strengthening national governments at the expense of the EU, subsidiarity ought to be defined in a far more positive way. Subsidiarity should mean that decisions are made at the most appropriate level of government, as close to the people as is practicable. Such a definition implies that the EU ought to have well-defined areas of competence, which cannot be eroded. But it also means that the EU should provide a framework within which power can be decentralised within the Member States. In other words, the EU should be built on the foundations of local and regional government, as well as on national government. If, in the European Treaty, subsidiarity were defined in this way, it could herald a serious move towards the creation of a decentralised 'Europe of the Regions'.

Creating a Europe of the Regions, where power rests with people in their communities and regions, must be a central part of a broader agenda to bring democracy to the EU. Throughout the EU there is a gaping democratic deficit, and nowhere is this more evident than in the institutions of the EU itself.

Although it is not evident from reading the British tabloid press, by far the most powerful of the European institutions is the Council of Ministers. It is here that the overwhelming majority of key and binding decisions are made about the EU. It will also be Europe's heads of government who will determine how the Maastricht Treaty is to be revised. Yet despite its obvious importance, the Council of Ministers is profoundly undemocratic. There is no other legislative body in the Western world which holds all its meetings in camera and which does not publish the minutes of those meetings. To make matters worse, most of the government ministers who attend do so without a mandate from their respective parliaments, and usually only report back in a selective and partial manner.

Reform of the Council of Ministers' practices is necessary if the EU is to gain greater support. But the agenda for reform has to go beyond the conduct of meetings and the mechanisms of accountability. It must also address the critical and sensitive issue of how the Council of Ministers makes its decisions – whether on the basis of unanimity or qualified majority voting.

Increasingly, over the past few years, the British government has exercised its veto over the adoption of progressive European legislation. This has meant that time and time again, Britain has found itself isolated and marginalised. Always seeking to block and obstruct; never attempting to influence and contribute constructively.

Few people would disagree that in some areas of decision-making, which are of vital national interest, the unanimity requirement should be retained. Such areas would include budgetary policy, taxation, changes to the Treaty, external border controls and foreign and security issues. However, Britain is not the only country to exercise its veto at the Council of Ministers. On various occasions other Member States have succeeded in blocking EU measures. Often other countries' actions have been against Britain's national interest. At best the veto is a double-edged sword; at worst it harms the United Kingdom more often than it helps.

A case in point concerns the restructuring of the steel industry. Today, the British steel industry is undoubtedly the most competitive in Europe. Yet it cannot achieve the success of which it is capable because competition is distorted in the EU by massive state subsidies, some of which are illegal, to steel producers in Spain, Germany and Italy. What is required is a fundamental restructuring of the European steel industry to create genuine parity. The reason why this has not happened is the need for unanimity in the Council of Ministers. In this area, therefore, an extension of qualified majority voting would be in Britain's national interest.

Equally, there is a sensible case to be made for extending qualified majority voting to such areas as social and environmental policy (excluding taxation), which are not already covered by QMV, and industrial, regional and cultural policy. In areas such as these, there is a sound pragmatic case to be made for change, and the case will be strengthened if the EU is to be enlarged. At present, with 15 Member States, it is difficult enough to achieve unanimity, with 25 or more Member States it will obviously be very much more difficult. In such a scenario, it most definitely will not be in Britain's interest to have important decisions blocked by even the smallest Member States.

If there is to be an extension of QMV, it follows that there should also be a change in the weighting of votes, so that the respective national population strengths are more accurately reflected. There will remain a need to have some measure of over-representation for the smallest of Member States, but the possibility has to be addressed that in an enlarged EU, Member States representing a minority of the population could block those representing the majority.

If the Council of Ministers needs to be reformed, so does the European Commission. Although the Commission is often unfairly criticised for its lack of sensitivity in decision-making, it is a bureaucracy which ought to be brought under greater democratic control. In particular, the Commission should be made more accountable to the European Parliament.

Under the Maastricht Treaty, the European Parliament was given substantially greater powers over the Commission.

During the past couple of years, those powers have been exercised responsibly and with good sense. It is, therefore, appropriate that the European Parliament should have the ability to nominate candidates for the Commission presidency on the same basis as national governments, and the Parliament ought to have not only the right to accept or reject the president-designate, but be able to exercise the same power over individual Commission nominees. Moreover, the European Parliament, by a convincing majority, should have the power to dismiss individual Commissioners when their performance falls well below that which is expected.

The EU's budgetary process generally needs to be reformed. The greater portion of EU expenditure is regarded as 'compulsory' and, as such, the European Parliament is unable to exercise any real influence over it. Creating a single budgetary procedure would enable the European Parliament to exercise influence over all areas of the budget, including the Common Agricultural Policy (CAP). For the first time, Parliament would be able to curtail wasteful agricultural expenditure, step up its efforts to end fraud and give real impetus to the long overdue reform of the CAP as a whole.

It is, however, in the area of Parliament's legislative role that some of the most far-reaching reforms need to be made. Our starting point has to be the simplification of the legislative procedure as it affects the European Parliament. At present, the Parliament is involved in five different legislative processes. These ought to be reduced to three: whenever there is a decision taken by QMV in the Council of Ministers, co-decision with the European Parliament ought to apply; when there is a unanimity requirement in the Council, a modified form of the current consultation procedure should be used in the European Parliament; and when there are international agreements in the name of the EU, the assent procedure ought to be used.

Tackling the democratic deficit must be one of the priorities at the 1996 IGC. But it is important to recognise that democracy has to be advanced within national legislatures, as well as at a European level. Just as the European Parliament ought to have greater powers, so national parliaments must be able to exercise greater control over their representatives at the Council of Ministers.

The degree of accountability varies from one national parliament to another. In Denmark and Finland, government ministers have to agree a negotiating mandate with a parliamentary committee before they attend a Council meeting. After Council meetings they are obliged to report back. Similarly, in Germany, France and Sweden, there is considerable influence over the negotiating positions put forward by government ministers.

There is nothing comparable in Britain. A straightforward 'mandating' of ministers would be anathema to the British parliamentary tradition, and yet there is a clear need for changes to ensure that there is increased accountability. Ministerial appearances before select committees would be a step forward, but there is also a need for a thorough overhaul of the system of European scrutiny. It is ridiculous that the Commons Select Committee on European Legislation often receives notice of European legislation just three days before it is due to consider that legislation. All the parliamentary committees concerned with European legislation have been currently examining their existing procedures and whatever conclusions are reached, they will have to be assessed in terms of the overall objective of increasing the influence of Parliament.

A final element of the democratic jigsaw is the EU's consultative bodies: the Committee of the Regions and the Economic and Social Committee. Both committees have an important role, in that they articulate the views of local and regional government, and of employers, trade unionists and other interested groups.

In the case of the Committee of the Regions, it is important for the representatives on that body to have a more clearly defined role. For example, the Committee ought to focus exclusively on issues of direct concern to local and regional government. It also ought to be able to express formal opinions to the European Parliament, and not merely the Council and the Commission. But most important of all, especially in the British context, the Treaty should specify that all the members of the Committee must be determined by local and regional government rather than by central government.

All these proposals are of enormous importance if Europe is to be made relevant to its citizens. There is, however, another issue which towers above them all, and that is the issue of 'peace' in Europe. The appalling conflict in the former Yugoslavia is a timely reminder of how fragile peace can be. Over the next few years the EU must do everything it can to ensure that there is increased stability in the Mediterranean region and in Central and Eastern Europe.

How best to achieve enlargement of the EU to the East is a difficult and complex question. Most of the former communist states are currently making great efforts to prepare themselves for EU membership. The EU has a responsibility to assist them in this process and not simply make exhortations about how they need to follow the Western example. This must mean that the EU's political declarations have to be matched by greater practical support. But before enlargement can be contemplated the EU itself must be prepared to change. An EU of 25 or more Member States will obviously have a profound impact on the its institutions. Without careful preparation we could find that the process of enlargement will undermine the EU's democratisation. Similarly, the CAP will have to be changed fundamentally, if agricultural support is not to assume astronomic proportions. And, at the same time, serious thought must be given to how the Structural Funds will operate, when all the countries of Central and Eastern Europe have a GDP that is far lower than that of even the poorest EU Member States.

To make these points is not to place obstacles in the path of enlargement. On the contrary, if progress is to be made, it is essential for there to be a realistic understanding of the problems which have to be tackled.

Six months after the conclusion of the IGC, negotiations should begin with Cyprus and Malta on the terms of their entry into the EU. This must be seen as the beginning of a continuous process, which will extend well into the next century. It is essential that the EU has the vision to extend its horizons to Central and Eastern Europe; it is in the interests of both the current and prospective EU Member States that this should take place according to a sensible timescale.

Linked to the issue of enlargement is the need to develop the EU's Common Foreign and Security Policy (CFSP). It is extremely unlikely that there will be agreement at the IGC to end the intergovernmental basis of either the CFSP 'pillar', or the Justice and Home Affairs 'pillar'. Member States, for obvious reasons, will be extremely reluctant to weaken their dominance in these areas. There is, nevertheless, an overwhelming case for the European Parliament to have a clear consultative role in relation to all areas of inter-governmental co-operation. With regard to the CFSP, there needs to be an increased role for its Secretariat within the Council of Ministers to provide an administrative continuity which currently does not exist. If such a Secretariat were able to analyse foreign policy trends and propose policy responses to perceived threats, it could provide the basis for the EU to respond quickly and effectively.

In the Maastricht Treaty it was suggested that, in the future, Europe might develop a 'common defence' policy. But giving the EU a defence role would substantially alter its character. It would also involve serious logistical problems and incur massive extra costs, and the creation of a European Army would certainly not receive public support in many of the European countries. Rather than embark on such a hazardous course, it is far more appropriate for the nations of Europe to work together so that they can develop a genuine capacity to co-ordinate their military operations in support of commonly agreed policies. In this respect, the Western European Union (WEU) ought to be given the ability to act effectively in missions of crisis intervention, whether it be humanitarian relief or peacekeeping missions. Whilst still remaining the European arm of NATO, the WEU could be given the means to support the foreign and security policies determined through the EU.

Fifty years after the Second World War, the EU has an onerous responsibility. Following the collapse of the communist bloc and the disintegration of the Soviet Union, many of the certainties of the Cold War era have been swept aside. In the past, the EU played an important role in encouraging democracy in Greece, Spain and Portugal. Now, the EU has to fulfil a different, but none the less important role in relation to the countries of Central and Eastern Europe. These countries are looking to us for support and guidance; we need to respond positively and in a spirit of solidarity.

The future of the EU depends, to a large extent, on whether it can successfully promote peace. The tragedy of the former

Yugoslavia has shown us what can happen when nationalism is allowed to grow unchecked to its full destructive capacity. If there is one lesson to be learned from the experience of that Balkan conflict, it is that without the essential bond of international and cross-cultural tolerance and co-operation, the future for Europe is bleak in the extreme.

If Europe can maintain peace and stability, then there will be the basis to create a Europe that is 'relevant'. The 1996 IGC could change the EU dramatically and profoundly. But for this to happen, Europe's national leaders will require enormous courage and determination. They will also have to listen to what the people of Europe are saying. The IGC could be subsumed under a mass of incomprehensible, esoteric, constitutional wrangling. Alternatively, it could focus on the issues that people are really concerned with. Politics is about choice, and the 1996 IGC is about the most important choices that Europe has to make.

2 Democracy and the European Union

Michael Newman

It is widely agreed that democracy is not one of the European Union's strong points. Indeed, the phrase 'democratic deficit' has passed into common usage to describe the problems that need to be addressed. Yet the discussion often appears to assume that the remedy lies in institutional reforms and that there is agreement about the causes of the 'deficit' and the nature of democracy. This chapter approaches the issues in a rather different way. It is based on the assumption that it is unhelpful to propose ways of strengthening democracy at the EU level without prior consideration of the kind of democracy which is to be applied. The first section therefore outlines a version of liberal democracy and then suggests the difficulties which this model is currently experiencing. Since one of these problems concerns the viability of the territorial state as the location for a liberal-democratic polity, this leads to a consideration, in section 2, of two ways in which the EU might be viewed in relation to the future of liberal democracy. It suggests that both represent unrealistic extremes and should be rejected. Finally, section 3 examines some views that avoid these failings and concludes by suggesting an alternative approach to the issues.

1. THE LIBERAL-DEMOCRATIC POLITY AND ITS DIFFICULTIES

'Democracy' is a multi-dimensional and contested phenomenon. Thousands of books and articles have discussed the differences between, and the relative merits of, 'direct' and 'representative' forms, and have disagreed as to whether capitalism is a precondition for, or a negation of, democracy.[1]

15

However, one model has dominated political thinking and practice in Western Europe and, with the collapse of the Soviet bloc, this now predominates throughout the continent: that is liberal democracy.

The general features of liberal-democratic theory are so familiar that it is unnecessary to discuss them in detail here, but it is worth recalling some of the key characteristics because they are now embedded in conventional thought about democracy itself. Despite considerable variations in practice, the system represented a marriage between pre-democratic liberalism, universal suffrage and the modern party system. From this there emerged a political order comprising at least two major parties, some degree of separation of power between the judiciary, legislature and executive, a relatively free press and comparatively free speech. The fundamental claim has been that democracy has been guaranteed by the fact that citizens make choices in elections, and that governments are subsequently directly accountable to parliaments and indirectly accountable to the people as a whole through the electoral process. Institutional checks and balances, pressure group activity and the free flow of information have been regarded as additional means of influencing the ways in which governments may act once they are in power.

This, of course, constitutes only a minimum definition, and the relative priorities within the constellation of values incorporated within the liberal-democratic model have always been a matter of fierce dispute. Although there is no space here to elaborate on such arguments, two of the contentious points must be discussed briefly since my position on these issues underlines the argument of the chapter. The first concerns the relationship between *liberty and equality.* Most theorists accept that, in some senses, both concepts are constituent elements of democracy, but also that there are tensions between them. The position taken here on liberty accepts the traditional catalogue of liberal values – freedom of expression, freedom of association, the right to vote, to join a political party and so on – but rejects the so-called 'libertarian' definitions of liberty, which uphold the notion of a minimal state. The assumption here is that libertarian theory effectively defends the rights of those who already possess power and privilege. In my view, public authorities do not simply have the right to use political power to redistribute in favour of the disadvantaged, but have a duty to do so. Otherwise they are curtailing the rights of others and negating equality, which is both a condition for, and a goal of, democracy. However, it is certainly also true that if equality is elevated to become the *sole* principle, it can lead to the elimination of fundamental liberties. It follows that democracy implies some form of balance between the goal of liberty and the goal of equality, but the argument here is based on the tradition that leans towards equality. It thus holds that inequalities must be justified, that is, an assumption that democratisation involves action on behalf of those without wealth and power.[2]

The second important tension is that between *elitism* and *participation* – that is, between those who favour the Schumpeterian model of democratic elitism and versions that emphasise the importance of active participation by the masses (Pateman 1970; Schumpeter 1976). The elitist model emphasises a strong leadership role for governments and parties with their policies endorsed by those 'below', while the participatory model emphasises wide-ranging discussion and action at the local level to influence the political elites. My own position is to favour some kind of synthesis between these competing models. I therefore assume that representation is indispensable, and that political parties are necessary agencies for articulating and implementing policies, but also that these must not be viewed as a substitute for active participation at all levels. Similarly, I accept that there is a role for leadership to highlight goals and values, but that change depends on pressure from below. Protest and participation must be regarded as legitimate aspects of political activity; organisations and channels for mass involvement should, therefore, be nurtured.[3]

However, the liberal-democratic model is now experiencing acute difficulties, both in its practice and in its underlying theoretical justifications. This statement may seem paradoxical: after all, in theory it has triumphed over all its rivals. It is also true that the system maintains its dominant position in thought and practice and is defended in the most robust manner by the European political elite, no doubt with the tacit support of the majority of the population. Yet there are clear signs of malaise in almost all states. Electoral support for the major parties has declined, there is growing cynicism about the political process, a marginalised, socially excluded under-class is growing, poverty, unemployment and underemployment are increasing, inequalities of class, gender and ethnicity persist, there is rampant racism, and neo-fascist and Far Right parties have secured support that would have been inconceivable in the 1950s and 1960s. Liberal-democratic systems may be surviving, but even their staunchest defenders can hardly regard them as wholly successful.

Of course, there have always been those who have disputed the claim that liberal-democratic states are democratic. Some of the critics who have adhered to the egalitarian and participatory models discussed above argue that liberal-democratic systems are not genuine democracies because of the unequal distribution of power within the polity, because they are elitist, because the parties offer no real choice, because governments assume mandates that they have not been given, and because the press and media barons manipulate public opinion. However, in the past egalitarian critics have often argued that Marxism or socialism could provide an alternative model of democracy.[4] With the crisis in Marxist theory and socialist practice, current debates have raised more fundamental questions about the nature of democracy and its relationship with the current liberal-democratic state. In effect, the weaknesses in practice have raised wide-ranging theoretical and normative questions.

One important element in the questioning of theory has concerned the economy. The conventional wisdom of the post-war era was that governments could maintain full employment and an adequate level of welfare benefits by demand management policies. The experience of the past 20 years has shaken belief in this post-war, Keynesian idea. On the Right, the growth of neo-liberalism as the new orthodoxy explicitly rejected this notion, arguing that it was economically counterproductive. Coupled with this was a whole range of political arguments which claimed that state intervention in the economy constituted 'creeping totalitarianism', that it arose from the vested interests of public officials, that it created a dependency culture and that the market itself constituted the most genuine form of democracy.[5] Such ideas have contributed to the partial dismantling of the mechanisms which had previously enabled states to intervene to bring about welfare goals.

On the Left the intellectual crisis has been far more agonising. In the first place, theorists and politicians have been forced to conceive of policies in a climate that is increasingly influenced by neo-liberal theories and practice. This has meant that they have found it ever more difficult to advocate the measures that they have traditionally favoured – progressive taxation, nationalisation, state-led regulation – with any likelihood of securing electoral support. However, they have also found it increasingly problematic to suggest viable alternatives (Anderson 1994). The second feature of the intellectual crisis concerns political agency, and in particular the role of political parties. For another fundamental assumption of the post-war era was that political parties could be instrumental in achieving change. In other words, it was believed that the election of a particular party (or party coalition) could result in a quite different policy outcome from the election of an alternative party. The supposition was that a government that had been elected on an explicit election manifesto would have sufficient support and determination to carry it out – at least in its essentials. Once again, experience has led to an erosion of faith in the validity of such propositions, particularly with regard to the parties of the Left, which have typically been forced to abandon major policy goals once in office.[6] Since parties have been regarded as the essential element in modern liberal democracy, their inability to deliver different policies from their political opponents inevitably calls into question another fundamental justification for the system.

The third major feature of the current conceptual crisis is the loss of belief that the territorial state can realistically be regarded as a separate polity in which decisions can be made and implemented. For liberal democracy has been based on a fundamental assumption: that is, the belief in the nation-state as the arena in which policy-making and implementation takes place. In other words, the state has been regarded as the polity, and, of course, this has been justified by doctrines of sovereignty and legitimised by forms of

nationalism and national integration. Thus the liberal-democratic state has been represented as a discrete polity, which
contained a democratic process.[7] Certainly, there have been
variations in the extent to which the systems were unitary
or decentralised, but even federal systems assumed that the
state had pivotal importance, and the agencies of socialisation
continued to mould – or tried to mould – national consciousness to engender a belief that democracy existed within
the state boundaries.[8] However, both the general processes
of globalisation and the specific impact of the EU have led
to an erosion of belief in this fundamental assumption of
liberal democracy.[9]

Such problems have revived and given new forms to traditions which had been squeezed out by the dominant liberal-
democratic conception.[10] Thus before the First World War
a variety of pluralists, federalists and anarchists condemned
the bureaucratic centralism and nationalism of the modern
state as anti-democratic and, in its early years, there was
considerable enthusiasm for the League of Nations as an
embryonic world government. The dominant state-centred
conception was then reinforced by the various processes of
national integration, the emerging Social Democratic parties focusing attention on reform through state action and,
above all, by the post-war Keynesian consensus. It is only
recently that such alternative perspectives have re-emerged
with particular salience in Western Europe.

The current problems in the dominant model – which
are reinforced by the fragmentation of traditional social and
political solidarities, the weakening in the support for major parties and the rise of new social movements – have
thus led many to question the extent to which state-centred
forms of liberal democracy are appropriate in terms of their
efficacy or their morality. If states are unable to provide for
their citizens' basic needs, their *raison d'être* must be called
into question. But many theorists and movements have also
attacked the state-centred view more generally, arguing that
states seek to legitimise themselves mobilising opinion through
forms of crude nationalism and xenophobia, that they op-
press minorities within their boundaries, that they discriminate against women in economic, social and political life,

and that they stifle local and regional forms of expression.[11] Whereas the post-war model of liberal democracy emphasised parties and governments as agencies for policy initiatives, many of the advocates of new forms of democracy place almost exclusive stress on the importance of representing interests, regions and identities through networking, lobbying and pressure politics. Similarly, while the earlier liberal-democratic model emphasised the territorial polity, much contemporary thinking proposes transnational democracy (Held 1993b; Goodman 1995). In other words, it is held that democratisation needs to be redirected both above the state and below it, in the regions and in local and functional communities.

What relevance does the EU have in relation to the problems of liberal democracy and the possible alternatives?[12]

2. DEMOCRACY AND THE EUROPEAN UNION: POSSIBLE FUTURES

Defence of the State-Centred System

The first position is to reject the arguments outlined above and to assert that the conventional state-centred model is still valid. The implications are that EU encroachment can and should be resisted or rolled back, and that the liberal-democratic state can and should be defended. The general features of the approach to the EU in this scenario are is as follows:

- An unwillingness to forgo veto power in the Council of Ministers;
- a reluctance to allow the EU to develop new areas of competence that may remove powers from the state;
- a desire to maintain control over the European Commission by means of the Council of Ministers to ensure that it does not challenge the power of the governments;
- a reluctance to allow the European Parliament legislative competence in any real sense – the assumption being that this is the preserve of domestic parliaments.

It is tempting to identify these opinions solely with the British Conservative government, but this would be a mistake, because it ignores the fact that these opinions are shared by other British political parties and analysts, and because it facts to acknowledge the extent to which such beliefs are held elsewhere in the EU, particularly at government level.[13] Yet this position is no longer tenable because of the extent of EU encroachment on the state system.

The Economy

The most obvious EU encroachment is in the economic sphere. Much of twentieth-century thought and practice, particularly in the Keynesian era, had been predicated on the assumption that there were national economies, which could be influenced by government policy. The extent of economic interdependence within the EU, and the removal of many of the levers of policy from domestic control, have therefore introduced a sea-change in the assumptions about liberal democracy.[14] The economy has traditionally been the overwhelming preoccupation of voters. But if an elected government is unable to implement a particular policy, because the extent of interdependence renders it unworkable or because it is incompatible with EU legislation, this necessarily negates a key assumption in conventional thinking about liberal democracy.[15]

EU Law and Domestic Law

The discussion of the economy demonstrates the second form of encroachment: that the attempt of a government to implement a different form of economic policy is *illegal*. The doctrines of the supremacy of EU law and direct effect, and the role of the European Court of Justice (ECJ) as the ultimate arbiter to which domestic courts must turn in the event of a dispute between domestic and EU legislation, have created a wholly different legal order. While it is true that the EU is restricted to certain fields of law (having only a minimal role in criminal law, for example), it has nevertheless transcended the traditional distinction between international law (which applies to states) and domestic law (which applies to individuals). In effect, states have become executive agents of the EU in carrying out its laws, and a new constitutional order has been created (Weiler 1995). This does not mean that states have become impotent actors, but the supremacy of EU law encroaches on the conventional doctrine of liberal democracy. For, in theory, a key function of a polity is law-making.

The EU and the Role of Domestic Parliaments

According to conventional liberal-democratic theory law-making is not simply based within the polity, but is a key responsibility of democratically elected legislatures. In reality, of course, governments rather than parliaments have been of primary importance in initiating legislation in most liberal democracies in the twentieth century. Nevertheless, parliamentary majorities have been necessary to pass laws. The fact that there is a whole body of EU legislation in which domestic parliaments have had no role at all clearly encroaches on the traditional interpretation of liberal democracy. However, this is only one way in which the EU has affected Member States' parliaments. Of equally significance is the fact that it has created a situation in which there is an overall reduction in parliamentary control over decision-making (Williams 1991).

This was inherent in the integration process from the outset, since decisions were made in camera by governments in the Council of Ministers. It is true that the Danish parliament alone secures policy commitments from their ministers *before* Council decisions are made (Nehring 1992; Sørensen and Waever 1992). Yet even the Danish parliament remains dissatisfied with the extent to which this amounts to real control, and most of the other legislatures remain dependent on the information that their governments choose to give them (European Parliament 1994). But each stage of EU development has intensified the problems for domestic parliaments. Thus the establishment of the European Council at the summit of the decision-making hierarchy reinforced Executive dominance, making it far more difficult for domestic parliaments to keep abreast of the policy-making process.[16] Instead, it acted as a secretive inter-governmental body without any real form of accountability. Similarly, the growth in importance of the Committee of Permanent Representatives (COREPER), and the increasingly sophisticated reorganisation of domestic administrations to advance the interests of the

Member States within the EU, has meant that civil services
are far more knowledgeable about the European policy process than most MPs. Moreover, the most powerful interest
groups – particularly international companies and farming
lobbies – are able to operate at both the European and
domestic levels, while parliaments are unable to do so (Mazey
and Richardson 1993).

Executive dominance, which played little part in conventional liberal-democratic theory, was already a feature of most
systems in the post-war period. Nevertheless, the policy-making
process of the EU made both a quantitative and qualitative
change in the situation. Domestic parliaments were completely excluded from some areas of legislation, and had
very limited access to legislative proposals at a sufficiently
early stage to influence them. They were also forced to
develop some understanding of a new esoteric system (leading
to a greater division of labour and expertise within parliaments), and were overwhelmed by ever-increasing amounts
of technical data which they could not scrutinise effectively.
The EU policy-making process thus further encroaches on
the conventional assumption of liberal democracy, that an
elected parliament is able to guarantee the accountability
of the government.

Majority Voting in the Council of Ministers
In practical terms the importance of the national veto has
been exaggerated and, even since the Single European Act
extended the use of majority voting, the policy process has
continued to depend on an ongoing bargaining process within
the Council.[17] In general, most governments have wished to
avoid raising the stakes by declaring a matter to be one of
supreme national interest, and the Council has not wanted
to override fundamental opposition to a particular policy,
thereby bringing about counterproductive polarisation. However, in the realm of theory, majority voting strikes at the
heart of the conventional notion of liberal democracy in
two key respects. First, it becomes difficult to represent the
political system as a self-contained polity if decisions about
policies may be taken by other states or an external entity
which it does not control. Secondly, the government can
no longer be accountable to parliament or other domestic

forces for a policy which it did not support. Thus, if parliaments were already operating at a disadvantage before the Single European Act, the introduction of majority voting since 1987 has increased the difficulties and calls into question a further assumption about liberal democracy.

The EU and Public Consciousness

Originally, the European Economic Community (EEC) was overwhelmingly the concern of political and economic elites and barely entered the public consciousness. For various reasons this is no longer the case. First, there have been concerted efforts to enhance public awareness of the EU. This has long been a policy of the Commission in order to elicit more support for the integration process. In particular, the Commission has seen the social and cultural dimensions of the EU as important means of instilling a European consciousness in the populations of the Member States and thereby of advancing the project through deepening its legitimacy. Some governments have shared this aim and, of course, the establishment of a directly elected parliament constituted a major step in providing the EU with greater democratic legitimation. Since then the EP and the Euroelections have certainly increased awareness of the EU, and this has also been reinforced by the growth of Community competences, and the impact of EU programmes in such areas as regional, environmental, gender equality and social policies. However, public attitudes may also be negative, particularly when political forces, including some governments, seek to mobilise opinion in opposition to 'Eurobureacuracy'. This obviously has relevance for the post-Maastricht ratification crisis and the negative attitudes which persist in many EU countries.

Yet in this context it is not important whether public attitudes are negative, positive or mixed. The relevant point is that if electorates *believe* that the EU is a major actor in policy-making – an actor which may sometimes rival or supersede the importance of their own governments – the conventional assumptions of liberal democracy are once again called into question. For the operating foundation for this system was that the citizens believed that they lived within a specific polity, which maintained autonomy over its own affairs.

The development of the EU has thus eroded the basis for many of the assumptions which underlay the idea of a liberal-democratic system. But this means that it is no longer realistic to claim that the state-centred model is intact. The governments are operating in an environment in which the degree of interpenetration between themselves and the Commission, and themselves and the other Member States, is so substantial that in some policy areas it is no longer possible to demarcate the boundaries between the domestic and EU spheres in any clear-cut way (Anderson and Eliassen 1993). It is certainly true that there are areas of policy in which EU encroachment is peripheral, but in some spheres, such as competition policy, agriculture and external trade, it is almost total. It is therefore sometimes impossible to determine whether policy proposals begin within Member States or within the layers of EU interactions. Of course, Eurosceptics may argue that this is precisely the basis of their objections, and that the way forward is to 'renationalise' policy-making by halting or reversing the interpenetration of the domestic and the external. However, this is an impractical suggestion and no major political party or movement in any Member State is calling for withdrawal from the EU. It is true that some forces – for example, the British Conservative Party – would like to limit further integration and reverse some stages that have already been agreed. However, because of the degree of interdependence that has already been established, this would not mean the restoration of the original operating assumptions of liberal democracy. It would simply mean that a particular policy was renationalised while others, such as control over capital movements, were not. This would not necessarily constitute a net gain for the process of democratisation and, given the current nature of the EU policy process, the state-centred doctrine actually justifies non-accountable government.

The EU as a Liberal-Democratic Polity

If the state-centred view refuses to acknowledge the significance of the impact of the EU on the traditional version of the liberal-democratic system, the second possibility is to draw the opposite conclusions; that is, to argue that the changes

brought about by 'globalisation' and European integration
are so fundamental that it is now necessary to transfer the
powers and prerogatives of the state to the EU. In effect,
this is to suggest that the EU should itself become a polity
– or state-like entity – comparable in nature to the Member
States which originally formed it. Such an approach might
result in the following institutional structure:

- an elected EU Executive responsible for policies affecting
  the EU as a whole;
- a bicameral legislature with the EP representing the EU
  electorate as a whole, and the Council of Ministers representing the Member States;
- other tiers of government with parliamentary assemblies
  at national, regional and local levels.

In this stark form the notion probably exists more fully
in the nightmare fantasies of Eurosceptics than as a proposal which is seriously suggested by proponents of the EU.
It is thus the bitter opponents of integration who argue that
the proposals for political union, EMU or the CFSP actually
constitute steps towards a 'United States of Europe' or that
federalism is a centralising project.[18] Most of those in favour of closer Union hold that their whole intention is to
avoid the reinvention of the state at EU level, and that, on
the contrary, the vision is one of decentralisation and diversity. Nevertheless, while these protestations are sincere, there
are, I believe, elements in some of the integrationist thinking which imply an assumption that significant powers which
previously existed at state level may simply be transferred
to the EU as an emergent polity. Such thinking is sometimes implicit in the suggestion that it is self-evident that
the EU should now replicate the institutional structures of
the liberal-democratic state.[19]

The first major objection to such views is immediately
evident: it is clear that, whether or not such a transformation is desirable, the EU is *not* a state-like entity. The governments, particularly those of the larger and more powerful
states, retain primacy in the decision-making process within
the EU, and exercise a range of powers in domestic and
foreign policy which differ very considerably from those of

regional governments within a federal state.[20] For while some
regional governments may have considerable autonomy, they
are still working within a hierarchical polity with the central state at its summit. Despite the EU encroachment on
the conventional liberal-democratic system, there is no real
comparability between the EU–Member State relationship
and the central government–regional government model.
For countries such as France, Germany and the United Kingdom not only retain a vast array of domestic powers, but
are also important actors in the international political, military and economic systems. In other words, they have powers,
relationships and networks – above all those involving the
United States – which are outside or even above the EU. It
is true that some states are more willing to cede significant
powers to the EU, but it is evident that the governments as
a whole would be utterly opposed to the transformation of
the EU into a super-state, and that they retain sufficient power
to block any such more in that direction.

The second reason for arguing that the EU cannot become a liberal-democratic entity is that it lacks the legitimacy for a metamorphosis of this kind. It can certainly be
argued, with some plausibility, that its relatively low popularity is partly the result of misrepresentations and misun-
derstandings, often engineered by national forces keen to
make the EU a scapegoat for their domestic failures. It is
also true that there is substantial support for Community
intervention in certain policy areas, such as the environment (Sinnott 1992). Nevertheless, the fact remains that in
most countries attitudes to the EU are lukewarm and in
some they are fairly hostile.[21] This provides no popular base
for the fundamental transformation which is necessary to
establish the EU as a liberal-democratic entity. This might
not matter if it were simply a temporary situation and
transnational European consciousness were to develop to
such an extent that a European state-like entity could be
grounded in popular legitimacy. Naturally, this is a matter
for speculation, but I do not see this as a realistic possibility, and it appears more probable that, for the majority
of people, political consciousness will remain more at local
or national level than at European.[22] For how would it be
possible for such a dramatic change to come about? After

all, many Member State governments are simultaneously doing their best to block any such development and, given their role in political socialisation and propaganda, their power in upholding national and even nationalist sentiments is liable to be far stronger than that of those seeking to engender a sense of European 'nation-statism'. Indeed, despite the problems of liberal democracy within the state system, and the reassertion of regional and minority national consciousness, subjective identification with the EU, or even Europe, is relatively weak (Branthwaite 1993).

Any conclusion that the nation, or existing nation-states, are to be regarded as the sole bases for identity must be resisted. However, the argument here is that there is no likelihood of an EU identity which will supersede or replace existing identities, and it is this which justifies the conclusion that the EU cannot be transformed into a liberal-democratic polity derived from a legitimacy rooted in a European consciousness. As Reif argues:

> any conceivable 'European Political Union' would be and will remain a multinational and multilingual political system for handling affairs no longer manageable at national or regional level; it would not be transformed into a one-nation-state aimed at homogenizing societies and cultures.
> (1993: 51)

Moreover, any attempt to create a 'one nation-state' identity at EU level would be undesirable since respect for existing identities (which is not the same thing as pandering to xenophobia or racism) is an important value in itself. It would also be counterproductive because it would be relatively easy for reactionary forces to exploit sentiments about the loss of identity in order to mobilise nationalist opposition to integration. It follows that any suggestion that the EU might be transformed into a democratic state-like entity is also mistaken.

3. THE EU AND DEMOCRACY: TOWARDS A SYNTHESIS?

The argument in section 2 has sought to establish that neither the conventional notion of the liberal-democratic state
nor that of the EU as an embryonic liberal democracy is
tenable. This suggests that the process of integration and
interdependence has created a mixed entity which has rendered anachronistic the idea of a discrete polity. However,
this interpretation may itself take many forms and, before
elaborating my own conclusions, it is necessary to examine
three others: those based in the doctrines of federalism,
subsidiarity and 'new democratic politics'.

Constitutional federalism conceives of the EU as an entity in which each tier of government is responsible only
for policies which need to be carried out at that particular
level. The underlying assumption is that there is an optimum level – on a mixture of democratic and efficiency criteria
– at which decisions should be made, and that the art of
constitution-building is to ensure the closest possible fit
between the optimum levels and the institutional structures.
In principle, this should avoid the danger of excessive centralisation by entrusting relatively few powers to the highest tier
of government – in this case, to the Executive of the EU
(Burgess 1989; Levi 1990). Subsidiarity is an ambiguous
concept, which is open to various interpretations, but it
resembles federalism in arguing that the levels of decision-
making should be determined in accordance with a combination of efficiency criteria and the need to ensure that they
are taken with the greatest possible proximity to the citizens whom they will affect.[23] The major difference between
this approach and that of federalism is that the concept of
subsidarity does not necessarily emphasise the importance
of constitution-making. Instead, it simply seeks to suggest
the appropriate level at which decisions should be made in
each policy area. The conclusions do not necessarily need
to be incorporated into a constitution, for the allocation of
responsibilities for policy-making in each sphere could be
agreed by convention or instituted into EU law without the
kind of overall constitutional settlement favoured by traditional
federalists. However, the common feature of both approaches

is that it suggests a polity in which power is divided and decentralised in accordance with some principles which are agreed to be rational.

The argument developed here differs from these views in two respects. First, both federalism and subsidiarity imply that there is an overall polity – the EU – in which powers and functions may be divided by agreement. However, there is no consensus that the EU is a polity (rather than a complex form of intergovernmentalism), and there is an unresolved conflict about the extent and nature of the competences which should be transferred to the supranational level. In my opinion it is impossible to go very far in reaching agreement about the distribution of powers and functions between the various tiers of government within the EU unless there is also agreement about the nature of the overall entity and the aspirations for its future. Otherwise each proposal for a transfer of competences from their existing level is likely to precipitate further conflict. For example, Eurosceptics will view any suggestion that the Commission should acquire additional responsibilities as embryonic federalism, while integrationist forces will regard a proposal that any existing EU powers should be renationalised as a threat to the EU. Secondly, both theories imply the possibility of a rational set of principles for making such decisions. However, this is questionable since it assumes, for example, that a socialist and a neo-liberal would agree about the level on which economic policy should be made, and would simply differ as to the nature of that policy. In fact, their disagreements as to the appropriate *agency* for policy-making (private or public), and the *nature* of the policy (interventionist or market-determined), are also likely to affect their views as to the appropriate *level* for policy-making. In established systems it is possible that they might accept the existing institutional framework as constituting the 'rules of the game', but this is very different from suggesting that they could agree about rational principles for *establishing* responsibilities for policy-making within the EU.

A third approach regarding the EU as a framework for democratisation avoids this emphasis on 'rationality'. Based in the perspective of 'new democratic politics', it tends rather to celebrate action and diversity.[24] The efforts of citizens, both as individuals and in new social movements, to gain greater control over their lives locally, regionally, nationally and transnationally will, it is suggested, lead to new forms of democracy and citizenship. These will be embodied in new structures and networks, both formal and informal, which will 'deconstruct' the state and constitute the EU as an arena in which multi-level and multi-mode governance may be established. According to this type of analysis, the EU is already an embryonic framework of this kind, but one which is stultified by bureaucracy and the dominance of the Member States. The task is to democratise the EU through active participation at the local, regional and transnational levels.

This reintroduces politics into the discussion. Unlike constitutional federalism, and the doctrine of subsidiarity, it is not implying that the distribution of power can be determined by 'rational' principles – or by such principles alone. Rather, the structure of the EU is held to depend upon conflict and co-operation between a whole range of groups and interests which will interact with one another in various ways. However, the element which proponents of 'new democratic politics' have in common with constitutional federalism and subsidiarity is in 'decentring' power. According to all three views, it is a mistake to believe that power is – or should be – located at either state or EU level. Instead power is – and should be – fragmented. Furthermore, the perspectives based in new democratic politics also emphasise participation at the local and transnational levels, highlighting the extent to which the traditional model of liberal democracy has been invalidated both by its hierarchy and by its geographical limitations, and signalling the potentially positive aspects of the EU.

Because of the interpenetration between the EU and the Member States, and because of the malaise of the liberal-democratic state, this multi-centred perspective appears to have some validity as a representation of the current situation and to offer an attractive vision. It also transcends the notion of a discrete polity – either at the state or EU level – which can become 'a democracy' and instead conceptualises the task as seeking democratisation in various ways and at various levels. Yet there are, I believe, certain weaknesses in the approach.

New democratic politics has been concerned, above all, with facilitating the opportunities for citizens to be involved in decision-making. Certainly, this is one fundamental goal of democracy. However, the notion of the EU as a framework for multi-centred, multi-mode democracy is based on a fragmented (post-modern?) paradigm, which treats power as an object of suspicion. At least some versions of the conventional state-centred model were based on the alternative notion that power could be beneficial so long as it was controlled and operated democratically. The history of twentieth-century liberal democracy may illustrate the importance of this point.

In many countries in inter-war Europe the procedures and constitutional conventions of liberal democracy were arguably as advanced as they were in the post-war era. However, as the Depression and the triumph of fascism demonstrated, liberal democracy was then a vulnerable system with comparatively weak legitimacy. The process by which it became embedded after the Second World War depended more on its *results* than on its underlying theory. Above all, stabilisation was achieved through the unparalleled economic growth of the so-called 'golden age' and by the development of welfare state and full employment systems which partly offset the persistent socioeconomic inequalities. Without these practical benefits, it would probably have been impossible to stabilise the system. This suggests that effective economic and welfare policies are again necessary to revitalise liberal democracy. But how can these be devised and implemented if power is fragmented and diffused? This problem is not always addressed by the advocates of new democratic politics, but it is surely crucial to any conception of democracy which considers goals and output as well as input. And it provides the final complicating aspect in any consideration of the democratisation of the EU. For it suggests an approach that takes a clear-cut attitude in favour of 'Europeanising' or 'regionalising' some issues, while seeking to safeguard other powers at state level.

In each case the relevant considerations are not simply locational, but concern the *content* of a particular policy and the probable implications, in relation to overall goals, of a transfer of power. For, ultimately, the ways in which democracy

is seen to apply depend on a combination of factual, theoretical and normative questions. Particular conclusions about
democracy and the EU entail analysis of how power is currently distributed, and this is a highly complex issue, which
involves both empirical observation and theoretical explo-
rations into the nature of power itself. But they also involve
normative analysis of democracy and of the relative importance of the various priorities and goals within it. It is not
possible to discuss the implications of this approach in detail, but the following section indicates the kinds of conclusion that flow from such an analysis.

Areas for which the Europeanisation would not Constitute a Democratic Advance

'Europeanisation' and 'democratisation' are not equivalents,
therefore some forms of 'Europeanisation' are unacceptable
and others should be treated with great caution. In particular, since the establishment of political control over
monetary policy constituted a fundamental democratic advance (even if governments have often abused this power
for electoral purposes), there is no democratic justification
for the establishment of an Economic and Monetary Union
(EMU) unless the Central Bank is subject to political control by elected bodies. Moreover, it is probable that the current
convergence criteria for EMU would exacerbate inequality
and poverty for much of the EU population and these are
therefore incompatible with the fundamental goals of democratisation (as defined in section 1).[25] This implies opposition to EMU, as envisaged in the Maastricht formula,
whatever the putative advantages of currency stability. On
the other hand, there are compelling arguments for suggesting that full-employment, Keynesian policies, under political control, would be more effective on an EU than on a
'national' level.[26] The goal of 'democratisation' would therefore be enhanced by common agreements on such policies
at this level. In other words, the issue is not whether economic affairs should be conducted at European, national or
regional level; it is the content and goals of the policies
and the nature of the decision-making processes that are
relevant.

Areas of Uncertainty

Other issues must be approached with caution since demo-cratic arguments can be advanced on both sides. It is often implied that democratisation involves a rapid advance in institutional development at the EU level, particularly by an extension of majority voting in the Council of Ministers and by an increase in the power of the EP. Yet this is surely far more complex than is suggested. It is, for example, no-table that the extension of majority voting is normally justi-fied in terms of an improvement in efficiency.[27] But expediting decision-making is not itself a democratic justification and, despite all the criticisms that may be advanced against the political systems of the Member States, most national govern-ments currently have much greater democratic legitimacy than the Council of Misters as a whole. Similarly, while it is clear that the EP is the most democratic of the EU institu-tions and that it has relatively strong claims to secure some increase in its powers, there is room for considerable scep-ticism about its ambition to achieve equality of status with the Council. Euro-elections tend to be based on domestic issues, turnouts are relatively low, the representational function of MEPs is comparatively weak and party cohesion is rather loose. In these circumstances, the democratic credentials of the EP are far less compelling than is customarily implied (Mather 1995).

Areas in which Democratisation Requires Action at EU Level

It seems clear, on basic liberal principles, that there can be no democratic justification for the current secrecy of the European Council and the Council of Ministers. Since it is a basic axiom of liberal democracy that control, account-ability and choice depend on the availability of informa-tion, any suppression of information by public authorities requires justification on the basis of a principle or princi-ples compatible with democracy.[28] This is certainly not the case with the argument that Council of Ministers' delibera-tions on legislative proposals need to be confidential to ensure frank discussion during the bargaining process. It is far more important that the EP, national parliaments and the Euro-pean peoples as a whole are aware of the positions taken by the various governments than that those governments are spared the embarrassment of justifying their positions publicly. Similarly, the formidable array of repressive measures against immigrants and asylum-seekers, which have been agreed in secret in such bodies as TREVI and the K4 Committee, without the relevant information being disclosed to the EP or national governments, demonstrates the need for a liberal EU Freedom of Information Act.[29] Basic democratic principles therefore suggest that there should be support at all levels for those who are seeking to ensure that openness of this kind is implemented in the EU policy-making process, and the recent European Court of Justice (ECJ) judgment in favour of *The Guardian* is a modest step in the right direction.[30]

An allied principle of liberal democracy is that public policies should be open to effective scrutiny and control, particularly by the parliamentary bodies through which legislation is enacted. This is clearly not the case in the EU. Almost all domestic parliaments and the EP are dissatisfied with their inability to control and scrutinise the Member States' governments effectively, despite the enhancement of the EP's legislative powers since the Single European Act, and despite the strengthening of scrutiny committees in most domestic parliaments. Indeed the latest report of the House of Commons European Legislation Committee is more scathing about the total ineffectiveness of democratic control over EU policy-making than it has ever been in the past.[31] There are, of course, differences in priority and attitude between the EP and many of the domestic parliaments, but they have a common democratic interest in demanding more adequate ways of scrutinising and influencing the legislative process.

The demands for a reduction in secrecy and an increase in control and accountability follow from basic liberal principles. But I would also argue that democratisation requires the development of a wider political consciousness to dismantle artificial boundaries. At present attitudes still tend to be fragmented by the frontiers of the separate nation-states, although it is evident that the peoples of the EU have some crucially important common interests – the economy, social policy or the environment, for example. It follows that their democratic power will be enhanced by a growth of transnational networks and an increase in the co-operation between parties, parliaments and non-governmental organisations. Moreover, since the process of integration has led to an increasing interpenetration between the domestic and the European, the peoples of the EU should seek to exploit the advantages that this offers. The development of EU citizenship under the Maastricht Treaty (weak though it is) effectively acknowledges that there is an EU public sphere in which such citizen rights are to be exercised.[32] This point is important because it is only if it is accepted that all those who have the legal right to live in the EU should have rights to full political participation throughout the EU that a transnational democratic culture may develop.[33] This might even lead to a charter of social and democratic rights, which could be incorporated into EU law and which all Member States would be required to observe. But the ultimate, and currently rather remote, aspiration would be the growth of democratic power to counteract the power currently wielded by governments and transnational economic and financial interests. This would depend on the development of a European consciousness to complement existing forms of consciousness, rather than replacing them or even rivalling them in intensity. It would be based on a recognition that the local, regional and national can no longer be insulated from the international, and that democracy needs to take account of the nature of the contemporary world.

The issues raised in this chapter are not intended to provide answers to the complex issues involved in assessing the future of democracy and the EU, but to contribute to the debate. For one purpose of this chapter is to suggest that there are no simple conclusions. Of course, it is more appealing to ordered minds to conceive of democracy in a final and holistic sense. But ultimately it is more helpful to recognise that there will be co-operation and conflict at all levels – in local communities, regions, states and EU institutions – and that such interactions will continue to shape the power configuration in Europe. The task is to ensure that the result is greater democratisation rather than the kind of fragmentation and chaos that could be exploited by anti-democratic forces.

NOTES

1. For useful recent analyses, see Arblaster (1987), Dunn (1992), Held (1993a) and Hyland (1995).
2. For the most influential modern view of this kind, see Rawls (1972). For an earlier version, see Laski (1938). For the libertarian notion, see Nozick (1974). For recent critiques of libertarian views, see Haworth (1994) and Hyland (1995).
3. Since the definition of liberal democracy is itself relatively fluid, it is a matter of judgement whether the position outlined above suggests a wholly different model or is a version of liberal democracy. In my view it remains 'liberal-democratic' since it adheres to the classical minimum definition, while wishing to extend it, and it is helpful to describe it in this way as this demonstrates that liberal freedoms are regarded as crucial even though a broader conception of democracy is also embraced.
4. For a recent thoughtful attempt to restate this position, see Miliband (1994).
5. For the most influential neo-liberal theories, see Hayek (1944) and Friedman (1962). For specific arguments against public officials arising from public choice theory, see Buchanan and Tullock (1962). For critiques of neo-liberalism, see Haworth (1994) and Hyland (1995); for a critique of public choice theory, see Stoker (1991).
6. For a useful comparative analysis, see Bell and Shaw (1994).
7. See Camilleri and Falk (1992).
8. Until the collapse of the Soviet bloc, the Cold War and American alliance also projected the image of an association of free, democratic states sharing the same fundamental values against the threat of 'totalitarianism'.
9. This will be argued at length in section 2.
10. For a detailed exposition of this view, see Hirst (1994).
11. For arguments of this kind, see Held (1993b), Hirst (1994), Camilleri and Falk (1992), Goodman (1995) and Meehan (1993).
12. For a more extensive discussion of the issues, see Newman (1996).
13. In effect, the British Labour Party took a similar position, albeit based in a different ideological perspective in the 1983 General Election, and it is maintained by some people on the British Left. See, for example, the intervention by Tony Benn in the European Communities (Amendment) Bill in the House of Commons, 20 May 1992, and for a more theoretical statement, see Miliband (1994: 179–90). A rather similar stance is taken in the Scandinavian Member States.
14. For discussion of such issues, from a variety of perspectives, see Brouwer *et al.* (1994).
15. It is, of course, quite possible that the traditional levers of policy would no longer be effective, whether or not the EU existed, so that the loss of domestic control constitutes a *theoretical* change rather than a practical one.
16. The fact that the European Council did not publish an agenda or

act as a legislative body intensified the problems of parliamentary control.

17. Quality majority voting (QMV) was applied to issues concerning the single market in the Single European Act and was extended in the Treaty on European Union to certain aspects of environment, development, consumer protection, education and public health policy and trans-European networks. It also stipulated that after January 1996 QMV would apply to visa policy.

18. See, for example, Cash (1991).

19. For example, in the well-known remark of David Martin, MEP and author of the influential EP reports on Political Union, that if the EU were a state and applied to join the EU it would be turned down since it was not a democracy (Dinan 1994: 228).

20. For an extensive discussion of federalist theories, see King (1982).

21. In 1990, when popular enthusiasm for the EU was far higher that it was after the Maastricht Treaty, 88 per cent of respondents felt attached to their country, 87 per cent to their region, 85 per cent to their own village, but only 48 per cent to the EC and 47 per cent to Europe as a whole; 46 per cent did not feel attached to the EC or Europe as a whole (Reif (1993: 138). For evidence of more negative attitudes to the EU in spring 1993, see Nugent (1994: 425).

22. For a different view, persuasively argued, see Meehan (1993).

23. For the statements in the Treaty on European Union, the 'clarifications' in Birmingham and Edinburgh in 1992, and a useful commentary, see Church and Phinnemore (1994). For other detailed analyses, see Endo (1994), Spicker (1993) and van Kersbergen and Verbeek (1994).

24. There is, of course, no agreed category of new democratic politics. The discussion here groups a variety of theorists including Held (1993), Meehan (1993), Hirst (1994), Goodman (1995) and Camilleri and Falk (1992). See also Kuper (1995). For a detailed sympathetic exposition of such perspectives, see Boggs (1995).

25. For critical analyses of the economic impact, see Michie and Grieve Smith (1994) and Holtham (1993). For an examination of the issue of political control, see Taylor (1994).

26. See Michie and Grieve-Smith (1994), Holland (1993) and Coates and Holland (1995); 'Put Europe to Work', *Report of the Parliamentary Group of the Party of European Socialists* (Brussels: 1993) and Lintner (1994).

27. See, for example, Progress Report from the Chairman of the Reflection Group on the 1996 Intergovernmental Conference (Madrid, 1 September 1995) SN509/1/95 REV1 (REFLEX 10), P.11.

28. For example, as a safeguard against libel and in demonstrable issues of security.

29. For a critique of such measures, see Bunyan (1993).

30. After more than a year of debate, the Council had finally agreed a code of conduct, which came into effect early in 1994, promising 'the widest possible access to documents'. *The Guardian* took action against the Council in May 1994 when the EU foreign ministers rejected

an appeal by one of its correspondents against the proceedings. The Court found in favour of *The Guardian,* which had been supported by the European Parliament and the governments of Denmark and the Netherlands, on 19 October 1995.
31. Select Committee (1995). For an analysis of the procedures of· parliaments of the EU 12, see European Parliament (1994).
32. The extension of such citizen rights to all those who are legally resident in the EU is also an urgent democratic imperative. See Dave Edye, this volume, chapter 4.
33. In this context the refusal by the French police to allow a party of Danish school students to wear T-shirts protesting about Chirac's nuclear policy constitutes exactly the same interference with the right to protest as it would if applied to French citizens. *The Guardian,* 13 October 1995.

REFERENCES

Anderson, P. (1994), Introduction, in Perry Anderson and Patrick Camilleri (eds.), *Mapping the West European Left,* Verso, London.
Anderson, S. and Eliassen, K.A. (eds.) (1993), *Making Policy in Europe: The Europeification of National Policy-Making,* Sage, London.
Arblaster, A. (1987), *Democracy,* Open University Press, Milton Keynes.
Bell, D.S. and Shaw, F. (1994), *Conflict and Cohesion in Western European Social Democratic Parties,* Pinter, London.
Branthwaite, A. (1993), 'The Psychological Basis of Independent Statehood', in Robert H. Jackson and Alan James (eds.), *States in a Changing World: A Contemporary Analysis,* Clarendon Press, Oxford.
Boggs, C. (1995), *The Socialist Tradition: From Crisis to Decline,* Routledge, London.
Brouwer, F., Lintner, V. and Newman F. (1994), *Economic Policy-Making and the European Union,* Federal Trust, London.
Buchanan, J. and Tullock, G. (1962), *The Calculus of Consent,* University of Michigan Press, Ann Arbor.
Bunyan, T. (ed.) (1993), *Statewatching in the new Europe: A Handbook on the European State,* Statewatch, London.
Burgess, M. (1989), *Federalism and European Union: Political Ideas, Influences and Strategies in the European Community,* Routledge, London.
Camilleri, J.A. and Falk, J. (1992), *The End of Sovereignty?,* Edward Elgar, Aldershot.
Cash, W. (1991), *Against a Federal Europe,* Duckworth, London.
Church C. and Phinnemore, D. (1994), *European Union and European Community: A Handbook and Commentary on the Post-Maastricht Treaties,* Harvester Wheatsheaf, Brighton.
Coates, K. and Holland, S. (1995), *Full Employment for Europe,* Spokesman, Nottingham.
Dinan, D. (1994), *Ever Closer Union?,* Macmillan, Basingstoke.

Dunn, J. (ed.) (1992), *Democracy – The Unfinished Journey*, London, Oxford University Press.

Endo, K. (1994), 'The Principle of Subsidiarity: From Johannes Althusius to Jacques Delors', *Ide Hokkaido Law Review*, Vol. 44, No. 6.

European Parliament (1994), *The European Parliament and the Parliaments of the Member States: Parliamentary Scrutiny and Arrangements for Cooperation, European Parliament*, Decision for Relations with the Parliaments of the Member States, Brussels/Luxembourg.

Friedman, M. (1962), *Capitalism and Freedom*, Chicago University Press, Chicago.

Goodman, J. (1995), 'The European Union: Towards a Transnational Politics of "Movement"', *Via Europa*, Summer, pp. 25–31.

Haworth, A. (1994), *Anti-Liberalism: Markets, Philosophy and Myth*, Routledge, London.

Hayek, F.A. (1944), *The Road to Serfdom*, George Routledge & Son, London.

Held, D. (ed.) (1993a), *Prospects for Democracy*, Polity Press, Cambridge.

Held, D. (1993b), 'Democracy: From City States to a Cosmopolitan Order?', in David Held (ed.), *Prospects for Democracy*, Polity Press, Cambridge.

Hirst, P. (1994), *Associative Democracy*, Polity Press, Cambridge.

Holland, S. (1993), *The European Imperative: Economic and Social Cohesion in the 1990s*, Spokesman, Nottingham.

Holtham, G. (1993), *Economic Integration after Maastricht*, IPPR, London.

Hyland, J.L. (1995), *Democratic Theory: The Philosophical Foundations*, Manchester University Press, Manchester.

King, P. (1982), *Federalism and Federation*, Croom Helm, Beckenham.

Kuper, R. (1995), 'Of Democracy and Deficits', Paper presented at UACES Research Conference, 18–19 September.

Laski, H. (1938), *A Grammar of Politics*, Allen & Unwin, London, 4th edn.

Levi, L. (ed.) (1990), *Altiero Spinelli and Federalism in Europe and the World*, Franco Angeli, Milan.

Lintner, V. (1994), 'National Economic Sovereignty and European Integration', in Brouwer *et al.* (1994).

Mathes, J. (1995), 'The European Parliament – A Model of Representative Democracy?' Paper presented to the UACPS Research, Conference, 18–19 September.

Mazey, S. and Richardson, J. (eds.) (1993), *Lobbying in the European Community*, Oxford University Press, Oxford.

Meehan, E. (1993), *Citizenship and the European Community*, Sage, London.

Michie, J. and Grieve Smith, J.A. (eds.) (1944), *Unemployment in Europe*, Academic Press, London.

Miliband, R. (1994), *Socialism for a Sceptical Age*, Polity Press, Cambridge.

Nehring, N.J. (1992), 'Parliamentary Control of the Executive', in Lise Lyck (ed.), *Denmark and EC Membership Evaluated*, Pinter, London.

Newman, M. (1996), *Democracy, Sovereignty and the European Union*, Hurst, London.

Nozick, R. (1974), *Anarchy, State and Utopia*, Basil Blackwell, Oxford.

Nugent, N. (1994), *The Government and Politics of the European Union*, Macmillan, London, 3rd edn.

Pateman, C. (1970), *Participation and Democratic Theory*, Cambridge University Press, Cambridge.

Rawls, J. (1972), *A Theory of Justice*, Oxford University Press, Oxford.

Reif, K. (1993), 'Cultural Convergence and Cultural Diversity as Factors in European Identity', in Soledad Garcia (ed.), *European Identity and the Search for Legitimacy*, Pinter, London.

Schumpeter, J.A. (1976), *Capitalism, Socialism and Democracy*, Allen & Unwin, London.

Select Committee, *The 1996 Inter-Governmental Conference: The Agenda: Democracy and Efficiency: the Role of National Parliaments*. 24th report. Volume 1; Select Committee on European Legislation: Session 1994–95, HMSO, London.

Sinnott, R. (1992), *Political Culture. Public Opinion and the Internationalization of Governance*, University College Centre for Europe Economic and Public Affairs, Dublin.

Spicker, P. (1993), 'Concepts of Subsidiarity in the European Community', Paper presented at the Conference on Democracy and Subsidiarity, 12 November, University of Manchester.

Sørensen, H. and Woever, O. (1992), 'State, Society and Democracy and the Effect of the EC', in Lise Lyck (ed.), *Denmark and EC Membership Evaluated*, Pinter, London.

Stoker, G. (1991), *The Politics of Local Government*, Macmillan, Basingstoke.

Taylor, C. (1994), 'Sovereignty and European Monetary Arrangements', in Brouwer *et al.* (1994).

van Kersbergen, K. and Verbeek, B. (1994), 'The Politics of Subsidiarity in the Union', *Journal of Common Market Studies*, Vol. 32, No. 2, pp. 215–36.

Weiler, J. (1995), 'The Reformation of European Constitutionalism', *Journal of Common Market Studies* Annual Lecture, UACES Research Conference, 18 September 1995, to be published in the *Journal of Common Market Studies* (forthcoming).

Williams, S. (1991), 'Sovereignty and Accountability in the European Community', in Robert and Stanley Hoffmann (eds.), *The New European Community: Decisionmaking and Institutional Change*, Westview Press, Boulder, Colorado.

3 Reinventing Government: The European Experience

Tony Butcher

Throughout Western Europe, governments have recognised the importance of improving the efficiency and effectiveness of the public sector in response to economic and financial pressures, consumer demands for better public services and other forces. In the words of two observers, 'a desire for management reform has been sweeping across the public sector in all West European countries' during the 1980s and 1990s (Eliassen and Kooiman 1993: 205). Such developments have not, of course, been confined to Western Europe. The reform of the public sector is seen by Osborne and Gaebler (1992: 328–30) as a global phenomenon, while Aucoin maintains that there has been an 'internationalization of public management' (Aucoin 1990: 134; see also Hood 1995: 104–5). A recent report on public management developments in industrialised countries concluded that 'efficiency and effectiveness in the public sector and the way governmental institutions are managed are now part of the policy agenda of almost all governments' (OECD 1990a: 7).

Across the world, governments have attempted to restructure the public sector in order to make it 'slimmer and fitter', as well as attempting to improve its management (OECD 1994: 7) Echoing Osborne and Gaebler's idea of public sector reform as a global phenomenon, Hughes (1994: ix) argues that there has been a paradigm shift from the traditional bureaucratic model of public administration – which has dominated West European countries for most of the twentieth century – to a new model of public sector management. There has been a trend towards post-bureaucratic forms of organisation and the marketisation of the public sector (see Hughes 1994: 20). Many of the ideas

underlying these developments were made popular in
Osborne and Gaebler's best-selling book, *Reinventing Government* (1992), which discusses the transformation of the public sector in the United States.

The aim of this chapter is to examine the reinvention of
government phenomenon with reference to Western Europe.
The chapter begins with a discussion of the pressures which
lie behind public sector reform. It then surveys recent developments in the reform of the public sector in the United
Kingdom – the recognised leader in this field in Western
Europe – before reviewing similar developments in the countries of continental Europe.

PRESSURES FOR PUBLIC SECTOR REFORM

The 'reinvention of government' label covers a wide range
of ideas and initiatives. Thus Osborne and Gaebler (1992:
xix) use the phrase 'entrepreneurial government' to describe
developments in the United States. The developments they
describe are built upon such key principles as catalysing the
contribution of the public, private and voluntary sectors;
injecting more competition between service providers; em-
powering citizens; using market mechanisms rather than
bureaucratic mechanisms; focusing on results rather than
inputs; redefining clients as customers; and decentralising
authority. There is a great deal of overlap between the principles advocated by Osborne and Gaebler and the ideas of
the so-called 'new public management', a term used to describe 'the set of broadly similar administrative doctrines
which dominated the bureaucratic reform agenda in many
of the OECD group of countries from the 1970s' (Hood
1991: 3–4). The central doctrines of the new public management consist of a concentration on management, performance appraisal and efficiency; the disaggregation of public
bureaucracies into separately managed units; the use of quasi-
markets and contracting out to promote competition; a stress
on cost-cutting; and a management style which emphasises
targets, short-term contracts, rewards linked to performance
and the 'freedom to manage' (Rhodes 1991: 1; Hood 1991:
4–5). A major element of the new public management has

also been a greater emphasis on the needs of the consumers of public services (see Pollitt 1993: 180).

Drawing on surveys of public management developments in industrialised countries produced by the OECD (see 1990a: 9–10 and 14; 1993: 9–10; see also Wright, 1994), it is possible to identify several driving forces behind the 'reinventing government' phenomenon. The first has been the economic and financial pressures facing the governments of Western Europe and other industrialised countries in the last quarter of the twentieth century. Public sector reform has been driven by pressures to control public expenditure and reduce budget deficits. Such demands have been described as 'probably the greatest single pressure' for public sector reform in the countries of Western Europe (Wright 1994: 105). Thus reforms in public management in the United Kingdom in the 1980s and 1990s have been heavily influenced by the Conservative government's policy of reducing the share of national resources absorbed by the public sector, while reform programmes in other West European countries – including Belgium, Denmark, France, Italy, the Netherlands and Sweden – have also been motivated by the need to introduce tighter controls on public expenditure. The recessionary economic climate has sharpened awareness – by both governments and the public – of the size and cost of the public sector (OECD 1993: 9).

Such pressures, together with the growing demand for better and more expensive public services, have reinforced demands for greater efficiency and value for money in the operations of the public sector. Cost-effectiveness has become a major concern of governments. As Osborne and Gaebler (1992: 15) put it, there is a need to get 'ever more bang out of every buck'. Or in the more measured words of the Head of the UK Home Civil Service: 'Governments throughout the world are . . . under intense pressure to use every resource which advancing technology or new management techniques can provide in order to squeeze out a greater return for the taxpayer's money' (Butler 1994: 264).

A second pressure for the reinvention of government has been the recognition in many countries that public sector reform is 'an important element of the structural adjustment necessary to enable their businesses to compete effectively

in international markets' (OECD 1993: 9–10). In the words
of the OECD (1990b: v), 'the private sector depends on the
efficient operations of the public sector so that, for instance,
administrative requirements necessary for the functioning
of a modern economy can be met with minimum cost and
delay.' Governments are increasingly aware of the impact
of such key public services as education, manpower training and health care on the competitiveness of their economies (see OECD 1990a: 10) – reform of the public sector
in France, for example, has been seen as contributing to
the wider objective of increasing economic competitiveness
(see OECD 1990a: 49).

A third factor underpinning the reinvention of government
movement has been the recognition that the government
organisations responsible for delivering public services have
been insufficiently responsive to the consumers of their services.
Thus the OECD (1990a: 10) refers to concerns about what
is seen as the 'excessive complexity' of the administrative
structures, rules and procedures that the users of services
encounter in their relationships with the public sector. Perhaps the most striking response to such concerns has been
the launching of the UK government's *Citizen's Charter* initiative in 1991, but other West European countries have also
been very aware of the importance of consumer responsiveness in improving the quality of public service delivery.

The increasing emphasis on greater consumer responsiveness is, of course, an idea which has its origins in the literature of private sector management. The influence of what
has been termed 'business-type "managerialism"' (Hood 1994:
134) represents a fourth important strand in the reinvention
of government movement. Public sector management, which
has been attacked for its inefficiency, waste and unbusiness-
like procedures, as well as for its lack of closeness to the
'customers' of services, has been seen as inferior to private
sector management. Underpinning the managerialism paradigm are the assumptions that 'the capacities of modern
complex organizations to realize their objectives can be
enhanced by management structures and practices which
debureaucratize organizational systems' (Aucoin 1990:
117). As Hood (1994: 134) puts it: 'the new principles of
good management were held to be portable across organ-

izations, policy fields and the public/private sector divide.'

A fifth strand in the debate about the reform of the public sector has been the growing awareness of the potential of information technology in contributing to the management of the public sector (see Bellamy and Taylor 1994). As the OECD (1990a: 14), has observed, the attention of both politicians and senior officials in industrialised countries has been sparked by 'an awareness of the potential of IT to contribute to effectiveness as well as to efficiency'. The use of information technology not only assists in the achievement of better value for money, but also helps in the realisation of more customer-oriented services. A major example is the completion in the early 1990s of the massive computerisation of the UK social security system, a project designed to facilitate the development of the 'whole person concept', thereby enabling an individual claimant's entitlements to social security benefits to be examined in a comprehensive manner (see Butcher 1995b: 146). France, Germany and Portugal have also recognised the potential of information technology as an instrument in improving the efficiency of their public sectors (see, for example, Wright 1990: 127).

Finally, in the particular circumstances of Western Europe, one must not forget the impact of the EU on public sector reform in its member states, The requirement to implement EU Directives and to harmonise legislation in the fields of social, monetary and economic policies – together with the involvement of their civil servants in negotiations in the EU decision-making processes – has meant that Member States have had to make changes to their administrative institutions and procedures (see OECD 1993: 10). For example, one aim of the restructuring of Spanish government ministries in 1991 was to adapt the central government system to meet the challenges presented by the Single European Market (OECD 1992: 81). Also – to paraphrase Nugent's (1993: 55) description of the impact of EC membership on the UK government – the civil services of member states are 'increasingly penetrated by an EC awareness and sensitivity'. In the case of the United Kingdom, some central government departments 'have had substantially to reorient and reorganize themselves in the light of Community requirements' (Drewry 1995: 463).

As a result of such forces, the public administration model of the public services traditionally associated with the countries of Western Europe is being superseded by new approaches to the organisation and procedures of the public sector. The clear leader in these developments is the United Kingdom, whose public service reform programme has been described as 'arguably the most radical in Western Europe' (Wright 1994: 109).

REINVENTING GOVERNMENT, UK-STYLE

In late 1994, the then Cabinet minister responsible for the public services, David Hunt (1994: 4), declared that 'reinventing government' was 'an idea whose time has come'. A year earlier, talking about the Osborne and Gaebler book, his predecessor, William Waldegrave (Waldegrave 1993: 12), had claimed that the Conservative government had 'got there first' and, in many respects, 'had gone much further'. The head of the UK Home Civil Service has also indicated how the themes of Osborne and Gaebler's book match many of the post-1979 management initiatives in UK government (Butler 1994).

Hunt (1994: 4) has described the 'start of the process of Reinventing Government in the United Kingdom' as the privatisation programme begun by the Conservative government in the early 1980s. Described by one writer as the 'most radical change in the management of public services' (Walsh 1995: xi), privatisation has had a major impact on the shape and size of the UK public sector. By the mid-1990s, nearly 50 public companies had been sold to the private sector, including the key utilities of gas, water and electricity. As a result of the privatisation programme, about two-thirds of the nationalised industry sector and well over 900 000 jobs had been transferred to the private sector. The programme has been seen by some commentators as a development which has recast the boundaries between the public and private sectors in a way comparable to the nationalisation programme of the 1945–51 Attlee government (see Butcher 1992: 101).

The Conservative government's privatisation programme has been just one, albeit extremely significant, element in a long-term policy of reducing the size of the UK public sector. There has also been a significant decline in the size of the UK civil service since the Conservative government came into office in 1979. As a result of the dropping of certain functions, the contracting out of other functions, general streamlining and the benefits of information technology, the number of civil servants had been reduced to 524 000 by 1995 – 28 per cent less than in 1979. The Major government expects the size of the civil service to have fallen significantly below 500 000 by the end of the century. Although employment in local government has remained steady, employment in the UK National Health Service has also fallen since the early 1980s. Total public sector employment in the United Kingdom had fallen from just over 7 million in 1981 to just over 5.25 million by the middle of 1994 (*Economic Trends*, January 1995: 14).

The privatisation programme and the reductions in the size of the public sector payroll are both examples of attempts to change the size and shape of the UK public sector. In their attempts to restructure the public sector, Conservative governments since 1979 have also developed Osborne and Gaebler's (1992: 35) notion of 'catalytic government' – separating policy-making and direction from service delivery. Thus, as a result of the Next Steps programme launched in 1988, the service delivery or executive functions of central government are being progressively hived off from the policy-making core of government departments (see Butcher 1995a). By the end of 1995, nearly two-thirds of the UK civil service worked in semi-autonomous executive agencies and other organisations working on Next Steps lines. Recent reforms in the National Health Service have been based on the separation of the funder and provider functions through the introduction of a quasi-market in which district health authorities and fund-holding general practitioners purchase health care on behalf of their patients from a variety of providers (see Butcher 1995b).

The reforms in the National Health Service are just one example of the important changes which have taken place in the structure of the UK public sector at the sub-national level. In 1986, a whole tier of elected local government was removed with the abolition of the Greater London Council and the six metropolitan county councils. The structure of local government is being further changed as a result of the creation of unitary authorities in various parts of the country. The shape of UK local government has also been transformed by the transfer of important local authority activities – notably in the areas of education, housing and urban development – to the various quasi-autonomous non-governmental organisations (quangos), which are a growing feature of what has been called a 'skeletal state' (see Wilson 1995).

There have also been changes in the management of the UK public sector. An important theme has been the emphasis on the delegation of managerial responsibilities to smaller operational units, of which Next Steps agencies are one example. This has been accompanied by the development of a more performance-based culture, as typified by the setting of targets, the introduction of performance measures and the provision of rewards for managers who meet targets – all manifestations of Osborne and Gaebler's principle of 'results-oriented government'. Thus Next Steps agencies are headed by chief executives, on short-term contracts and salaries linked to performance, who are set performance targets and given important financial and managerial freedoms. Performance-related pay is increasingly used in the UK civil service. The use of performance indicators and performance-related pay is also an important feature in the management of the National Health Service and local government (see Butcher 1995b).

Competitive systems have been introduced into UK government – 'competitive government'. One particularly important initiative has been central government's market-testing programme, whereby certain functions are put out to tender to private contractors (see Butcher 1995c). The introduction of market-type mechanisms into central government emulates the process of compulsory competitive tendering, which has been such an important feature of recent reforms in the other two major types of UK public service delivery agency – local authorities and the National Health Service (see Butcher 1995b).

The 1980s and 1990s have also seen the introduction of a number of initiatives intended to empower the customers of public services – Osborne and Gaebler's notion of 'customer-driven government'. The centrepiece of this approach in the UK public sector has been the *Citizen's Charter*, underpinned by principles of public service, introduced by the Conservative government in 1991, and followed by the publication of a series of individual charters for particular public services. The accompanying Charter Mark scheme rewards those organisations that demonstrate excellence in meeting the principles of the Charter (see Butcher 1995c).

Thus a series of significant developments has taken place in the 'reinvention' of the UK public sector since the early 1980s. As Ridley (1995: 387) observes, these developments add up to a set of changes which go far beyond the introduction of new management techniques – they are 'a new model of the state'. It is a programme of reform which has involved the 'rolling back' of public administration (Ridley 1995: 388). For some commentators, however, this programme has failed to 'roll back the state'. On the contrary, critics point to the centralisation of functions formerly carried out by elected local authorities and the proliferation of unelected quangos as evidence of the 'nationalisation' of the state. In the words of one commentator, 'the Leviathan of the modern state has been streamlined and reinvigorated rather than shrunk' (Jenkins 1995a; see also Jenkins 1995b).

DEVELOPMENTS IN PUBLIC SECTOR REFORM IN CONTINENTAL EUROPE

The United Kingdom has not been alone in its attempts to reinvent the public sector. A study of the series of reports on public sector management produced by the Public Management Committee of the OECD since 1990 reveals that the governments of other West European countries have also made the reform of the structure and management of the public sector a major plank in their policies. A brief listing of some of the programmes launched, and documents published, by these countries since the early 1980s provides an indication of the importance attached to the reform of public sector management in the countries of continental Europe (for fuller details, see the various OECD reports published since 1990; see also Wright 1994).

In 1983 the Danish government launched its *Modernisation Programme on the Public Service,* which was followed eight years later by the submission of *The Public Sector in the Year 2000* programme to the Danish Parliament. The Irish government published a White Paper on public sector reform entitled *Serving the Country Better* in 1985. In 1988 the Austrian Council of Ministers introduced the *Administrative Management Project,* whose aims included reductions in the cost of administrative activity, a concentration on management tasks and an improvement in the 'citizen orientation' of public administration. A year later, the French government committed itself to a major reform of public sector management with the publication of a prime ministerial circular entitled *Renewal of the Public Service,* which was followed two years later by the setting up of a committee with the same title, chaired by the Minister for the Public Service. Also in 1989, the Spanish government published a discussion document on *Reflections on Modernisation of the Public Administration.* The Swedish government's *Administrative Reform Programme* was announced in 1990. In the same year, the Italian government launched a project entitled *Functionality and Efficiency of the Public Administration.* Greece introduced a *Programme of Administrative Modernisation: 1993–95* in 1992. Also in 1992, the Finnish government launched the *Government Programme for Public Sector Reform* and the Dutch government published a report entitled *Towards Results-oriented Management.* In the late 1980s and early 1990s, Norway appointed Royal Commissions on the reorganisation and adaptation of managerial and control systems; organisational and budgetary reforms; and a better organisational model for state-owned enterprises. The Swiss government introduced the *Management Control Project* in the early 1990s.

This growing concern with public sector reform in the countries of continental Europe has been reflected in a series of significant developments. Following the discussion of initiatives in the United Kingdom in the previous section of this chapter, these developments will be discussed under three main headings: (1) attempts to change the size and shape of the public sector; (2) efforts to improve the management of the public sector; and (3) attempts to improve the responsiveness of public services to users. (This section draws on the regular surveys undertaken since 1990 by the Public

Management Committee of the OECD on the key initiatives to improve public sector management: OECD, 1990a; 1991; 1992; 1993; 1994.)

Restructuring the public sector in Western Europe has been manifested in a number of ways. Economic and financial pressures have meant that an important goal of many countries has been to limit the size of their public sectors. Thus, in 1992, the Dutch government – which has the slogan 'Fewer civil servants but a better service' (OECD 1990a: 74) – set targets for staff reductions in each government ministry. In 1990, the Swedish government announced a policy of reducing its national administration by 10 per cent over a three-year period. Finland has also set specific targets for reducing the size of its civil service. Restrictions have also been introduced on the replacement of Italian civil servants. In 1991 the Greek government introduced a policy of freezing public sector recruitment as part of a policy of reducing public expenditure. In 1993, the French government announced a freeze on civil service salaries and the reduction of posts by 1.5 per cent per year (see Stevens 1994: 70).

The privatisation of state assets has also been an important approach in attempts to change the size and shape of the public sector in many countries (see Vickers and Wright 1988). The most radical exponent of privatisation in continental Europe has been France. A privatisation programme was established by the Chirac government in the late 1980s (see Bauer 1988). A new round was launched in 1993, involving the sale of all or part of some 21 public sector groups. Other West European countries have also launched privatisation programmes. In the early 1990s, Italy introduced an ambitious privatisation programme involving the sale of banks, insurance companies and the part-sale of the holding organisation for the country's telecommunications industry. Although privatisation in Germany in the 1980s has been described as 'timid' (Essen 1988: 70), the Treuhand agency – the body charged in 1990–4 with the restructuring of the industries of the former East Germany and arranging their disposal to the private sector – sold over 8000 firms (see Konig 1993: 142–4). The German government has subsequently restructured the state-owned post and telecommunications services in preparation for their privatisation.

In 1989 the Portugese government initiated a large-scale privatisation programme covering the majority of the companies nationalised by the previous socialist governments, notably in the banking and insurance sectors. In Denmark the 'Postgiro' – the postal banking and payment services – was partially privatised in 1993. Finland launched a large privatisation programme in 1991. Austria, Belgium, Ireland, Greece, the Netherlands, Norway and Spain have also introduced privatisation initiatives. Even in Sweden, the traditional home of social democracy, the privatisation of state-owned assets was a central component of the public sector reform programme when the centre-right coalition government was in office from 1991–4. Twenty company groups were privatised during this period. Although the Social Democratic government elected at the end of 1994 has stated that the policy of 'ideological' privatisation is at an end, it 'has not ruled out the policy as such should the advantages be there' (Stein 1995: 156).

Although the concept of privatisation is generally used to refer to the sale of state-owned assets, it is also used to describe the use of market-type mechanisms in the public sector. A key feature of the 'new public management', such mechanisms have been an important feature of public sector reforms in many West European countries. The Scandinavian countries have been particularly associated with developments of this kind. Thus Sweden has increased competition between the public and private sectors in the delivery of services, especially in education and health care. In neighbouring Denmark, central government departments and agencies are required to market test all activities suitable for contracting out. Finland has encouraged the market testing of support services.

As we saw earlier, a key feature of the reform of central government in the United Kingdom has been the separation of the policy-making and executive functions through the creation of executive agencies – a concept which has affinities with the ministerial agency concept found in the Swedish administrative system. Since the early 1990s one aim of the Dutch government has been the creation of a 'policy-oriented central government', including the establishment of agencies. Some Scandinavian countries are reassessing their use of the agency concept (OECD 1993: 10). In the early 1990s, Denmark established a number of 'free agencies' with four-year budgets and increased managerial freedoms.

Another major theme of the restructuring of the public sector in many West European countries has been the decentralisation of authority and responsibility from central government to lower levels of government. The decentralisation programme introduced in France during 1982–6 – described as 'a decisive reform toward the modernization of the state' (de Montricher 1995: 416) – gave more responsibilities to sub-national authorities, with an accompanying transfer of financial resources (see Mazey 1990). Since 1992, the focus has shifted to the administrative deconcentration of government ministries. Italy has continued its policy of devolving responsibilities to authorities at the regional and local levels (see, for example, Weiss 1989). In Spain, there has been a significant transfer of powers from central government to the Autonomous Communities (regions) in education and other fields.

Since the mid-1980s, all four Scandinavian countries have introduced so-called 'free local government' experiments, designed to give local authorities more freedom to meet local needs (see Stewart and Stoker 1989). In 1993, the Swedish government introduced a new system of government grants designed to put local authorities on 'an equal financial footing'. Local authorities are also to be given 'all possible freedom to shape their own activities' (OECD 1994: 65). In 1991, the Dutch government introduced what has been described as a 'decentralization impulse' (OECD 1992: 63), involving the devolution of central government responsibilities to local authorities, provinces and regional bodies. Belgium has had a far-reaching programme of decentralising major powers from central government to sub-national authorities since 1988. The early 1990s saw the devolution of powers in the fields of education, health and industrial policy, with the result that the powers of central government are now refocused on the traditional functions of 'oversight and security (fiscal, economic, social, physical)' (OECD 1993: 37).

The reinvention of government in Western Europe has not been restricted to restructuring the size and shape of the public sector. Like the United Kingdom, many continental

European countries have also introduced a public sector management style which emphasises targets, short-term contracts, incentives and the freedom to manage. Performance-based pay regimes have been introduced for the civil services in Denmark, Germany, Norway and Switzerland. Ireland has introduced a performance-related pay scheme for certain senior civil servants and the chief executives of commercial state-sponsored bodies. The Netherlands has introduced bonus payments across the public service to reward performance. Fixed-term contracts have been established for the directors-general of agencies in Sweden.

Another important manifestation of the managerial approach has been the delegation of managerial responsibility to units and managers – what the OECD (1992: 12) refers to as 'managing for results'. Thus, a results-oriented approach to budgeting was introduced in Finland in 1993 . In 1992, the Norwegian government introduced a programme to develop performance indicators and performance monitoring systems across the public sector. Devolved budgeting has been taken up by the French government, which has established cost centres ('centres of accountability') to allow more flexible management. However, the effect of this particular initiative does not seem to have been very significant; by 1992, there were only 85 such centres, involving only about 33 000 officials (see Stevens 1994: 71).

As we saw in the previous section, a key initiative in the creation of a more responsive and customer-friendly public service in the United Kingdom has been the *Citizen's Charter* programme. A similar initiative has been introduced in France, with the *Public Service Charter* launched in 1992. Like its UK counterpart, the French *Charter* has the aim of making public services more 'user-centred' (OECD 1993: 70). Also, like the *Citizen's Charter*, the French *Charter* stresses the key principles of public service. There have been similar developments in other EC countries. In Belgium, a *Public Service Users' Charter* was formulated at the end of 1992. The Portugese government set up a *Public Services Quality Charter* a year later, along with *Quality in Public Services Awards*.

There are, of course, other mechanisms for emphasising the customer orientation. Thus Scandinavian countries have experimented in the setting up of so-called 'one stop shops'.

The Norwegian government has integrated the field services of a number of central government and local government agencies through the establishment of 'public administration service offices'. Neighbouring Sweden is experimenting with 'citizens' bureaux', which gather all central and local government services under one roof. Developments in information technology have allowed the Portugese government to set up multi-media, computerised kiosks designed to provide members of the public with clear and up-to-date information about public services.

CONCLUSIONS

Thus a series of important developments have taken place in the reform of the public sector in the countries of Western Europe. The reinvention of government has encompassed a wide range of initiatives – the privatisation of state-owned companies, the greater use of market-type mechanisms, cuts in public service staff, the decentralisation of authority to more autonomous units, the development of a performance-based culture, the emphasis on greater responsiveness in the delivery of public services, etc. As we have seen, these approaches to public sector reform are increasingly shared by a number of West European countries.

Having said this, however, it is important to recognise that there are differences in emphasis in the reform programmes of these countries. Indeed, it is possible to categorise the countries of Western Europe according to the extent to which they have developed their public sectors along the lines of the principles of the 'new public management'. Thus, Hood (1994: 132–3) identifies the United Kingdom and Sweden as countries which have given 'a particularly strong emphasis' to some aspects of this set of administrative doctrines. Denmark, France, Ireland, the Netherlands and Norway are countries which have provided some 'marked shifts' in this direction. Germany, Greece, Spain and Switzerland, however, are classified as countries which have given only a low emphasis to the principles of the new public management.

A clear example of the differences in emphasis in public sector reform can be found in the area of privatisation.

Although the sale of state-owned assets has been an important theme of developments across Western Europe, this process has been much more pronounced in the United Kingdom and France than in other countries. Also, as Vickers and Wright (1988: 5) point out, whereas privatisation in the United Kingdom, France, Greece and Portugal has been influenced by anti-statist views – the desire to roll back the frontiers of state activity – this has not been a major factor in the privatisation programmes of other countries. Thus privatisation in Germany is based on 'a broad consensus of all sectors and social groups involved' (Von Freyend 1995: 129). The sale of state-owned companies in Belgium has also been based on political and social consensus rather than on ideological pressures (Schrans 1994: 117). Both Germany and Belgium are, of course, coalition-based countries with a tradition of consensual policy-making.

Differences are also apparent in the emphasis given to other aspects of public sector reform. As we have seen, a major feature of the reinvention of government in the United Kingdom has been in the organisation of central government, notably the Next Steps programme and the market testing initiative. Germany, however, has left the form of its public service at its federal level 'largely intact' (Hood 1995: 109). Public sector initiatives at the federal level in Germany have emphasised personnel management – in-service training, recruitment, flexible working time, etc. – and the use of information technology (OECD 1990a: 55; 1993: 79). Public sector reform in Germany during the 1990s has also been especially concerned with 'rebuilding public administration in the East' (Sturm 1992: 112), setting up state and local administrations, and improving public management, in the five eastern Länder in the wake of German unification (OECD 1993: 76) .

Also, as Jones (1993: 11–12) has pointed out, although such traditionally highly centralised countries as France, Spain and Italy, together with the Scandinavian countries, have decentralised powers from central government to sub-national authorities, the United Kingdom has experienced the increasing centralisation of power in the hands of central government ministers and quasi-governmental bodies appointed by ministers. A recent examination of current trends in local government in various West European countries concludes that local government in continental Europe and the United Kingdom is 'moving in quite different directions' (Blair 1991: 56).

The idea that the responsibility for performing tasks should be taken at the lowest effective level of government – the principle of subsidiarity – was a central theme of the 1992 Maastricht Treaty on European Union (see Peterson 1994). The Treaty was followed by the establishment of the Committee of the Regions, an advisory body set up to provide sub-national authorities with a greater say in the development of the Community. Cram and Richardson (1994: 21) have observed that the 'logical conclusion' of the principle of subsidiarity is an enlarged role for local and regional bodies. As Jones (1993: 12) puts it, however, 'The theory of subsidiarity is more commonly understood and practised in the rest of Europe than in the UK.'

Despite such differences, there are common elements in the reform programmes of many West European countries. As Hughes (1994: 19), writing about public sector reforms in industrialised countries, observes, a key feature of such initiatives is the similarity across countries. The reform programmes of the 1980s and 1990s, with their emphasis on improving efficiency and effectiveness and the way governmental organisations are managed, have clearly had significant implications for both the structure and management of the public sectors of the countries of Western Europe. The 'reinvention of government' in Western Europe may also have a wider significance – its possible relevance for the countries of Eastern Europe. As one writer observes, the experience of public sector reform in Western Europe (and other Western countries) could well hold 'some pertinent and profitable lessons' for the new European democracies (see Jones 1995: 17).

60   *The Future of Europe*

REFERENCES

Aucoin, P. (1990), 'Administrative Reform in Public Management: Paradigms, Principles, Paradoxes and Pendulums', *Governance*, Vol. 3, No. 2, pp. 115–37.
Bauer, M. (1988), 'The Politics of State-directed Privatisation: The Case of France 1986–88', *West European Politics*, Vol. 11, No. 1, pp. 49–60.
Bellamy, C. and Taylor, J. (1994), 'Reinventing Government in the Information Age', *Public Money and Management*, Vol. 14, No. 3, pp. 59–62.
Blair, P. (1991), 'Trends in Local Autonomy and Democracy: Reflections from a European Perspective', in R. Batley and G. Stoker (eds.), *Local Government in Europe: Trends and Developments*, Macmillan, Basingstoke.
Butcher, T. (1992), 'Rolling Back the State: The Conservative Governments and Privatisation 1979–91', *Talking Politics*, Vol. 4, No. 2, pp. 101–5.
Butcher, T. (1995a), 'A New Civil Service? The Next Steps Agencies', in R. Pyper and L. Robins (eds.), *Governing the UK in the 1990s*, Macmillan, Basingstoke.
Butcher, T. (1995b), *Delivering Welfare*, Open University Press, Buckingham.
Butcher, T. (1995c), 'The Major Government and Whitehall: The Civil Service at the Crossroads', *Teaching Public Administration*, Vol. XV, No. 1, pp. 19–31.
Butler, Sir R. (1994), 'Reinventing British Government', *Public Administration*, Vol. 72, No. 2, pp. 263–70.
Cram, L. and Richardson, J. (1994), 'Citizenship and Local Democracy: A European Perspective', *Public Money and Management*, Vol. 14, No. 4, pp. 17–24.
de Montricher, N. (1995), 'Decentralization in France', *Governance*, Vol. 8, No. 3, pp. 405–18.
Drewry, G. (1995), 'The Case of the United Kingdom', in S.A. Pappas (ed.), *National Administrative Procedures for the Preparation and Implementation of Community Decisions*, European Institute of Public Administration, Maastricht.
Eliassen, K.A. and Kooiman, J. (eds.) (1993), *Managing Public Organizations: Lessons from Contemporary European Experience*, 2nd edn, Sage, London.
Essen, J. (1988), '"Symbolic Privatisation": The Politics of Privatisation in West Germany', *West European Politics*, Vol. 11, No. 1, pp. 61–73.
Hood, C. (1991), 'A Public Management for all Seasons?', *Public Administration*, Vol. 69, No. 1, pp. 3–19.
Hood, C. (1994), *Explaining Economic Policy Reversals*, Open University Press, Buckingham.
Hood, C. (1995), 'Contemporary Public Management: A New Global Paradigm?', *Public Policy and Administration*, Vol. 10, No. 2, pp. 104–17.
Hughes, O. (1994), *Public Management and Administration: An Introduction*, Macmillan, Basingstoke.

Hunt, D. (1994), 'Reinventing Government', speech to the *Reinventing Government Conference* at The Merchant Centre, London, 1 December.

Jenkins, S. (1995a), 'Party of Freedom has Shackled us all to the State', *The Sunday Times*, 8 October.

Jenkins, S. (1995b), *Accountable to None: The Tory Nationalisation of Britain*, Hamish and Hamilton, London.

Jones, G.W. (1993), *International Trends in Public Administration*, LSE Public Policy Paper No. 7, Department of Government, London School of Economics.

Jones, R. (1995), 'Reinventing Government in Transition Economies: The New Public Administration in Eastern Europe', *Teaching Public Administration*, Vol. XV, No. 1, pp. 1–18.

Konig, K. (1993), 'Administrative Transformation in Eastern Germany', *Public Administration*, Vol. 71, Nos 1/2, pp. 135–49.

Mazey, S. (1990), 'Power outside Paris', in P. A. Hall, J. Hayward and H. Machin (eds.), *Developments in French Politics*, Macmillan, Basingstoke.

Nugent, N. (1993), 'The European Dimension', in P. Dunleavy, A. Gamble, I. Holliday and G. Peele (eds.), *Developments in British Politics 4*, Macmillan, Basingstoke.

Organisation for Economic Cooperation and Development (1990a), *Public Management Developments: Survey 1990*, OECD, Paris.

Organisation for Economic Cooperation and Development (1990b), *Financing Public Expenditures Through User Charges*, Occasional Papers on Public Management, OECD, Paris.

Organisation for Economic Cooperation and Development (1991), *Public Management Developments: Update 1991*, OECD, Paris.

Organisation for Economic Cooperation and Development (1992), *Public Management Developments: Update 1992*, OECD, Paris.

Organisation for Economic Cooperation and Development (1993), *Public Management Developments: Survey 1993*, OECD, Paris.

Organisation for Economic Cooperation and Development (1994), *Public Management Developments: Update 1994*, OECD, Paris.

Osborne, D. and Gaebler, T. (1992), *Reinventing Government: How the Entrepreneurial Spirit is Transforming the Public Sector*, Addison-Wesley, Reading, Massachusetts.

Peterson, J. (1994), 'Subsidiarity: A Definition to Suit any Vision', *Parliamentary Affairs*, Vol. 47, No. 1, pp. 119–32.

Pollitt, C. (1993), *Managerialism and the Public Services*, 2nd edn, Blackwell, Oxford.

Rhodes, R.A.W. (1991), 'Introduction', *Public Administration*, Vol. 69, No. 1, pp. 1–2.

Ridley, F.F. (1995), 'Reinventing British Government', *Parliamentary Affairs*, Vol. 48, No. 3, pp. 387–400.

Schrans, H. (1994), 'Belgium: Asset Transfers Get Under Way', in R. Lord (ed.), *Privatisation Yearbook 1994*, Privatisation International, London.

Stein, P. (1995), 'Sweden: Hiatus after Sales', in H. Gibbon (ed.), *Privatisation Yearbook 1995*, Privatisation International, London.

Stevens, A. (1994), 'The French Civil Service: Some Comparative Aspects', Appendix 20 in Treasury and Civil Service Committee, Fifth Report, Session 1993–94, *The Role of the Civil Service*, Vol. III, HC 27–III, HMSO, London.

Stewart, J. and Stoker, G. (1989), 'The "Free Local Government" Experiments and the Programme of Public Service Reform in Scandanvia', in C. Crouch and D. Marquand (eds.), *The New Centralism: Britain Out of Step in Europe?*, Blackwell, Oxford.

Sturm, R. (1992), 'Government at the Centre', in G. Smith, W.E. Patterson, P.H. Merkl and S. Padgett (eds.), *Developments in German Politics*, Macmillan, Basingstoke.

Treasury and Civil Service Committee (1994), Fifth Report, Session 1993–94, *The Role of the Civil Service*, Vol. 1, HC. 27–1, HMSO, London.

Vickers, J. and Wright, V. (1988), 'The Politics of Industrial Privatisation in Western Europe: An Overview', *West European Politics*, Vol. 11, No. 1, pp. 1–30.

Von Freyend, E.J. (1995), 'Germany: Pursuing Private Enterprise', in H. Gibbon (ed.), *Privatisation Yearbook 1995*, Privatisation International, London.

Waldegrave, W. (1993), *Public Service and the Future: Reforming Britain's Bureaucracies*, Conservative Political Centre, London.

Walsh, K. (1995), *Public Services and Market Mechanisms: Competition, Contracting Out and the New Public Management*, Macmillan, Basingstoke.

Weiss, L. (1989), 'Regional Economic Policy in Italy', in C. Crouch and D. Marquand (eds.), *The New Centralism: Britain Out of Step in Europe?*, Blackwell, Oxford.

Wilson, D. (1995), 'Quangos in the Skeletal State', *Parliamentary Affairs*, Vol. 48, No. 2, pp. 181–91.

Wright, V. (1990), 'The Administrative Machine: Old Problems and New Dilemmas', in P.A. Hall, J. Hayward and H. Machin (eds.), *Developments in French Politics*, Macmillan, Basingstoke.

Wright, V. (1994), 'Reshaping the State: The Implications for Public Administration', *West European Politics*, Vol. 17, No. 1, pp. 102–37.

4 Citizenship in the European Union: The Post-Maastricht Scenario
Dave Edye

INTRODUCTION

The Maastricht Treaty states that all nationals of the member states are now citizens of the European Union (EU). The inclusion of the notion of an EU citizenship, is at the core of an attempt by the EU to bring its predominantly elite-driven integration project closer to the people. This is part of a wider movement throughout Europe in recent years, which has seen politicians of all hues and persuasions embracing the notion of 'citizenship' as the way to renew their appeal to the voters. In the last 20 years, citizens have been active in Western Europe in providing, for example, much of the initial impetus leading to the formation of the Green Party in the Federal Republic of Germany. Citizens Action Groups (*Bürgerinitiativen*) were set up to oppose the building of nuclear power plants, and the decision in the late 1970s to station Cruise and Pershing missiles on their soil. Many of the opposition groups in East and Central Europe pre-1989 too were grouped under umbrella organisations called citizens' groups. The demise of communism and the apparent triumph of liberal democracy has also resulted in a shift of focus from the undemocratic nature of regimes in East/Central Europe and the Soviet Union, to questions about the nature and operation of political institutions and practices in Western Europe at national and supra-national (EU) level.

The new impetus towards closer economic and political integration in the European Community, which began with the Single European Act (SEA) in 1987 and continued with the signing of the Maastricht Treaty (Treaty on European

Union – TEU) in 1991, has come up against the rocks of citizens' scepticism and opposition. The Danish 'No' in their first referendum on Maastricht in 1992, followed by the close result in the French referendum later that year, has been followed by the Norwegian rejection of EU membership in 1994. All these expressions of popular dissatisfaction and opposition have forced Member States and the European Commission to attempt to close the distance between the EU policy processes and institutions and their constituents.

This chapter begins by considering some of the theoretical issues surrounding the general concept of citizenship, and then focuses on some of those issues in relation to EU citizenship, and particularly in light of its inclusion in the Maastricht Treaty. The specific kinds of rights that may be described as forming the basis of citizenship of the EU are then critically considered. In addition, some comment is made on the EU's attempt to create a 'sense of belonging'. Finally, there is an assessment of possible future developments concerning the whole issue of citizenship as the integration process widens and deepens.

THEORY OF CITIZENSHIP

For Marshall (1950), citizenship has three crucial components: civil rights, political rights and social rights. Each of these rights has developed out of particular historical circumstances:

1. Civil rights refer to those individual rights like freedom of speech and faith, and the right to own property, which writers such as John Locke championed against the absolutist state in the seventeenth century. It took until the last decades of the eighteenth century for these rights to be codified, for example in the US Constitution, and the Declaration of Rights that accompanied the French Revolution. Marshall argues that the development of these rights laid the basis for the rise of capitalism and the formation of new class inequalities.
2. Political rights arose during the nineteenth century, when struggles were fought to ensure a greater franchise and greater representation for the people in elected assemblies.

3. Social rights refer to all those rights, such as health care education and benefits, that citizens have demanded under the provisions of the welfare state in the twentieth century.

For Marshall, these rights have gone a long way to mitigating the worst effects of capitalism and, although they have not brought about full equality, they have at least improved all citizens' participation in the social world. Critics of Marshall have focused on his rather rosy view of the way in which rights have evolved and may continue to evolve, and their apparent basis on the position of *men* in society, and insistence on the relationship between citizenship and social class rather than other forms of stratification such as gender, race or age (Jones and Wallace 1992). Walby (1994) and Lister (1990) have questioned whether women have unrestricted rights as citizens or only as dependants of men. Smith (1989) and Harrison (1991) suggest, also, that there may be differential access to citizenship rights on the basis of race. But all have agreed on the importance of stressing the link and interdependence of these rights (Walby 1994).

THE EU AND CITIZENSHIP: THEORETICAL CONSIDERATIONS

There are two schools of thought on whether citizenship can have any real meaning beyond the nation-state level in Europe. Meehan (1993) and Close (1995) take a guardedly optimistic view that the EU (formerly the EEC/EC) has been and is engaged in a process in which there is a slow but steady accretion of citizenship rights. Aron (1974) took the opposite view, arguing that it was not possible to envisage a European citizenship.[1] Meehan's more confident view is based on a refutation Aron (1974).

The main elements of Aron's argument are first, that national and Community authorities provide a group of rights that are of a different order from one another. Secondly, European citizenship would entail the transfer of legal and political powers from national to EC level (in a similar fashion to the transfer of Scottish and English citizenship to a single

British citizenship with the 1707 Act of Union). Thirdly, citizens can insist that a nation-state respect their rights because the state can demand that citizens fulfil their duties to defend the state, but no multinational polity has the same authority. Finally, Aron argues that when he was writing, the early 1970s, there was no popular demand for a European federation which would take responsibility for legal-political rights and economic regulation, and which could command the duties of citizens.[2]

Meehan takes Aron to task for his over-reliance on the nation-state as the sole guardian and promoter of citizenship. Quoting Heater, she emphasises that citizenship can adhere to any unit from the 'small town to the whole globe'.[3] Meehan's view is not that EU citizenship will replace Member State citizenship, but that it has already extended and strengthened in a significant way a range of rights for citizens. The model is the Roman Empire in which citizens were able to rely on more than one source of legal protection when claiming their rights. Meehan points out that the nation-state and the EU developed at different historical times, and most people now accept the connection between the three sets of rights outlined by Marshall.

The effect of all this has been that the EU has become increasingly active in establishing a measure of social rights, which can be considered as having enhanced the notion of citizenship. The promotion of social rights detaches them from any Member State locus and so contributes in Meehan's view to the creation of 'multiple identities', whereby citizens may appeal to a European set of rights as well as to their own national set of rights. Another aspect of this situation is that judgments made by the European Court of Justice (ECJ) have acted as catalysts in forcing member states to introduce national legislation to conform to EU norms or amend conflicting domestic practice.[4]

CITIZENSHIP AND THE MAASTRICHT TREATY

Although the EEC was concerned initially with workers not citizens, citizenship was mentioned even in the early years. Levi-Sandri, the Commissioner responsible for overseeing the implementation of the Articles concerning free movement of labour in the Rome Treaty, commented that the idea of a migrant worker would soon be replaced by a 'European worker', which represented an 'incipient form of European citizenship' (Levi-Sandri 1961). The next mention appears at the Paris Summit in 1974 with the attempt to establish some kind of social rights for citizens.[5] In 1976 the Tindemans Report, 'Towards European Citizenship', set up a working party to study whether social rights could be extended to EC nationals resident in other Member States.

The major impetus, however began in the 1980s with the decision by the Council of Ministers to set up an ad hoc committee, chaired by Pietro Adonnino, whose subsequent report (1985) asked the Council to invite EC institutions to bring into existence 'the citizen as a participant in the political process in the Community' (Meehan 1993: 147).

This was the background to the establishment of 'Citizenship of the Union' in Part Two of the TEU. It is useful to outline the main points of the Treaty Articles before considering their significance:

Article 8 establishes 'citizenship of the Union', and 'every person holding the nationality of a Member State shall be a citizen of the Union'. Article 8(2), declares 'citizens of the Union shall enjoy the right conferred by this Treaty and shall be subject to the duties imposed thereby'.

Article 8a: Citizens 'shall have the right to move and reside freely' within the Union, subject to 'the limitations and conditions' laid down in the Treaty.

Article 8b: Every citizen shall have the right to vote and stand as candidates in municipal elections in any Member State on the same basis as nationals of that state, and also the right to vote and stand as a candidate in elections to the European Parliament (EP) on the same basis as nationals of that state.

Article 8c: Citizens residing in a country where their national government is not represented can seek and expect the same degree of diplomatic or consular protection as nationals of that Member State.

Article 8d: Citizens shall have the right to petition the EP and apply to the Ombudsman, in conjunction with Articles 138d and 138e respectively.

Article 8e: The Commission would report by 31 December 1993, and every three years thereafter, to the EP, the Council and the Economic and Social Committee on the application of the provisions on citizenship.

The Right to Vote and Stand for Election

As the Commission noted in its Reflection Report, the right to vote and stand as a candidate in European and municipal elections is 'the most noteworthy and visible application' of the concept of citizenship, as a way of creating a 'sense of belonging'.[6]

There are at present just under 4 million EU nationals resident in another Member State. The granting of the right to vote and stand as a candidate in municipal and European elections only poses the question why the same rights were not extended to national elections. It may be that Member States do not attach the same importance to municipal and European elections as they do to national elections, and so this qualified right presented no difficulty. But there is a certain illogicality in the position. The practical difficulties of ensuring this right are enormous and its exercise so far has been minimal (see Tables 4.1 and 4.2).

The right to vote and stand in an election has been probably the most contentious issue concerning citizenship within member states, and was one of the principal reasons for the close result in the French referendum on the Maastricht Treaty. The main reason for this controversy stems from the requirement in most Member States that only nationals may vote in elections.[7] Although some member states (Ireland, Denmark, the Netherlands and Sweden) allow long-term residents the right to vote in local elections, the extension of this right to national elections was unacceptable.[8] The United Kingdom is, perhaps, unique in this regard, allowing not only Republic of Ireland citizens but also Commonwealth citizens (in both cases non-nationals) the same rights to vote and stand as candidates as British nationals in all UK elec-

Table 4.1 Elections to the European Parliament, June 1994: Participation of Non-national Voters[1]

	Potential Voters among Non-national Residents	Non-national Voters Registered
Belgium	471 000	24 000 (5.1%)
Denmark	27 042	6 719 (24.5%)
Germany	1 369 863	80 000 (5.84%)
Greece	40 000	628 (1.57%)
Spain	172 466	24 227 (14.5%)
France	1 100 000	47 632 (4.35%)
Ireland (excluding UK nationals)	approx. 17 000	6 000 (35.29%)
Italy	99 100	2 000 (2.02%)
Luxembourg	105 000	6 907 (6.58%)
Netherlands	160 000	15 000 (9.37%)
Portugal	30 519	715 (2.34%)
United Kingdom (excluding Irish nationals)	approx. 400 000	7 755 (1.94%)

Source: European Commission (1995).

Table 4.2 Elections to the European Parliament, June 1994: Non-national Candidates

	Non-national Union Candidates	Candidates Elected
Belgium	18	
Denmark	1	
Germany	12	1
Greece	5	
Spain	1	
France	5	
Ireland	1	
Italy	2	
Luxembourg	8	
Netherlands	2	
Portugal	0	
United Kingdom	2	

Source: European Commission (1995).

tions. The question of nationality and whether this new right from the TEU will lead to a greater sense of belonging is discussed below.

Free Movement

The importance of this right was stressed by Advocate-General Jacobs in the case of Collins:

> The nationals of each Member State are entitled to live, work, and do business in all other Member States on the same basis as the local population. They must not simply be tolerated as aliens, but welcomed by the authorities of the host state as Community nationals who are entitled, within the scope of application of the Treaty 'to all privileges and advantages enjoyed by the nationals of the host state'. No other aspect of Community law touches the individual more directly or does more to foster the sense of common identity and shared destiny without which 'the ever-closer union among the peoples of Europe' proclaimed by the preamble to the Treaty would be an empty slogan.[9]

It is nationals of the EU Member States that enjoy the rights of free movement within the EU. The right to free movement as envisaged in the 1957 Rome Treaty was designed to ease labour market tensions, particularly in southern Italy. It applied to workers not citizens, but subsequent regulations and directives extended that right to a worker's dependants, and now to all EU nationals.[10]

But the right to free movement is not unlimited. Nationals of EU Member States who are not economically active may have their rights to free movement curtailed and may be refused entry to a Member State or be deported from it (Macdonald and Blake 1995: 217–27). Member States are permitted to curtail free movement on the grounds of public policy, public security or public health.[11] However, the European Court of Justice (ECJ) has ruled that the general use of an exclusion order from mainland Britain against a person from Northern Ireland is contrary to free movement provisions contained within the Treaty.

Other Rights

The remaining rights that the TEU provides relate to diplomatic and consular protection, and the right to petition Parliament and apply to the Ombudsman. It is not clear, however, exactly how the right to diplomatic and consular protection is being put into effect – the evacuation of EU citizens from Rwanda in 1994 was organised through ad hoc bilateral arrangements. According to the Commission Report the second right (of petition), and its application, has not improved significantly on previous practice. Indeed, as a result of procedural difficulties, the recently appointed Ombudsman, J. Söderman of Finland, whose period of appointment coincides with the election of each new European Parliament was much delayed.

Non-EU nationals who have become permanently settled in a Member State, do not enjoy the same rights as EU nationals. As Spencer notes, 'the position of non-EU nationals living and working in the Union is grossly unsatisfactory. Their second-class status becomes more and more of a handicap as the concept of citizenship is developed to give more rights to the nationals of Member States' (Spencer 1995: 116).

For both EU nationals and particularly non-EU nationals, the enjoyment of full rights as European citizens is a distant reality. In terms of Marshall's three categories, civil rights may be fully established for EU citizens if and when the European Convention on Human Rights is enshrined as part of EU law. Even then, the exclusion of non-EU nationals would still present a formidable challenge to the EU's own definition of itself as the promoter and protector of basic human rights.

Political rights have been partly introduced, and recent years have seen a much more concerted move by the Commission to widen the definition of the 'social'. One other important factor to be considered is the strength of nationalism, still rooted in the nation-state, which may militate against this attempt to create a 'Euro-citizenship'.

IS BEING THE SAME AS FEELING? IDENTITY AND LOYALTY IN THE EUROPEAN UNION

If the EU is interested in creating some kind of identity or 'sense of belonging', then the question is raised whether it is engaged in an exercise akin to that undertaken by nation-states from the early days of their formation, albeit in different circumstances. Anderson has shown how nation-states were able to secure the allegiance of their citizens on the basis of an imagined political community, 'conceived as a deep, horizontal comradeship' (Anderson 1991: 6–8). This sense of belonging has been based on developing a shared common culture that has served as the main dynamic for nationalism. Furthermore, nation-states have been able to replace religion as the main focus of loyalty. Millions have been prepared to give their lives in defending the idea of the nation, in terms of motherland or fatherland. The most potent symbols of this force being the tomb to the unknown soldier and war memorials in every village.

Will the development of these citizenship rights, together with the incremental steps towards deepening and widening the EU, be able to create some kind of 'imagined community'? It may be that the EU can avoid the worst excesses of virulent nationalism, precisely because it is being built up in a different way and in different historical circumstances from the traditional nation-states. There is a clear set of rationally based constructs which underlies this project. But is it possible to create a 'sense of belonging' without some kind of emotional attachment? Will Europe finally mean something only when there is a tomb to the unknown (European) soldier in Brussels?

Jackson and Penrose (1993) argue that nationalism is the motivating ideology of the modern world, based on the idea of a common culture.[12] There are two cultural bases: primary, which includes language, religion and tradition; and ancillary, which refers to history, its symbols and shared meanings. The use of the ancillary base to legitimise a nationalist movement may increase substantially when primary bases are under threat or diminishing. The key factor is nation and nationalism, but nationalism legitimises only specific elements of culture. Cultural bases are very powerful motivators, but the way in which they are operationalised and ideologically essentialised is directly linked to power, and in particular the elite's need to maintain power.

Culture is essential, and therefore nations too are essential, since culture forms the basis of nation. Both sources are seen as necessary and inevitable. So claims of common ancestry based on pseudo-biological grounds are used, as the German case illustrates (see below). Within Europe, both East and West, the prominence of all these nationalist groups is perhaps one indication of the decline of the traditional nation-state's cultural homogeneity. The problem is, however, that all human beings need fixed categories of some kind to make sense of the world and to have some sense of belonging in it. Ideas about culture are important in motivating and legitimising human behaviour, but cultural bases are not natural, essential or immutable; they are constructed and promoted as being essential to human beings. The wholescale dismissal of essentialism is problematic because many human beings believe some things are essential, and further, the processes which give rise to categories are essential to human beings. There is a continual process of generating a sense of identity through the in-group/out-group dichotomy, which is present in most human relationships. Language, religion and traditions are all examples of categories which become cultures, and which are then defined, named and take on a life of their own; they become taken-for-granted aspects of our world, are almost 'natural'.

The EU does not have a common language and so it lacks one of the chief components of culture. There is a shared dominant religion, but it is both a divided and diminished dynamic in terms of a common European identity. Other religions, moreover, now, as always, are practised in Western Europe – for example, Judaism, Islam and Hinduism. There may also be a tendency to impose an unnecessary urgency on the EU to develop a strong sense of belonging, without appreciating that this process may take decades. Most people's primary focus of identity remains the nation-state, and it is likely to continue to be so for the foreseeable future.

On the other hand, as the nation-state is declining in importance as the main locus of capital accumulation (Ohmae 1995), and is being replaced by regional economic loci, so its political institutions and national forms of social development and attachment may weaken, together with its traditional role of creating a sense of belonging. Undying loyalty may, therefore, be refocused on supranational institutions (e.g. the EU) and local or regional territorial units (e.g.

northern Italy, Catalonia or Scotland) to forge or revive new identities.

FUTURE PROSPECTS

The issue of citizenship formed a key part of the *Commission Report for the Reflection Group* in the run-up to the Intergovernmental Conference (IGC) in 1996.[13] This report focuses on the two major challenges that the EU faces: (1) to 'make Europe the business of every citizen', and (2) to make a success of the future enlargement of the EU. The prioritising of the Maastricht Treaty's objective of creating a Union closer to the citizens reflects the concern that further European integration is threatened by citizens' disenchantment at the distance that exists between their concerns and the policies and programmes of the Commission and other institutions of the EU.

The Report emphasises that the concept of European citizenship is one of the basic innovations in terms of democracy of the Maastricht Treaty. The object is not to replace national citizenship, but to give Europe's citizens an additional benefit and strengthen their sense of belonging to the Union.[14]

Finally, the Commission calls for a fundamental text, presumably like the European Convention on Human Rights (which the TEU refers to in Article F(2)), which could be invoked by citizens as a summary of their rights and duties, and would be a 'powerful means of promoting equal opportunities and combating racism and xenophobia'.[15]

Part of the emphasis is structural, that is it tries to create more accountable institutions (for example, the Committee of the Regions), which may breathe new life into notions of subsidiarity, and recognise that decisions should be taken with as much transparency as possible. The problem with subsidiarity is that it means different things to different Member States. First, the notion contains a principle to bring decision-making as close to the people as possible, but secondly, it implies a certain institutional mechanism to deliver that process. No Member State disagrees with the basic philosophy, but the institutional means of realising the principle differ markedly.

To the British government, subsidiarity implies decisions being relocated to the national government level, whereas the German view is that decision-making should devolve down to the regional level. In Denmark, which has no regional structure but has a powerful tier of local government, subsidiarity means taking decisions down to the very local level. This is also strengthened by the 'power of general competence', which allows local and regional authorities in continental Europe, wide-ranging discretion in all areas, provided that their actions do not contravene the Constitution. This compares favourably with the very restrictive notion of local government that now operates in the United Kingdom, where local authorities may only do what central government allows them to do. Together with the inexorable rise of quangos, the increasing centralisation of the British state makes the implementation of any meaningful kind of subsidiarity very problematic.

Transparency poses another problem in that the main decision-making body of the EU, the Council of Ministers, is reluctant to become more open in its working. Some governments in the EU are notorious for their wide definition of what constitutes an official secret. At the EU level, the question of official secrecy is becoming an issue in the way that member states conduct their business, whether in the Council of Ministers or in matters concerning civil rights – for example, in the secret discussions that take place on asylum and immigration matters in the Ad Hoc Committee on Immigration. The Dutch government, supported by the EP, took a case before the ECJ in Luxembourg to demand more openness in EU proceedings, particularly in the deliberations of the Council.[16]

The Code of Public Access to Documents, which was drawn up by the EU's Council of Ministers meeting in December 1993, favoured disclosure of documents unless there were special reasons to keep them secret – for example if they concerned public safety, monetary stability or personal privacy. However, there was a catch-all clause, which allowed for material to be withheld to protect the confidentiality of the Council's deliberations.[17]

Given the reluctance of most Member States to open their deliberations to wider scrutiny, the possibility of greater transparency may have to wait some time longer. But there are indications that the ECJ may take a more active role in these areas. In the area of transparency this may mean greater access to Council deliberations, and in terms of subsidiarity, may mean that member states no longer have exclusive competence over their individual local governments (Neuwahl 1995).

As far as nationality is concerned, most member states seem to be moving towards a restrictive *jus sanguinis* position and away from a more open *jus soli* as the basis for granting nationality (Baldwin-Edwards and Schain 1994). Germany's nationality laws, for example, are based on an ethno-cultural definition of nationality using the notion of *jus sanguinis*. It is extremely difficult to become a German national unless a blood link to Germany can be demonstrated. Consequently, after the break-up of the Soviet Union, many ethnic Germans from the Volga region claimed German citizenship, even though neither they nor their ancestors had lived in Germany for centuries. In many cases they did not even speak German. Compare this situation to the community of some 3 million Turks who are permanently settled in Germany, but to whom full citizenship is denied. Germany continues to maintain the difficult fiction that it is not 'a country of immigration' despite having received more immigrants since 1945 than the United States.[18]

During the civil war in the former Yugoslavia, the EU had its own negotiators and monitors, and expressed outrage at the horrors of ethnic cleansing.[19] If ethnic cleansing is considered so abhorrent as an idea and practice, then the EU must have another set of values on which a society can be based. If it is not to be mono-cultural or mono-ethnic, then it has to be multi-cultural or multi-ethnic, the ideal that the Bosnian government was attempting to defend. If we accept the logic of this position, then it has implications for the EU in the way, for example, nationality is defined, and immigration and asylum laws are drafted and implemented.[20] Unfortunately, it appears that the most restrictive and exclusive set of rules and regulations are in the process of being instituted.

It may be that in time a new form of identity or sense of belonging can be created whereby people may see themselves as Franco-European, Anglo-European or Hispano-European. Interestingly, or perhaps notoriously, the one country where the label European had a specific meaning was South Africa under the apartheid regime, where it meant white. In order to avoid the same kind of exclusivity, Member States have to consider how Europe may be defined in terms of values, such as respect for the democratic process, rule of law and protection of human rights.[21] However, if a significant number of people living within its borders are denied some of the basic rights of citizenship, then it is difficult to see how a pan-European identity and sense of belonging can be securely and fully developed. This form of exclusion discriminates against not only non-EU nationals, but EU nationals who are unemployed, women, members of ethnic communities, the elderly and gay men and women.[22]

Overall, an assessment of citizenship rights post-Maastricht must conclude that they are a minor but potentially significant step along the road to providing some kind of meaningful basis for a more developed notion of European citizenship. This conclusion is qualified by the considerations outlined above in terms of the need for the concept to become more inclusive. An authentic notion of citizenship should aim to avoid the creation of a 'Fortress Europe', where large numbers of people who reside within its borders languish in the dungeon of restricted rights.

NOTES

1. Aron (1974). For a more detailed discussion of this debate, see Newman (1996, chapter 6).
2. This outline is based on Meehan (1993: 3).
3. Heater (1990) and Meehan (1993: 4).
4. As a result of the ECJ's decision in the case of *Defrenne* v. *Sabena* (No. 2) case 43/75 (equal pay), [1976] ECR 455, the British government was concerned to hasten the introduction of its parallel legislation.
5. Bulletin EC 12–1974/7, item 11.
6. Reflection Report (1995: 21).
7. The Second Declaration, annexed to the Final Act of the TEU, made it quite clear that 'the question whether an individual possesses the nationality of a Member State shall be settled solely by reference to the national law of the Member State concerned'. For a fuller dis-

cussion of all these issues, see Koslowski (1994).

8. Ireland, unlike most other EU countries, does not allow its nationals resident abroad to vote in its national elections.

9. *Phil Collins* v *IMTRAT Handelsgesellschaft mbH* [1993] 3 CMLR 773 at 785, in Macdonald and Blake (1995: 204).

10. Directive 64/221. Public policy, public security and public health. Regulation 1612/68 Regulation 1251/70.

11. Directive 64/221.

12. Jackson and Penrose (1993). See also Penrose (1995).

13. *Commission Report for the Reflection Group*, Brussels, European Commission. May 1995.

14. Commission Report (1995), p. 6.

15. Ibid. See also Chapter 1 in the Report entitled 'Heightening the Sense of Belonging to the Union and enhancing its Legitimacy'.

16. *The Guardian*, 28 April 1994, 7 March 1995. In November 1995, the Council of Ministers agreed to abide by a decision of the ECJ, which outlawed prevailing official secrecy (*The Guardian*, 27 November 1995). But see also *Independent on Sunday* (26 November 1995), which highlights the continuing way in which major decisions by the Council of Ministers are subject to little, if none, of the usual parliamentary or media scrutiny.

17. *The Guardian*, 17 May 1994, and 8 September 1994.

18. Recent statements by the Federal government indicate that there may be some relaxation in its tough nationalisation criteria; see Faist (1994).

19. In terms of creating a feeling of belonging together as Europeans in the EU, it would be interesting to ascertain whether the fact that it was EU monitors who were detained in 1995 that really concerned Member States, or only their own particular nationals.

20. The creation of a 'white' list of countries from which asylum-seekers will not be considered to be genuine refugees, and the restrictive definition of a 'refugee', in the face of opposition from the UNHCR and Amnesty International, reflects an arbitrary approach, which throws doubt on the EU's commitment to universal human rights (*Independent on Sunday*, 26 November 1995).

21. For a discussion of similar issues in terms of Western Europe's treatment of its migrant workers in the 1960s and 1970s, see Miller (1981).

22. See Newman (1996) for more discussion on the way in which these groups are excluded.

REFERENCES

Anderson, B. (1991), *Imagined Communities*, London, Verso.

Andrews, G. (ed.) (1993), *Citizenship*, London, Lawrence & Wishart.

Aron, R. (1974), 'Is Multinational Citizenship Possible?', *Social Research*, Vol. 4, 41, No. 4, pp. 638–56.

Baldwin-Edwards, M. and Schain, M. (ed.) (1994), *The Politics of Immigration in Europe*, London, Frank Cass.
Bauböck, R. (1991), 'Migration and Citizenship', *New Community*, Vol. 18, No. 1, pp. 27–48.
Bauböck, R. (1994), *Transnational Citizenship. Membership and Rights in International Migration*, Cheltenham, Edward Elgar.
Castles, S. and Miller, M.J. (1993), *The Age of Migration: International Population Movements in the Modern World*, New York, The Guilford Press.
Close, P. (1995), *Citizenship, Europe and Change*, London, Macmillan.
de Wenden, C. (1987), *Citoyenneté, nationalité et immigration*, Paris, Arcantère Editions.
Costa-Lascoux, J. (1989), *De l'immigré au citoyen*, Paris, La Documentation Française.
Dummett, A. and Nicol, A. (1990), *Subjects, Citizens, Aliens and Others*, London, Weidenfeld and Nicolson.
Faist, T. (1994), 'How to Define a Foreigner. The Symbolic Politics of Immigration in Germany. Partisan Discourse, 1978–92', in Baldwin-Edwards and Schain (1994).
Gordon, M. (1978), *Human Nature, Class and Ethnicity*, New York, Oxford University Press.
Hammar, T. (1990), *Democracy and the Nation-State: Aliens, Denizens and Citizens in a World of International Migration*, Aldershot, Avebury.
Harrison, M.L. (1991), 'Citizenship, Consumption and Rights: A Comment on B.S. Turner's Theory of citizenship', *Sociology*, Vol. 25, No. 2, pp. 209–13.
Heater, D. (1990), *Citizenship. The Civil Ideal in World History, Politics and Education*, London, Longman.
International Migration Review (1985), Special Issue on Civil Rights and the Sociopolitical Participation of Migrants, Vol. 19, No. 3.
Jackson, P. and Penrose, J. (1993), *Constructions of Race, Place and Nation*, London, UCL Press.
Jones, L. and Wallace, C. (1992), *Youth, Family and Citizenship*, Buckingham, Open University Press.
Koslowski, R. (1994), 'Intra-EU Migratory Citizenship and Political Union', *Journal of Common Market Studies* Vol. 32, No. 3, September, pp. 369–402.
Levi-Sandri, L. (1961), *La libre circulation des travailleurs dans les pays de la Communauté Européenne*, Brussels, European Commission.
Lister, R. (1990), 'Women, Economic Dependency and Citizenship', *Journal of Social Policy*, Vol. 19, No. 4, pp. 445–67.
Macdonald, I. and Blake, N. (1995), *Immigration Law and Practice in the United Kingdom*, London, Butterworths.
Marshall, T.H. (1950), *Citizenship and Social Class*, Cambridge, Cambridge University Press.
Meehan, E. (1993), *Citizenship and the European Community*, London, Sage.
Miller, M.J. (1981), *Foreign Workers in Europe. An Emerging Political Force*, New York, Praeger.
Neuwahl, N. (1995), 'A Europe Close to the Citizen? The "Trinity Concepts" of Subsidiarity, Transparency and Democracy', in Allan Rosas and Esko

Antola (eds.), *A Citizens' Europe in Search of a New Order*, London, Sage.
Newman, M. (1996), *Democracy, Sovereignty and the European Union*, London, Hurst.
Ohmae, K. (1995), *The End of the Nation State*, London, Hayes Collins.
Penrose, J. (1995), 'Essential Constructions? The "Cultural Bases" of Nationalist Movements', *Nations and Nationalism*, Vol. 1, part 3, pp. 391–417.
Rosas, A. and Antola, E. (1995), *A Citizens' Europe. In Search of a New Order*, London, Sage.
Smith, S.J. (1989), *The Politics of 'Race' and Residence*, Oxford, Polity Press.
Spencer, M. (1995), *States of Injustice. A Guide to Human Rights and Civil Liberties in the European Union*, London, Pluto Press.
Spencer, S. (ed.) (1994), *Strangers and Citizens: A Positive Approach to Migrants and Refugees* Sevenoaks, IPPR/Rivers Oram Press.
Turner, B.S. (1986), *Citizenship and Capitalism*, London, Allen and Unwin.
van Steenburgen, B. (1994), *The Condition of Citizenship*, London, Sage.
Walby, S. (1994), 'Is Citizenship Gendered?' *Sociology* Vol. 28, No. 2, pp. 379–95.

5 Crime and Policing
Frances Heidensohn

INTRODUCTION

Crime and criminal justice are not mentioned in the Treaty of Rome of 1957. Nor did these topics become part of the new social agenda which developed later in the history of the European Community. In the 1990s, however, justice and home affairs have at last come to the fore and are now forming part of one of the key structures of the future design for the European Union (EU). In practice, there were several organisations which dealt with policing matters between European nations before the Treaty of European Union (Maastricht Treaty) included the 'third pillar' of justice and home affairs.

In this chapter I shall outline the histories of these formations and their influences on current policies, indicate current trends in the European Policing Office (Europol) and consider what directions these may take in the future. To do this it will also be essential to review the state of crime in Europe and what responses this may evoke at the European level.

This will not merely be a descriptive account. I shall also analyse the distinctive features of these policies and consider various views on the directions they have taken and to where they might be moving. Explanations offered by various commentators emphasise either the policing agenda or the political as key factors, but they also note the complexity of the issues involved. First, however, it is necessary to trace some of the prehistory of the current position in Europe.

TOWARDS TRANSNATIONAL POLICING

Defining what constitutes policing and what makes the police distinctive has generated endless debate (Bittner 1990; Bayley 1994). One succinct version in a text on policing

Europe proposes that 'police is the label and policing the means used by the state when asserting its exclusive title to the use or threat of force against dangers emanating from within its boundaries' (Hebenton and Thomas 1995: 2).

The origin of the word 'police' (from the Greek *polis*, the word for city-state) is shared with the words 'policy' and 'politics', and these links reveal an important aspect of modern policing, namely that it has, on the whole, been identified with the nation-state, especially in the major European countries.

In comparing different systems of modern policing, Mawby (1992) distinguishes four types of early modern police systems, those of England and Wales, the United States, the Continental and the Colonial. He describes the Continental model, of which France was the template both before the French Revolution and under Napoleon and Fouché, his Minister of General Police, as being centralised, armed and militaristic, with crime control only one function and an emphasis on political and administrative functions. This he contrasts with England and Wales and the United States, which were local government-based, decentralised and civilian and, in the case of the former, unarmed, with responsibilities for crime and some welfare and administrative responsibilities.

Mawby concludes his comparative analysis by saying 'there is clearly no one continental system', noting variations *within* Europe and within the British Isles (1992: 125). By contrast, Hebenton and Thomas argue that

> over the last 200 years [in Europe] . . . the original idea of a 'police-state' regulating all kinds of civic activities has given way to the idea of policing being directed at more specific anti-social criminal activities. The organisation of police forces has moved along from centralisation to decentralisation.
>
> (1995: 36)

There are, nevertheless, many and continuing debates about the nature and role of the state in relation to policing today. However, one feature soon becomes clear in examining the development of international policing in Europe: moves towards transnational policing have a long history.

INTERPOL

The International Criminal Police Organisation was first discussed at an International Police Congress held in Monaco in 1914 when lawyers, police officers and other professionals resolved 'to improve direct police-to-police cooperation . . . and give it a more systematic and official character', including centralised and standardised criminal records (Anderson *et al.*, 1989: 38–9). These aims still remain to be achieved. The outbreak of the First World War prevented the plans being taken further, but in 1923 the second International Police Congress met in Vienna and set up the International Criminal Police Commission (ICPC) with its headquarters and bureau in Vienna, which held information about both individuals and offences (Kendal 1993). This survived until the Anschluss of 1938, when Germany entered Austria, and the headquarters were moved to Berlin.

In 1946, at a conference in Brussels, the ICPC and the whole idea of international policing were revived and a new organisation was set up in Paris. Eventually, in 1956, the body was renamed the International Criminal Police Organisation – Interpol for short – and now has its headquarters in Lyons. There are also National Central Bureaux in each of the member countries; there are currently some 175. Contrary to some fictional portrayals, in practice Interpol 'is a police information and intelligence exchange system that also advises police officers having to visit other countries, and carries out research and analysis of international crime patterns' (Hebenton and Thomas 1995: 64–5). Discussions of the history and role of Interpol can be found in Anderson *et al.* (1989), Fijnaut (1991) and Kendall (1993).

For the purposes of this chapter there are three significant factors to note about Interpol, all of which contributed in some way to its *not* becoming the key body for European security. Interpol is notable for its European origins, strongly linked to France; non-governmental status, and its alleged insecurity in handling records.

Interpol was extensively and increasingly criticised during the 1970s (Fijnaut 1991), especially by the United Kindom, (the then) West Germany and the Netherlands. As well as the features noted above, several governments were frustrated by its focus on 'ordinary' criminal offences and the consequences of Article 3 of its Constitution. This precludes political, military, religious or racial intervention of any kind (Kendall 1993) and thus Interpol did not assist the police in those states, particularly West Germany and the United Kingdom, that were affected by terrorism in the 1970s. This, among other factors, led directly to the founding of TREVI, which can most neatly be described as 'the consultative body of the European Community dealing with matters of internal security' (Fijnaut 1991: 105).

TREVI

TREVI is the name given to the European inter-governmental group holding regular meetings and forming networks 'to discuss cooperation on the policing of drugs and serious crime, terrorism, football hooliganism' (Hebenton and Thomas 1995: 70). In addition, TREVI members worked on the consequences and implementation of the Single European Act in 1992. As we shall see, TREVI has been an important influence in the setting up of Europol. Yet its history is somewhat shadowy because of the secrecy of its proceedings. Even the origin of its name is controversial and unclear:

> Some see TREVI as an acromym for Terrorism, Radicalism, Extremism and Violence International. This is denied by the UK Home Office who claim that the name derives from a pun on the names of a famous Roman fountain and the Chair of the first meeting, Mr. Fontejne.
> (Woodward 1994: 9)

True or not, the more extravagant title does embody the main concerns of the founders of TREVI in 1975.

All 12 EC countries were members of TREVI, while other nations, e.g. the United States, Canada, Norway and Sweden, had observer status. Crises, such as the taking hostage of Israeli competitors at the Munich Olympic Games in 1972 and the hijacking of airliners in that period, were stimuli to its formation, as well as helping to set its agenda, influence its structure and determine its closed nature (Benyon *et al.* 1993).

Despite its EC focus and membership, TREVI was in fact outside the formal constitution of the EC. It had no permanent base or staff, but rotated amongst them. TREVI operated principally at three main levels. Ministerial groups met regularly and set up working groups TREVI I, II and III, which covered terrorism and security, training and public order, drugs, organised crime and money laundering. A fourth group, often called TREVI '92, prepared for the implementation of border control reduction as the Single European Act came into force in 1992. Various ad hoc groups – on international organised crime, refugees and asylum, extradition etc. – were also formed. TREVI clearly met with some success in furthering both transnational policing and some degree of European co-operation and integration.

Some of the secrecy covering TREVI and its activities was lifted in 1990 with the publication of their Programme of Action on terrorism, drug trafficking and illegal immigration. Among the developments then revealed were that 'the TREVI group already had its own rapid and protected communications system' (Hebenton and Thomas 1995: 84). It is also clear that by the time TREVI ceased to exist as it metamorphosed into part of the new European Union structure as soon as the Treaty on European Union came into force on 1 November 1993 the group had enormously extended the range of its activities. Better policing of international football matches is cited as one positive outcome of TREVI group co-operation.

Views about the success of TREVI vary, although they use the same benchmark of achievement, the group's own demise/transformation. Benyon *et al.* (1993 and 1995) cite several widely voiced criticisms from their own researches, in particular the group's lack of accountability and transparency, its constitutional and organisational weakness, having had no formal status with the EC and lacking a permanent secretariat and base. On the other hand, Ahnfelt and From (1993) argue that its very informal status enabled it to play a 'significant role by accentuating the importance of police cooperation' (1993: 109). Benyon and his colleagues raise questions as to whether TREVI was effective at an operational level, stressing instead its promotion of 'the principle of increased police cooperation'. They see its major achievement as reducing 'national rivalries in the field of law enforcement and [promoting] mutual respect and trust, the culmination of which has been the agreement for the establishment of Europe' (Benyon *et al.* 1993: 165).

Before outlining the origins and structure of the latter, we should consider the other key formation within the EC which has had an important, if controversial, influence on the building of the 'third pillar' of the EU: the Schengen Convention.

SCHENGEN

Under an Agreement signed at the small (and symbolically placed) border town of Schengen in 1985, five EC nations, France, Germany and the Benelux countries, pledged to remove all internal borders and controls. This was explicitly linked to the Single European Act and the aim of founding a 'citizens' Europe in which freedom of movement could be achieved. In 1990, the Schengen Convention was ratified by a wider membership, which then included all the EC member states except Denmark, Ireland and the United Kingdom.

It is important to stress that while its effects have been, amongst other things, an increase in police co-operation, Schengen has

> a completely different point of departure from TREVI . . .
> the rationale behind the Schengen Agreement is the notion of *compensatory measures*; when the borders are opened for the free flow of people and goods, internal security can only be maintained if the border controls are compensated for by the introduction of alternative measures. Conversely, compensatory measures in the form of intensified internal controls should not be implemented until the external border controls have been removed.
> (Ahnfelt and From 1993: 199)

The Schengen Agreement, and the Convention for its implementation, have been described as 'the most ambitious attempts to date to promote practical police cooperation on a large scale in Europe' (Benyon *et al.* 1993: 146). At the time of writing six member states (the Benelux countries, Germany, Spain and Portugal) are subject to the Convention. Under it, internal frontier controls are abolished and external frontier controls strengthened. France resolved to lift border controls by the end of 1995, with other states planning to join in. The United Kingdom, however, remains opposed, for three main reasons: the 'natural' frontiers of the British Isles are deemed to be sensible and appropriate for border controls; intensive checks and the carrying of identity papers, etc. for internal movements are seen as alien; and finally, there is doubt about the real strength of the 'ring of steel' around 'Schengen land'.

Implementing Schengen has proved difficult and has been subject to delay even among those nations without Britain's reservations about it. Nevertheless, it is regarded even by its critics as the prime example of transnational policing in Europe and as a possible model for the future, although considerable doubts and difficulties remain. These can be summarised under the headings of delays, borders and democracy.

Delays

Schengen has proved complex and troublesome to implement; visa and asylum questions proved very controversial. Several signatories (e.g. Germany and France) had to enact changes to their constitutions in order to implement it. France halted implementation at one stage and German reunification slowed its progress. More importantly, since the Agreement which was due to aid the 1992 barrier removal missed that target by several years, its significance has perhaps been diminished.

Borders

While the Agreement is intended to provide a ring of steel or hard shell border around the whole of Europe, the concept has proved simpler than the practice. Most obviously, several Member States remain outside Schengen and some intend to do so indefinitely. On the other hand, existing ties with countries outside the EU, or simple geographical proximity, mean that the 'shell' is not as hard as it might be.

Democracy

By far the most serious criticisms voiced about this aspect of European policing concern a range of questions to do with accountability, rights and democracy. McLaughlin (1992) has discussed the 'democratic deficit' produced by structures such as Schengen whose deliberations are secret yet whose impact on the civil rights of citizens and non-citizens can be very considerable. Moreover, as he and other commentators point out, no possibility for judicial review of the Agreement exists. Of particular concern is the 'jewel' at the heart of Schengen, its computerised information system and how well its data, including material on migrants and asylum-seekers, are safeguarded.

Schengen is often described as a laboratory or an experiment intended to produce designs for co-operation in Europe, to be adopted later by the whole Community. In practice, however, the arrangements remain a purely intergovernmental affair (Anderson *et al.* 1994). Under the Maastricht Treaty, a new notion of citizenship was introduced, although it may appear to be more radical than it will be in practice. In considering the Schengen Agreement, it must be noted that the Treaty notion of citizenship is one of free movement across 'a space without frontiers' and that the key preconditions for this are the Schengen issues of border controls, etc. These matters are dealt with under the separate third pillar of the Treaty (Title VI or Article K) and this in turn has a problematic relation to the Commission (Anderson *et al.* 1994) and will be handled at intergovernmental levels, except for visas. The new IGC-level co-operation on Justice and Home Affairs resembles Schengen in several respects (Ahnfelt and From 1993) and could possibly replace it. However, at present the one firm development in the dialectical cycle of transnational policing in Europe which we are tracing here has been Europol.

EUROPOL AND EDU

Writing about the future of crime in Europe in 1989, I speculated on the possibility of Eurocops being a reality in the 1990s (Heidensohn 1991) and saw them as one potential Eurocrime body, along with Eurojustice and Europrisons. In fact, Eurocops may still be some way off, in the sense of an FBI-style agency doing hands-on investigations. What we have nevertheless is the inheritor of the experiences, and mistakes, of the developments set out above. Commentators variously stress that '"Europol" is an old idea' (e.g. Woodward 1993). Yet also that its introduction was something of a surprise and a coup achieved by the German Chancellor, Helmut Kohl, who tabled a motion at the European Council at its Luxembourg meeting in June 1991 proposing a European Criminal Police Office: 'The original intent was to establish a framework for a fully operational Euro-police akin to the Federal Bureau of Investigation in the USA' (Sheptycki 1995a: 623).

Fijnaut traces the idea of a European policing agency back to the 1970s, and also to Germany where the head of the German CID Association proposed 'the "Europol" idea within the EC... this meant that the EC would not only have to harmonise criminal law... but also have to create a supranational criminal investigation department... and be able to launch investigations in its own right' (1991, p. 106). Writing in the late 1980s, Fijnaut presciently identified the two key sources for Europol. One was the long discussion, mostly led by senior German police officers and already noted. Second was the development of TREVI III. Launched in June 1985, TREVI III was a study group focused on the fight against 'international crime', notably armed robbery and drug trafficking. Of the European Council resolution at the Hague, adopted in April 1986, which urged increased police cooperation and a more formal 'troika' structure for TREVI, Fijnaut suggested: 'The resolution... contained the seeds out of which an independent "Europol" could grow within the European Community' (Fijnaut, 1991, p. 110).

In her detailed description of establishing Europol, Woodward (1993) links these two 'strands of action', the strong *political* drive from Germany and the growing influence, and success, of TREVI in its later and wider forms. The structures under which Europe is to operate are complex and some issues remain to be resolved at the 1996 Inter-governmental Conference.

Broadly, the Maastricht Treaty (Treaty on European Union, or TEU) provides a legal basis for a Europol and a basis for European police co-operation. Under its 'third pillar' the Treaty makes provision for co-operation on matters of justice and home affairs between member states (Title VI, Article K1-9). Areas of common interest for achieving EU objectives are not set out in this part of the Treaty and include police co-operation and the organisation of Europol. Article K4 also establishes an official structure (to be put in place after full ratification), which will cover fields similar to or broader than TREVI, which it will effectively replace. It should be stressed that the 'third pillar' is outside Community competence and, although the European Commission is closely associated with the work of the K4 Committee, this will operate *intergovernmentally* (Benyon *et al.* 1993; Woodward, 1993).

As yet it is the European Drugs Unit, opened at the Hague in 1994, which is the one functioning arm of Europol (Valls Russell 1995). In an account of the Unit's activities thus far, its Assistant Director stressed how much was already being done without formal legal status or power. He specifically noted co-operation and co-ordination over intelligence (although personal data may not be stored) and its capacity 'to facilitate multiagency operations' (ibid.). This is likely to be just the beginning. In his analysis of the growth of transnational policing in Europe, Sheptycki quotes from an EU report that

> the scope of Europol can be progressively widened so that . . . it is likely that money laundering and aspects of organised crime linked to drug trafficking would be included at an early stage in the responsibilities of Europol
> (1995a, p. 624)

With Europol still in its infancy, it is too early to judge its success. As, however, the debate about policing Europe has now spread from within professional groups to a much more public arena, many observers have been prepared to offer comments. Woodward, for instance, speculates on three possible benefits:

1. enhanced information co-ordination and exchange;
2. political capital;
3. the development of a legal basis for a European police co-operation.

Her list of practical problems, however, is longer and finds parallels in the commentaries of other writers, who also take issue with some of the possible benefits. Thus several point to the lack of clarity in Europol's formation (Ahnfelt and From 1993; Walker 1995). Hebenton and Terry go further in questioning the claims to 'knowledge/expertise and organisational effectiveness', which form the core basis of Europol. The major doubts voiced by Woodward (and also by her former colleagues at the Centre for the Study of Public Order at Leicester University (Benyon *et al.* 1993; Benyon 1995)) and echoed by others are practical, but also include serious reservations about democracy and accountability.

Practicality is often raised as an issue for Europol, with both professionals and academics pointing to lack of harmonisation in judicial systems, language and policing practices. A further problem is the duplication of agencies in Europe, with Interpol now taking a fuller role (Kendall 1993), as well as a range of other organisations operating in what has been described as a 'crowded policy space' (Raab 1994; Benyon *et al.* 1993; and Hebenton and Terry, 1995, all provide descriptions of other agencies).

Nevertheless, despite all the considerable concerns expressed by the authors cited, and by politicians and police officers, it does seem to be widely agreed that structures are now in place 'for transnational police co-operation in Europe' (Sheptycki 1995a: 624) and what others describe as some 'measure of Europeification of police collaboration between the member states' (Ahnfelt and From 1993). Why this has come about when crime and policing were marginalised for so long as European issues (Heidensohn, 1991) is the subject of a wide range of interpretations. Some of these are lengthy, complex and sophisticated (e.g. Fijnaut

1993; Walker 1995). They are relevant for the purposes of this chapter in so far as they can help us to predict the possible developments in the field. For this purpose, the explanations can be grouped under two headings: those that emphasise political imperatives, and those that link events to questions of crime and control.

An example of the first is Ahnfelt and From's assertion: 'this study confirms the significance of EC integration as a driving force in the evolution of police cooperation within the Community' (1993: 211). They argue that politicians set the agenda and thus sovereignty – sensitive issues such as terrorism are left off the agenda while drug trafficking is included because it is a low policing task. Whilst also stressing the importance of political influence, Walker (1995) and Sheptycki (1995a) take very different approaches. Walker examines various political discourses in the post-Hobbesian state, arguing that the whole process has been, and is likely in the future to be, 'overdetermined', with almost every trend pushing towards internationalisation. Sheptycki, however, foresees a 'Fourth Epoch' of postmodernity in Europe of 'fragmentation and unity' (1995a: 631).

More schematically, Benyon (1995), who has directed the most comprehensive and systematic research and reviews of police co-operation in Europe, concluded a recent paper with a summary of the respective factors which provide impetus or impediments to further progress. He divides the forces promoting co-operation into *political impetus* at the macro level and *practitioner demands* at the meso level. The former he describes as the *unionist* or federal impetus and links it to political mutual interests but also suggests that 'some of the political momentum arises from an idealistic belief in constructing and consolidating institutions of the European "state"' (Benyon 1995: 25). Practitioner demands come from powerful professional bodies which raise a parallel agenda of urgent policing issues. These he particularly relates to the professionalisation of policing and to increasing demands for training, equipment and the capacity to use networks and access information. Amongst impediments to these transnational developments he notes similar political factors, e.g. concerns about legitimacy, accountability and democracy, which see supranational or federal institutions as threatening the sovereignty of individual nation states.

The Europeanisation of policing may well become a reality in the twenty-first century. At present formal structures exist for the achievement of that goal. It seems clear that they have been constructed as part of the political development of the EU and, in particular, to enable certain aspects of integration to be achieved more speedily. More precisely, the implementation of a Europe without frontiers under the Single European Act meant that external borders had to be strengthened and internal barriers removed. Given the assumptions made about European policies, it is hardly surprising that this became a policing matter (Schengen). Recent developments in relation to migration, refugees and asylum have, for the most part, also hardened this part of the agenda.

It can be argued that some features of the trends in Europe-wide policing have their origins in patterns of crime and policies to combat these. As Walker (1995) points out, many official reports put forward variants of the argument that, with frontiers falling, traditional filters to international crime are removed and hence, if they are to keep up with the new jet-set crook, the police too must mobilise. As an official of Europol put it: 'increased travel and freedom of movement; rising levels of crime – local, national and international – all feed on each other' (Valls-Russell 1995: 27). Yet, as various sources suggest, there are considerable difficulties with this argument. In the next section I shall briefly outline what can be said about crime in Europe, especially about its future patterns, and suggest how far these will relate to the trends in policing which we have already considered as well as with other European developments.

CRIME IN EUROPE

When I co-edited a book on this topic some years ago, it was striking how sparse the published material was on the subject and how little it seemed to relate to the then European agenda on which 1992 loomed large (Heidensohn and Farrell 1991). A comparison I made then with the current European images of butter mountains and wine lakes has since been cited as evidence of considerable change (e.g.

Hebenton and Terry 1995; Sheptycki 1995b). Certainly, as I hope I have made clear in the first section of this chapter, crime issues have become EU topics through developments in the field of policing. Policing Europe has been given additional priority because of perceptions of a range of 'new' problems to do with migration and other issues, or that, at least, is how they are presented (McLaughlin 1992).

There is now a very considerable literature, some of which I have quoted above, detailing the history of the growth and organisation of Europe-wide policing and endeavouring to account for it. There can be little doubt, then, that 'crime' is now a proper and permanent topic for Europe. Yet there are still considerable gaps in our knowledge of the topic. These are significant in that much of the rhetoric justifying transnational policing and specific forms of organisation and management of law enforcement cites trends in crime.

In practice, it is usually only certain types of crime and groups of criminals who have become the objects of this attention. These include crimes categorised by their *cross-border* or *international* features and also those 'perceived as a serious threat to the "fabric of the state". These include large scale drug trafficking, terrorism and, latterly, the issue of illegal immigration' (Levi and Maguire 1992: 167).

As we saw earlier, concerns about all these topics and wishes to try to control them and their effects lay behind the initiatives already discussed towards European police co-operation. Yet, as Levi (1993) argues in a later article, it is first of all exceptionally difficult to define what is meant by 'international' crime and also near-impossible to categorise 'cross-border' crime. A UK Parliamentary Report (1990) outlines four main types of crime suitable for Europe-wide police co-operation: the illicit drug trade, terrorism, fraud and football hooliganism. As Sheptycki points out:

> this document did not so much provide a definition of transnational crime as list various types of crime which might have an international dimension. Indeed, it was argued by the Home Office that 'there may be a need for international cooperation on almost any type of crime.'
>
> (1995a: 3)

Later official documents broaden the categories to include cases as diverse as sexual slavery, piracy, illicit currency dealing and non-specific claims about the likely impact of technological innovation (United Nations 1990). Another UK document focused on a further preoccupation: organised crime with an international basis (House of Commons, 1994).

A further dimension which has been added to such material in Europe in recent years is that of the removal of border controls and hence of one set of barriers to illicit movement. Benyon *et al.* (1993) quote several claims about this threat:

> A single European Market without boundaries and without a consistent policing policy would be an open invitation to them (the South American drug barons).
>
> (Chairman of the Police Federation, ibid.: 26)

> The drugs traffickers have been winning the battle; they are organising an increasingly efficient network for the distribution of cocaine across western Europe; their resources are mounting relentlessly.
>
> (MEP, ibid.: 26)

Yet as increasing numbers of researchers and some professionals have pointed out, much of this is purely assertion and speculation. Partly this is because of the lack of clarity indicated above, as to what constitutes either cross-border or international crime. In addition, 'there is almost no hard information about cross-border crime for gain in Europe' (Levi and Maguire 1992: 171).

Some of the most sensational accounts amount to no more than predictions. Carter, for example, 'hypothesized that organized crime groups from Eastern Europe will aggressively spread into Western Europe during the present decade. Their involvement will be in drug trafficking, information-related crimes . . . and black marketeering' (1993: 62). Writing from within the European justice system, however, others are more sceptical:

> When a few years ago the first prospects of an integrated Europe without internal border controls became clear, many

law enforcement agencies were worried that this would enormously enhance the opportunities for drug traffickers. *However, there are reasons to consider these worries as being premature.* Professional drug entrepreneurs have never been that much impressed by border controls as to be frightened out of business.

(van Duyne, 1993, p. 12)

Benyon *et al.* (1993) reviewed all the evidence available to them, as well as interviewing key police and official personnel Europe-wide. They conclude that there is 'a serious lack of knowledge and understanding about crime in Europe' (ibid.: 60) and that this has led to moral panics about it. Moreover, those tentative predictions that can be made about future European crime trends include:

- International terrorism will neither increase nor decrease.
- The relaxation of internal border controls is unlikely to see the pattern of organised drugs trafficking within the EU change significantly.
- The main 'growth areas' are likely to be:
    drugs from Eastern Europe,
    low-level property crime, especially car theft,
    art and antique thefts,
    fraud, including credit card fraud and fraud against the
      EC itself
    ecocrimes (Benyon *et al.* 1993: 60–1).

Such cautious judgements have also been made about doom-laden scenarios which predict that migrant flows from 'economically disadvantaged and politically destabilised regions in the South and East of the EU, and [emphasise] the importance of limiting and policing that flow in order that new problems of crime and public security are not imported' (Walker 1995: 12). Walker goes on to point out this is not so much a 'self-evident problem', but *one* response to the socially constructed issue of crime.

Sheptycki takes a similar view, insisting that 'the message [that] organised crime is a clear and present danger and requires a high level police response. . . . To criminologists this . . . should be as material ripe for deconstruction' (1995b:

p 5). While not necessarily adopting a criminological approach, Walker (1993) has explored several of the dimensions of this issue. In a chapter on the international aspects of accountable policing he identifies four aspects of it. First,

> the *absolute* level of, or threat of international crime remains deeply obscure . . . a second argument points to the *relative seriousness* with which many international crimes are viewed . . . thirdly there is the question of *overall trends* . . . a key imponderable. Finally there is a fundamental *discursive problem*. Should the issues which tend to be addressed in predominantly law enforcement terms be viewed through such a conceptual grid at all?
>
> (Walker 1993: 126–7, original emphasis)

He cites other European commentators who have fundamentally challenged this approach, which brings disparate, discrete issues such as asylum and immigration policies as well as crime so that

> the constant association of different themes in the language and practice of European politicians has created a mutually reinforcive 'internal security ideology', with each substantive topic across a broad spectrum presented as but one component of an indivisible 'security deficit'.
>
> (ibid.: 128)

He concludes this analysis, as well as a later one, by arguing that the problems of international crime are by no means self-evident and follows a similar argument in a later paper (Walker 1995), where he also develops the idea of the security deficit, stressing that 'there is . . . an important economic agenda at work in the reinforcement of Europe as a security community', and noting the way 'the new status of European citizenship, introduced by the Treaty of Maastricht, emphasizes this exclusionary logic by narrowly confining [such] citizenship . . . and thus consigning those who do not have it to a process of double marginalisation' (Walker, 1995: 21).

In their account of policing Europe, Hebenton and Thomas (1995) note the parallels between the doom scenarios and risk analyses of some observers and participants in the crime debates and the defence terms of the Cold War. They also cite den Boer (1992), who has discerned a '"reiterative pattern" in which politicians and senior officials produce stereotypical accounts of crime which are in essence "rhetorical statements without a substantiating context"' (Hebenton and Thomas 1995: 161).

Those attempts which have been made to assess the level of cross-border or international crime have shown how complex it is to assess and how difficult to determine whether rates are rising, falling or stable (Levi 1993).

Two things thus seem clear: on the one hand police co-operation in Europe is planned and poised for serious development, yet on the other, the claims about crime associated with this remain unsubstantiated. In predicting the future of Europe, then, it may be that trends in crime will be much less important than political situation and associated rhetoric. The questions then to be answered are those to do with what forms Europolicing will take, and how effective it may be.

Almost all commentators agree that the future looks uncertain. Some of this uncertainty is the result of organisational, operational, linguistic and cultural matters (the opening of the Channel Tunnel between England and France epitomises these (Policespeak 1993)). Other factors also play a part: social and economic changes, and political will or the lack of it (Hebenton and Thomas 1995). So many uncertainties adhere to these that prophecy is unsafe. Much wider issues, such as those concerning democracy and accountability, also remain to be resolved.

PROPOSALS FOR THE FUTURE

All those who have studied this topic have recommendations, sometimes in the form of lengthy lists, about what should happen in future policies focused on this area. I have selected three major focus areas: research and training, social policy and welfare, and citizenship.

Research and Training

It is remarkable that the inter-governmental agencies with the prime responsibility for promoting police cooperation

do not undertake, or commission, more detailed research
of the problems with which they are dealing.

(Benyon *et al.* 1993: 332)

The Council of Europe is the one body which has carried
out this task (Heidensohn and Farrell 1991). The scope of
such projects should not be confined to policing, but should
also include basic data on trends (Levi 1993) as well as conceptually more sophisticated work. At a 1995 conference on
crime prevention van Dijk proposed that

the European Union should organise a Euro-barometer
of crime. The professionals and the public deserve to have
credible comparative crime statistics. It is really absurd
that this is the only policy area where the European
Union does not provide any credible comparative statistics.

(1995: 16)

One might add that the official publication of the EU (*Eurostat
Yearbook '95*) contains very limited data on crime and that
most of that comes from Interpol.

The Leicester group suggest that there should be a European Centre for Research into Crime (1993). A considerable number of commentators agree on the need for
evaluative projects on changes in policing (Hebenton and
Thomas 1995), exemplary projects on crime prevention (van
Dijk 1995) or innovatory drugs control regimes (Clutterbuck
1995). Several writers insist on a necessary and major change
of focus in crime and law enforcement research because of
Europeanisation (Hebenton and Thomas 1995; Sheptycki
1995b). Benyon *et al.* (1993) press the need for much more
joint and common training across Europe.

Social Policy and Welfare

It is a mark, perhaps, of the most recent evolution of the
EU that policing and control have come so much to the
fore in the 1990s. Yet as Walker points out, 'security' is only
one way in which some of the post-1992 issues could be
perceived and addressed. Thus the 'threat' and 'deficit' posed
by the disparities of income and wealth within and outside

the EU can be addressed in ways other than through law enforcement. In an earlier paper, while acknowledging some of these problems, Martin Farrell and I (1991b) suggested solutions directed at supporting the truly disadvantaged, improving employment and welfare policies (while dismantling the CAP). There have been some signs of this happening (Nacinovic 1995), although there has been reluctance to accept links between poverty, inequality and disorder and to provide suitable responses.

Citizenship

All the developments in this field in one way or another connect with questions about citizenship. If European policing becomes a more serious reality, then issues about citizens' rights will become more significant. Schengen, the other side of this agenda, raises many more questions about the rights of EU citizens and of non-citizens, both those resident within member states and those who wish to visit, to come to work or settle, or to seek refuge. There are also questions about the respective and relative rights of citizens in different Member States: those in Schengen land and those outside it, for instance. Another difficulty arises where changes in one nation's law enforcement policies are exacted as a price for implementing the Schengen Agreement. The Netherlands' relatively tolerant approach to soft drugs is under pressure from other member states, who see it as a threat to their own, more restrictive régimes (*The Guardian*, 31 October 1995).

Judicial and home affairs form the third pillar of the Maastricht Treaty. This is a new domain for the EU and remains at an inter-governmental level. The maintenance of good order and internal security are central tasks for all forms of stable government. Because they affect the lives and liberties of so many individuals they can be matters of great sensitivity and complexity. As yet this pillar is scarcely in place; its mortar hardly dry. How well it holds up, how central it becomes to the new Europe, will be developments worthy of intense scrutiny for all its citizens.

REFERENCES

Ahnfelt, E. and From, J. (1993), 'European Policing' in S. Vein, *Making Policy in Europe. The Europeification of National Policy-Making*, Sage, London.

Anderson, M., den Bogr, M. and Mkller, G. (1989), *Policing the World – Interpol and the Politics of International Police Co-operation*, Clarendon Press, Oxford.

Anderson, M. *et al.* (1994), 'European Citizenship and Cooperation in Justice and Home Affairs', in A. Duff, Pindare and R. Pryce (eds.), *Maastricht and Beyond*, Routledge, London.

Barnes, I. and Barnes, P.M. (1995), *The Enlarged European Union*, Longman, London.

Bayley, D.H. (1994), *Police for the Future*, Oxford University Press, Oxford.

Benyon, J. (1995), 'The Developing System of Police Co-operation in the European Union' (mimeo), Centre for the Study of Public Order, University of Leicester, Leicester.

Benyon, J., Turnbull, L., Willis, A., Woodward, R. and Beck, A. (1993), *Police Co-operation in Europe: An Investigation*, Centre for the Study of Public Order, University of Leicester, Leicester.

Benyon, J., Morris, S., Toye, M., Willis, A. and Beck, A. (1995), *Police Forces in the New European Union: A Conspectus*. Centre for the Study of Public Order, University of Leicester, Leicester.

Bittner, E., (1990), *Aspects of Police Work*, Northeastern University Press, Boston.

Carter, D.L. (1993), 'A Forecast of Growth in Organized Crime in Europe: New Challenges for Law Enforcement', *Criminal Justice International*, Vol. 9, No. 2, pp. 62–74.

Clutterbuck, R. (1995), *Drugs, Crime and Corruption*, Macmillan, Basingstoke.

van Dijk, J.M. (1995), 'Towards a European Partnership Strategy at the Macro and Local Level in E.U.D.A.C.C.', Wandsworth Borough Council, pp. 12–16, London.

van Duyne, P. (1993), 'Organized Crime Markets in a Turbulent Europe', *European Journal on Criminal Policy and Research*, Vol. 3, pp. 10–30.

The European Commission, Background Reports (1994/5a), EC, Storey's Gate, London SW1P 3AT.

The European Commission (1994/5b), *The Week in Europe*, EC, Storey's Gate, London SW1P 3AT.

Fijnaut, C. (1991), 'Police Co-operation within Western Europe', in F.M. Heidensohn and M. Farrell (eds.), *Crime in Europe*, Routledge, London.

Fijnaut, C. (ed.) (1993), *The Internationalization of Police Co-operation in Western Europe*, Kluwer Law and Taxation Publishers, Doventer.

Hebenton, B. and Thomas, T. (1995), *Policing Europe – Co-operation, Conflict and Control*, Macmillan, Basingstoke.

Heidensohn, F.M. (1991), 'Introduction: Convergence, Diversity and Change', in F.M. Heidensohn and M. Farrell (eds.), *Crime in Europe*, Routledge, London.

Heidensohn, F.M. and Farrell, M. (eds.) (1991a), *Crime in Europe*, Routledge, London.
Heidensohn, F.M. and Farrell, M. (1991b), 'Social Welfare and Social Change in Europe', in G. Room (ed.), *Towards a European Welfare State?* SAUS, Bristol.
House of Commons (1990), Home Affairs Committee Seventh Report, *Practical Police Co-operation in the European Community*, HMSO, London.
House of Commons (1994), Select Committee on Home Affairs Inquiry into Organized Crime, London.
Jones, L.J. (1994), *The Social Context of Health and Health Work*, Macmillan, Basingstoke.
Kendall, R. (1993), 'Interpol Today – Interpol's Place in European Policing', *Policing*, pp. 279–85.
Leffler, M.P. and Painter, D.S. (eds.) (1994), *Origins of the Cold War – An International History*, Routledge, London.
Levi, M. (1993), 'The Extent of Cross Border Crime in Europe', *European Journal of Criminal Policy and Research*, Vol. 1, No. 3, pp. 57–77.
Levi, M. and Maguire, M. (1992), 'Crime and Cross-Border Policing in Europe', in J. Bailey (ed.), *Social Europe*, Longman, Harlow.
McLaughlin, E. (1992), 'The Democratic Deficit: European Union and the Accountability of the British Police', *British Journal of Criminology*, Vol. 32, No. 4, pp. 473–87.
Mawby, R. (1992), 'Comparative Police Systems: Searching for a Continental Model . . .', in K. Bottomley *et al.* (eds.), *Criminal Justice: Theory and Practice. British Journal of Criminology*, London.
Nacinovic, M. (1995), Presentation to European Urban Delinquency and Crime Conference, London, March.
Policespeak (1993), *Police Communications and Language and the Channel Tunnel: Report*. Policespeak Publications, Cambridge.
Raab, C. (1994), 'Police Co-operation: The Prospect for Privacy', in M. Anderson and M. Den Boer (eds.), *Policing Across National Boundaries*, Pinter, New York.
Reiner, R. and Spencer, S. (eds.) (1993), *Accountable Policing – Effectiveness, Empowerment and Equity*, Institute for Public Policy Research, London.
Sheptycki, J.W.E. (1995a), 'Transnational Policing and the Makings of a Postmodern State', *British Journal of Criminology*, Vol. 35, No. 4, pp. 613–35.
Sheptycki, J.W.E. (1995b), 'Folk Devils and Eurocops: Criminological Problems and Prospects for Understanding Transnational Crime and Policing in Europe', Paper delivered at British Criminology Conference, Loughborough.
Sheptycki, J.W.E. (1995c) Review, *British Journal of Criminology*, vol. 35, No. 2, pp. 302–7.
United Nations (1990), *Crime Prevention and Criminal Justice Newsletter*. Special Issue on the Eighth UN Congress on the Prevention of Crime and the Treatment of Offenders, United Nations Office, Vienna.
Valls-Russell, D, (1995), 'Pan European and Local Crime in the EU and in E.U.D.A.C.C.', Wandsworth Borough Council, pp. 27–30, London.

Valls-Russell, D. (1995), 'Pan European and Local Crime in the EU – The Role of EUROPOL', in *Europartners Against Crime*. Report of a Conference, Wandsworth Partnership and European Commission, London.

de Waard, J. (ed.), (1995), 'Crime Prevention in the Netherlands: Policies, Research and Practice', *Security Journal 6*, The Hague, Ministry of Justice.

Walker, N. (1993), 'The International Dimension', in R. Reiner and S. Spencer (1993).

Walker, N. (1993), 'The Accountability of European Police Institutions', *European Journal of Criminal Policy and Research*, Vol. 1, No. 4, pp. 34–53.

Walker, N. (1995), Evidence to the European Communities Sub-Commitee and (Law and Institutions) Inquiry into the Draft Convention on Europe.

Walker, N. (1995), 'Policing the European Union: The Politics of Transition', in O. Maremin (ed.), *Changing Police: Policing Change*.

Warr, P. (1987), *Work, Unemployment and Mental Health*. Clarendon Press, Oxford.

Wilzing, J. and Mangelaars, F. (1994), 'Establishing Europe', *European Journal on Criminal Policy and Research*, Vol. 1, No. 4, pp. 71–81.

Woodward, R. (1994), 'Establishing Europe', *European Journal on Criminal Policy and Research*, Vol. 1, No. 4, pp. 7–31.

6 The European Union's Common Foreign and Security Policy Conundrum

Jussi M. Hanhimäki

Defining a common foreign and security policy (CFSP) for the European Union (EU) is one of the hardest tasks the Member States are and will be facing. The problems are obvious. First, there is a sheer logistical concern: how do you get the foreign services of 15 Member States to co-operate with each other effectively? Secondly, there is an institutional problem: where is CFSP going to be 'made', and who will be responsible for implementing any decisions – the Western European Union (WEU), the North Atlantic Treaty Organisation (NATO), or the Conference on Security and Co-operation in Europe (CSCE)? Thirdly, there is the problem of defining what 'security' means in the second half of the 1990s and what should be placed under the general rubric of 'foreign policy' – is security simply a question of national security/defence, or does it involve such issues as the protection of the environment and the regulation of immigration from non-member countries? Lastly, how does one find a common thread to unite the historically divergent members of the EU, some of which have been allied with each other as members of NATO, others that remained neutral throughout the Cold War.

The Maastricht Treaty itself offers little help in narrowing down the definition of security. According to the Treaty on European Union (TEU), the Member States would simply 'safeguard the common values, fundamental interests and independence of the Union' and pledged to 'strengthen the security of the Union and its Member States in all ways'. Indeed, according to the TEU, CFSP was to include 'all questions relating to the security of the Union, including the eventual framing of the common defence policy, which might in time lead to a common defence'. Although relatively vague on institutional arrangements, the Maastricht Treaty identified the WEU as the central institution that was to 'implement decisions and actions of the Union which have defence implications'.

That was the CFSP as defined in the TEU. It was broadly-based and vague, and effective implementation has, thus far, proved difficult. This chapter outlines some of the major difficulties that have complicated the definition and implementation of a common European external policy before and after the Maastricht Treaty came into force in 1993. I shall begin by exploring the historical context of the Cold War (and détente), move on to the institutional and national rivalries and problems, and present a brief outline of some of the major current foreign and security policy concerns. In conclusion, I shall offer a prognosis as to why, at least in this author's opinion, the likelihood of a meaningful CFSP appears a very dim prospect in the near term.

FROM COLD WAR TO DÉTENTE

While the Cold War persisted the issue of common and foreign security policy was relatively simple. Between 1945 and 1989 the core countries of Western Europe (Britain, France, West Germany and Italy) essentially defined their foreign and security policy interests in terms of East–West confrontation. The division of the continent and the threat seen to be emanating from the USSR were the common threads that allowed for general unity to develop in the late 1940s and 1950s as these countries joined the US-led anti-Soviet coalition. This leadership role, and the differing interests and priorities of the Europeans, however, became contentious issues as the Cold War went through several stages of development.

Within a few years following Germany's surrender in May 1945, West Europeans had relatively quickly unified behind the United States to face the Soviet threat. Whilst there was concern, particularly in France, about the possibility of a

resurgent Germany, Soviet actions in Eastern Europe and
the American offer to help rebuild Europe, financed by the
Marshall Plan, had led to a broad anti-Soviet consensus by
the late 1940s. As the Soviet threat became even more omi-
nous with the Berlin blockade (1948–9), ten West European
countries (the Benelux countries, France, United Kingdom,
Iceland, Italy, Portugal, Norway and Denmark) joined the
United States and Canada to form NATO in the spring of
1949. Thus, the postwar security system that originated with
the Brussels Pact in the spring of 1948 (Benelux, France
and the United Kingdom) was given an Atlantic, rather than
a European, character. In practice, this meant that the United
States adopted a leadership role and assumed, in effect,
primary responsibility for the containment of the Soviet threat
in Europe. Moreover, as, for example, Geir Lundestad has
argued, West Europeans not only accepted this, but to a
large extent 'invited' Washington to play a leading role. With
Great Britain weakened by the war, France in internal political turmoil and Germany divided and economically shat-
tered, the United States provided the common link, and
argued the common purpose. For at least a decade after its
founding, there was little question that NATO was the predominant foreign and security policy institution in Western
Europe.[2]

Even during this period of relative unity, however, there
were disagreements and rivalries within Europe. The failure
of the European Defence Community (EDC) offers a good
example. In 1950 the Korean War placed an additional burden
on the United States and led to the conclusion that the
Americans did not have sufficient resources to fight a land
war in Asia and simultaneously counter a possible Soviet
attack in Western Europe. Thus, in September 1950, Washington proposed that West Germany be rearmed and invited to join NATO. The prospect was, however, particularly
distasteful to France, which was still deeply concerned at
the possibility of a military threat from Germany. The idea
that was put forward to counter such fears was the EDC, a
military organisation with a common army, budget and institutions. Placing West German and the other signatories'
(Benelux, France and Italy) military units under an integrated command structure, the European Defence Commu-

nity (EDC) – which founding treaty was signed in Paris on 27 May 1952 – was designed to keep the possibility of German militarism in check. Ironically, after two years of haggling and the ratification of the EDC treaty by the Benelux countries and West Germany, the French National Assembly rejected the treaty in August 1954.[3]

Great Britain, which had refused to join the EDC because of its supranational nature, stepped in to pick up the pieces. The prime minister, Anthony Eden, suggested that the best way of satisfying US demands for German rearmament on the one hand, and French fears of renewed German militarism on the other, was to revitalise the 1948 Treaty of Brussels and bring West Germany into NATO. In 1955, Italy and West Germany thus joined with the Brussels Treaty powers to establish the Western European Union (WEU), a loose coalition that was directly incorporated into NATO. In the end, the WEU had no significant independent structure and could not serve as a body defining effective political cooperation.[4]

During the next three decades the WEU's significance thus remained marginal; its main function was to ensure smoother European co-operation within the Atlantic organisation. In this regard the WEU did serve a dual purpose: it provided a link between Britain and the Rome Treaty powers after 1957, and a bridge between France and NATO after President de Gaulle's decision to withdraw France from NATO's integrated military structure in 1966. Like so many European institutions it remained, however, primarily consultative in nature.[5]

In the 1960s and 1970s the Cold War underwent a significant qualitative change which fundamentally affected the role of the superpowers in Europe. The 1962 Cuban missile crisis brought to the fore the growing fear of a nuclear holocaust; and at the same time, the United States' failure to consult its NATO partners during the crisis concerned many European leaders. During the 1960s the United States' protracted war in Vietnam, along with its relative decline as the world, economic hegemon, further shaped the Atlantic relationship. In addition, France's show of independence – de Gaulle's independent initiatives with the USSR and France's rift with NATO – and West Germany's *Ostpolitik* helped to usher in the era of détente and, to some degree, signified increasing European independence from the constraints of superpower confrontation. At the same time, the economic success of the Rome Treaty powers brought France and West Germany closer together. Another major dividing issue, at least in theory, was solved when Great Britain, with Denmark and Ireland, joined the EEC in January 1973. While de Gaulle's talk of a 'Europe from the Atlantic to the Urals' was premature – and effectively negated by the Warsaw Pact invasion of Czechoslovakia in August 1968 – the success of *Ostpolitik*, the CSCE process and the subsequent survival of European détente independent of the decline of Soviet–American détente, showed that by the mid-1970s political relationships within Europe were becoming less determined by the bipolar conditions of the Cold War.[6]

FROM EPC TO CFSP

European Political Co-operation (EPC) is, in some ways, a by-product of détente. During the 1969 EC summit in the Hague – the meeting that also launched the processes of enlargement and monetary union – the participants agreed to have their foreign ministers report on the potential for foreign policy co-operation. In 1970 the Davignon Report outlined the first major EC-based effort to coordinate foreign policy. EPC was launched as a process that consisted of regular meetings, starting in October 1970, of the Member States' foreign ministers and senior foreign service officials. Among its early successes was the co-ordination of Western European approaches to the CSCE process and bringing human rights prominently to the agenda of the 1975 Helsinki Final Act. However, the EPC was not an effective vehicle for solving the issues that divided the member countries (such as sanctions against South Africa) or bringing single countries in line with the others (e.g. Greece and Cyprus). Indeed, one could argue that even the issue of human rights at the CSCE may have owed a great deal more to US persistence on the matter than the EPC.[7]

The EPC suffered a significant setback when the Genscher–Columbo Plan (named after the West German and Italian foreign ministers), which was designed to strengthen the

EC's decision-making structure, was all but rejected in 1983. At the time the EC was undergoing one of its enlargement phases: Greece joined in 1981 and negotiations on the membership of Spain and Portugal were progressing. (Spain and Portugal eventually joined in 1986.) The political and economic implications of the South European enlargement were obviously significant, but all that the 1983 Stuttgart Heads of Government meeting could agree upon was a broad statement that promised to review progress in foreign, social and cultural matters in five years' time. It was, by and large, empty rhetoric which avoided making complicated and potentially unpopular decisions.

In addition to the EPC, the 1980s saw the reinvigoration of the WEU, when the French president, François Mitterrand, frustrated over the fate of the Genscher–Columbo Plan and the slow progress of the EPC, started pushing for an enhanced role for the virtually defunct institution. In part Mitterrand's efforts were a response to the New Cold War, the resurrection of Soviet–US tensions during Ronald Reagan's first term in office. Unless Western Europe wished simply to be dragged along with the United States – a fact the French had resented throughout most of the Cold War era – it needed a strong body to co-ordinate security and defence policy within, and outside of, NATO.[8] After all, by the mid-1980s Western Europe was economically strong enough to assume a larger role in its own defence. Thus, the WEU became a significant part of the European security structure with the Rome Declaration of October 1984. WEU was given a role as the body through which Member States would consult each other on matters related to joint defence, arms control and other security matters, including their relationships with each other and their role in the East–West confrontation. In addition, the WEU was to be a true European pillar within NATO. Whilst the WEU could not override NATO as the pre-eminent defence and security organisation in Western Europe, it was bound to become, at least on paper, the most significant EC (that is without outside members) vehicle for collaboration in foreign policy.[9]

In the late 1980s EPC was considered sufficiently successful to be formalised as part of the Single European Act (SEA) process. When the SEA came into force in June 1987, it set down formal procedures for EPC and established a small Secretariat in Brussels. In addition, the SEA included political and economic aspects of security under the EPC, provided for an association between the EPC and the European Parliament (EP), and established that the EP's assent was necessary before new associates or members could be included in the Community. In effect, the SEA significantly strengthened EPC. There were two problems, however. As is the case with most declarations during the history of European integration, the SEA, particularly regarding its provision on foreign and security policy, was extremely vague. In part this is quite understandable; when Mikhail Gorbachev embarked on his reforms in the USSR, the Cold War was still in force and security issues remained subject to the restraints of the East–West confrontation. The second problem was the lack of a significant institutional framework that could be used in order to coordinate and/or integrate the Member States' foreign and security policies effectively. Add to these the divergent views of the signatories, and the effective end-results of the SEA in terms of security and foreign policy co-operation were far from unifying.

The end of the Cold War opened a Pandora's box. With the coming to power of Mikhail Gorbachev in 1985 *glasnost* and *perestroika* had clearly exposed the intractable problems within the Eastern bloc, which led to the rapid dissolution of the Eastern European communist dictatorships in 1989 and the collapse of the Soviet Union in 1991.[10] At the same time Germany, the country that had symbolised the division of postwar Europe, was reunified. Thus collapsed the postwar international and European security system, and thus was freed an underlying current of nationalism and ethnic rivalries which had been overshadowed by the Cold War. The effects of this lack of restraint were soon felt in the Balkans, as the Yugoslav Federation came apart and descended into an orgy of violence.[11] Meanwhile, Europeans had to contend with another unsettling conflict of the post-Cold War world as the Iraqis invaded Kuwait and the US president, George Bush, in between discussions about the 'new world order', mustered an impressive coalition, which eventually had little trouble in pushing the Iraqis back to

Baghdad.[12] In short, the 1989 'Year of Miracles' was followed by years of unanswered problems, tough challenges and a need to rethink common principles and institutional arrangements regarding security and foreign policy.

INSTITUTIONAL RECONFIGURATION

As the Soviet threat faded away, Western Europe was rapidly faced with new, exciting opportunities and unsure prospects. For all its unpleasantness and wasteful spending on a nuclear arms race, the Cold War had made security and foreign policy decisions relatively straightforward. While living in the shadow of a nuclear holocaust, most West Europeans had at least agreed on their 'vital' security interests. But with the threat that produced such relative uninamity gone, the search for a new common denominator proved difficult. In the years 1989–92 trying to find agreement was further hampered by the institutional rivalries between the CSCE, NATO and the WEU – all creations of the Cold War. A further problem was that the major decision-makers involved in the process were all children of the Cold War, with little vision about how to adjust to a chaotic new world. While Bush may have spoken of 'a new world order', the reality consisted mostly of disorder, competition, distrust and, inevitably, incoherent policies and institutional readjustments.

Initially, the end of the Cold War seemed to enhance the role of the CSCE. After all, it was the only European-based security organisation to include NATO members, the neutrals and the former Soviet bloc. The CSCE was viewed, briefly, as an institution that offered a chance to resolve the many security issues – political, economic and military – that were rapidly coming to the fore. Its stated aims of promoting human rights and economic co-operation between East and West appeared particularly appealing to the emerging democracies in Eastern Europe. Nevertheless, hopes were high in November 1990 when the Member States signed the Paris Charter, which emphasised co-operation in a broad field of issues, ranging from human rights and democracy to economic liberty and environmental responsibility. Notable was the absence of stress on military security – a reflection, perhaps, of the optimism of the times.[13]

In the summer of 1991, however, military security became a major European issue as the turmoil in Yugoslavia erupted after Slovenia and Croatia announced that they were leaving the Yugoslav Federation. The CSCE was quickly paralysed as the Yugoslav vote (and thus veto right) in the CSCE was controlled by the Serbs. In addition, during the early 1992 meeting of CSCE foreign ministers, the German proposal for the creation of a CSCE peacekeeping force was rejected and the CSCE was relegated to a minor, indeed, an all but insignificant, role. At best, it could provide a moral voice as the atrocities mounted and the frustration grew.

Meanwhile, a limited rivalry between NATO and the WEU developed. In essence the issue was the redefinition of the relationship between the United States and Western Europe in the post-Cold War era. In the spirit of Europhoria, the French in particular hoped that the WEU would overtake NATO as the pre-eminent institutional framework for European security and defence matters. During the Gulf War the WEU, in fact, co-ordinated the military contributions of its member countries, albeit within the general framework of NATO.

The seeming enhancement of the WEU's role in 1989–91 was partly a result of NATO's, and particularly the United States', concern with the major issues unfolding at the time. While NATO's initial reaction to the collapse of the Soviet empire was rather muted, the main focus was on the impact of German unification and the still outstanding arms control negotiations. Throughout the early 1990s NATO, in fact, seemed to be relinquishing the major role for post-Cold War European security to CSCE. In 1990–1 NATO's main concerns were the Gulf War and the relationship with the former Soviet bloc, particularly the future control over the vast nuclear arsenal stationed in the various former Soviet republics.[14]

It has become clear, however, that NATO continues to be the pre-eminent security organisation, and the United States still has great leverage over the making of security policy in Europe. The Gulf War, for example, served as a reminder to the Europeans that without US participation, effective

European military action was likely to remain a pipedream and that the WEU to a large extent was still a paper organisation. In addition, CSCE's impotence in the Bosnian crisis meant that NATO quickly re-emerged as the primary security institution in 1992–3. An agreement was reached in early 1993, for example, that the Franco-German Eurocorps would be placed under NATO command in the event of crisis. In January 1994, the Clinton administration's 'Partnership for Peace' (PfP) formula could be seen as a US effort to seize control over establishing a future pan-European security framework. Its success seemed guaranteed when, in May 1994, Russia, after its western neighbours had already done so, indicated its willingness to participate in PfP.[15] Moreover, it was the Clinton administration's pressure that finally helped to end the bloodshed in Bosnia. Although the Dayton Agreement, reached on 21 November 1995, was hardly a foolproof formula, it is far more than the combined efforts of various European peace missions had achieved.[16]

So far the post-Cold War reinvigoration of the WEU has, in short, been more or less impotent. In contrast to NATO, an alliance with well-established bureaucracies and institutional structures, the WEU is an unstructured newcomer caught in the whirlwind of a rapidly changing international environment. It can hardly be said to have a set agenda, not to mention the capability of actually imposing effective pressure, whether political or military, in a crisis.

Some of this relative impotence was to be resolved by the Maastricht Treaty. In December 1991, the European Council decided to move WEU's headquarters from London to Brussels, an act that was meant to stress the symbolic significance of the WEU as part of an institutional framework of a more closely integrated post-Cold War Europe. The Maastricht Treaty also enhanced the WEU's role as the central institution that would 'implement decisions and actions of the Union which have defence implications'.[17] Indeed, the TEU, which came into force after ratification in 1993, seemed to raise the WEU to the central institutional framework under which defence and security policy was to be made.

At the same time, it was clear that the TEU's broad principles of CFSP concealed the continued difficulty of reconciling the problem between national and EU foreign and security policies. The treaty itself states that the two – national capitals and Brussels – will act in unison to define and implement CFSP. Both goals are beset with problems. The difficulty with achieving the first of the tasks, 'defining' CFSP, appears to be virtually impossible, particularly if the EU goes through yet another stage of enlargement. On the other hand, the implementation of CFSP again raises the question of a proper institutional framework and decision-making structure; not all members of the EU, for example, are currently members of the WEU. Moreover, because the TEU covered all areas of security policy, it suggested that a redefinition of the relationship between the WEU, NATO and CSCE was needed. Because the TEU still endorsed the unanimity rule within the Council, the problem of national differences remained a major problem. To be sure, the TEU charged the Council with defining issues that would be decided by majority rulings, but the practical implications of that are likely to be meagre in the near future, although the Intergovernmental Conference scheduled for 1996 may provide some clarification. It is, however, highly unlikely that the EU will force its majority will (if such were to develop) against the interests or needs of one of its 'major' countries (the United Kingdom, Germany, France). While internal divisions are likely to continue to hamper CFSP, other tests are likely to arise from external sources.

CHALLENGES EAST AND SOUTH

As in the past, the potential for unity in the future may lie, unfortunately, in the aggravation of new or potential threats. If the issues of nationalism and divergent security concerns of the member countries are the major dividing forces with the EU's quest for CFSP, the relationship *vis-à-vis* the outside world may provide some common threads. Yet, even in this case the fact that these real and potential threats are, in the end, geographically determined means that their gravity to the various union members differ significantly. It is by no means certain that a unified front can easily be established. Two specific geographic regions, the Mediterranean and the former Soviet bloc, are likely to remain problems regardless of the institutional frameworks that are adopted.

The Maghreb states of North Africa (Algeria, Morocco, Tunisia, Libya, Mauretania) have all concluded protocols on financial and technical co-operation with the EC/EU, the present (fourth) being in force until October 1996. A similar protocol has been concluded with a number of Middle East, or Mashreq, states (Egypt, Jordan, Lebanon and Syria). Under these pacts, the Maghreb and Mashreq countries are eligible for low-interest loans from the European Investment Bank (EIB) and for grants from the EU Budget to help the economic development of the area. Although there have been disagreements over whether the aid to these countries should be in the form of loans and grants (preferred by southern EU states) or simply in the form of preferential treatment in trade (as the northern members, who end up bearing much of the cost of loans and grants, would hope), there is relative unanimity that the Mediterranean countries are a priority area.

Why is this the case? Sadly, the answer is fear. It is fear of migration prompted by economic and political instability; fear of terrorism prompted by the rise of Islamic fundamentalism; fear, in short, of the type of 'clash of civilisations' Samuel P. Huntington wrote about in his controversial 1993 essay.[18] In 1995, the main issue in relations with the Mediterranean countries was on one of the Maghreb countries, Algeria, and its relations with France, the colonial power until 1962. In 1989 the National Liberation Front (FLN), which had ruled the country since independence, faced a crisis brought about by a horrendous economy, a rapidly growing population and ethnic strife. The FLN agreed to suggestions for democratisation; and a new constitution allowed for alternative political parties to organise. More than 50 were formed, but in the 1990 elections the most successful of them turned out to be the Islamic Salvation Front (FIS), a radical fundamentalist coalition. The next election, held in December 1991, was annulled in January 1992 by the Algerian army, and the FIS was banned. In June 1992 FIS extremists assassinated the President, Mohamed Boudiaf, and civil unrest turned into a war that claimed approximately 30 000 lives between 1992 and 1995. Assassination campaigns against foreigners in Algeria and terrorism abroad, most visibly in

France, became a part of the FIS's strategy, although following the November 1995 elections, in which a weary nation lent its support to President Liamine Zeroual, the FIS called for a peaceful settlement of the four-year crisis.[19]

The civil conflict in Algeria has become the most visible symbol of a growing fear that affects the Mediterranean EU countries in particular, that is, France, Greece, Italy and Spain. All four, as well as Tunisia, have offered assistance to the current Algerian government by using their security forces to monitor and at times arrest suspected militants. The fear of Muslim fundamentalism, which might lead to the creation of regimes in North Africa similar to that of Iran, is further heightened by the fact that the fundamentalist governments of Iran and Sudan support the FIS. On the other hand, the combination of a rapid increase in population in the 'Muslim Crescent' (from Iran to Morocco) and stagnant economies – in Algeria, for example, almost three-quarters of people under the age of 25 are unemployed – heightens the spectre of future waves of immigrants coming across the Mediterranean. Millions of Maghrebis, for example, already live in different parts of southern Europe. The flashpoint has been evident in recent years as anti-immigrant sentiments have become popular political tools within EU countries, perhaps most prominently in France, where the Minister of the, Interior Charles Pasqua, announced 'zero migration' as his goal in 1993. The FIS has responded by a series of terrorist attacks, most notably in France. The fear is that any sort of unrest in North Africa, such as the current crisis in Algeria, would result in a further influx of refugees across the Mediterranean.[20] The only sensible solution, it seems, is for the EU to act to raise prosperity in the region. The EU's recent Customs Union agreement with Turkey should be seen in the same light.

The Middle East presents another problem. While fear of migration may not appear to be such a pressing concern, one of the greatest nightmares for the EU (and the United States) is that the rise of Islamic fundamentalism will lead to a situation in which the EU is cut off from the region's oil reserves, a fear that was made all the more real by the Gulf War in 1990–1.[21] The EU therefore has a great stake in the peace process in the Middle East, and the prevention of conflicts that might erupt between Middle East states (not necessarily between the Arab states and Israel) in the future. The dilemma is that stability in the Middle East is endlessly challenged, not least by the large economic gap between the oil-rich and the poor Arab states, the militancy and the unpredictability of such regimes as Iran and Iraq, and the persistent opposition to the peace process, evidenced by, for example, the assassination of Israel's prime minister, Yitzhak Rabin, in November 1995 and fundamentalist terrorist attacks in Saudi Arabia later that month.[22]

The fear of Islamic fundamentalism is likely to remain one of the central problems for the CFSP in the future. When the European Council decided, in June 1994, to include Malta and Cyprus in the next stage of enlargement this meant that Israel and Egypt would eventually become EU neighbours. With the chaotic state of Egypt and the fragile progress of the Israeli–Palestinian peace process, EU's stake in the promotion of stability will be enhanced. In essence, the challenge is for the EU to: (a) involve itself more in the reconciliation between Arabs and Jews (an arena in which the EU has traditionally been overshadowed by the United States); (b) expand its economic links with the Middle East and Maghreb; and (c) do this whilst at the same time becoming increasingly exposed to further terrorist attacks on its own territory.

If the Maghreb states present serious migrationary prospects, the same applies certainly to the countries of the former Soviet bloc. While France has felt the brunt of North African migration, Germany has experienced a great flux of asylum-seekers, mostly from the former Soviet bloc and former Yugoslavia. In 1989–92, for example, Germany accepted approximately 1.2 million refugees . During the early 1990s these refugees were met by a population suffering from an economic reunification hangover and a simultaneous rise in neo-Nazism and attacks on immigrant populations. While Germany has not yet announced 'zero migration', and probably never will, the Bundestag, in a controversial decision that evoked some ugly memories of the nation's Nazi past, voted to change the country's liberal asylum laws in 1993.[23]

Whilst migration from Eastern Europe is a major issue, the prospect that civil unrest in one of the former Soviet republics would, at some time in the future, push another flood of refugees towards the West, raises critical prospects for the future. With the accession of Finland to the EU on 1 January 1995, the EU now shares a common border with Russia over 1000 km long, a border that is relatively unguarded. With the possibility of such countries as Poland, Slovakia and Hungary joining the EU, it would then have borders with two of the most densely populated, non-Russian former Soviet republics, namely Belarus and Ukraine. Should Hungary, Romania and Bulgaria join, the EU would share a border with Serbia and, unless the Dayton Peace Plan of November 1995 succeeds in bringing a lasting peace to the Balkans, the EU would be compelled to act more decisively in that region than has been the case thus far.

Although the challenges may be clear, there are hardly any non-controversial solutions. The obvious, and all but confirmed, approach is to have these potential members gradually integrated into the EU. Their troubled economies and the endemic ethnic tensions in the former Soviet bloc, however, provide little reason to expect that even the most successful of the Visegrad states (the Czech Republic, Poland) will be granted EU membership by the year 2000, as some optimists had hoped in the early 1990s.[24] At the same time, keeping them continuously on a waiting list will, most likely, only exacerbate the problems. Making these countries 'acceptable' for EU membership calls, naturally, for generous economic aid. Here, the EU is bound to run into an internal dilemma over which is the more important region to be concerned with: the Mediterranean countries, led by France, will probably push for helping the Maghreb states, while the northern countries, led by Germany, are more likely to focus on Eastern Europe.[25]

There is, of course, nothing new in expansion. Since the 1957 Rome Treaty Western European integration has gone through several stages of enlargement. In 1973 Britain, Denmark and the Irish Republic joined the Community; in the 1980s Greece, Portugal and Spain became members in the southern stage of enlargement. In the first post-Soviet era expansion three neutral countries – Austria, Finland and Sweden – joined the EU in January 1995. Currently, talk about expanding further East in order to include all or some of the East/Central European, countries of the former Soviet bloc is a frequent topic of discussion and speculation. The problem, in terms of CFSP, is that, as with the previous enlargements (with the exception, perhaps, of the 1973 case), the additional members bring with them added national needs and security concerns which are hard to reconcile with the needs of all the Member States.

Whilst the end of the Cold War may have made neutrality obsolete by removing the conflict that these countries were neutral from, each has a specific problem that they need to address. Austrian neutrality, for example, is based on the country's 1955 constitution. However, as that in itself was a Cold War by-product, the Austrians may be quite willing to abandon their 40-year tradition in a new international environment. On the other hand, Swedish neutrality dates back to the early nineteenth century and is, in many ways, part of the country's cherished political tradition. With unhappiness over the economic cost of joining the EU growing, one can expect that serious opposition to abandoning neutrality in favour of CFSP will rise. In the case of Finland the situation is even more difficult. Having placed prime importance on satisfying the USSR's security concerns and modifying its neutrality to meet the Kremlin's foreign policy goals, the Finns are faced with a new, potentially more serious, 'eastern question'. Having the unenviable position as the border state of an unpredictable Russia, the Finns may find it virtually impossible to join in a CFSP that is likely to provoke the brewing nationalism in their eastern neighbour even further. The Finnish position has, ironically, become far more unpredictable than it was a few years ago. At the same time, although Finland has suffered economically from the reduction in cross-border trade with the former Soviet Union, the greatest disparity in living standards between an EU country and its eastern neighbour is the one between Finland and Russia.[26]

Even with the possible inclusion of the countries from the former Soviet bloc, however, the question of further enlargement is bound to continue to haunt the EU. The great dilemma of CFSP is that in the end the problems seem to have solutions that are not only expensive but are likely to be solved, if at all, only temporarily: if you expand to Poland, will you draw the line there? For if you stop expanding, you run the risk of creating a strong new border – potentially, indeed, a new Iron Curtain – between a 'Fortress Europe' and the CIS. But if you do expand, every step on the expansionary course will add yet another distinctive element to the structure and complicate, possibly jeopardise, any prospect of unified decision-making. In short, in terms of CFSP the EU might become like the CSCE, unable to act effectively and decisively when faced with a major challenge. Even if expansion may, to some, amount to added external security, at the same time it brings more internal dissent.

THE CFSP CONUNDRUM

The problem of defining and implementing CFSP is truly a multifaceted one. In part it is one of the legacies of the sudden collapse of the Cold War order, which whilst removing a major threat to Western Europe, has opened up a multitude of other threats. In part the problem is linked to the changing and increasingly complex nature of security in the late twentieth century; it incorporates not only the 'traditional' issues of military threats and economic-political relationships, but environmental, immigration and social issues. In addition, the decision-making process has yet to be clarified and enlargement to East/Central Europe, if it is to take place, is likely to produce yet more dilemmas and complications.

This is not to overlook the fact that there are, of course, new, real and potential security threats which may actually help in the construction of a common foreign and security policy for the EU in the future. The prospect of a post-Yeltsin nationalist Russia, the continued sorry state of affairs in former Yugoslavia and the rise of Islamic fundamentalism present only the most obvious negative building blocks for CFSP. The problem is, however, that most of these issues are as much 'national' as they are 'pan-European'. It is hard to see that, say, the Finns and the Portuguese will interpret the significance of a sudden change in the internal political situation in Russia with similar urgency. In other words, most (probably all) EU Member States still see national security as far more important than supranational security. As Noel Malcolm puts it: 'On each separate security issue, individual states may have concerns of their own that are not shared by their fellow [EU] members. To try to form a single "European" policy on such issues, whether by unanimity, consensus, or majority voting, is to guarantee at best ineffective compromise and at worst self-paralysis.'[27] Indeed, the possibility that national policies can be standardised and organised into an effective CFSP appears slim.

They appear naturally even slimmer if the EU continues to expand: 'widening' will certainly do little to improve the 'deepening' of CFSP. While enlargement may, on the one hand, enhance security in the short term and help in reducing the migratory prospects from the former Soviet bloc, the fact is that there has to be a physical limit to expansion if the EU is to retain any significant 'European' function. This, in turn, is bound to raise concerns in the regions that will be excluded, perhaps most significantly in Russia and the former Soviet republics, lest a European fortress of some sort be established. Given that internal EC/EU liberalism has traditionally been accompanied by protective 'neo-mercantilist' attitudes towards the outside world, such fears are, naturally, well-founded.[28] In a world where economic security has gained added prominence in contrast to military security, and in the case of an EU that has, thus far, found it easier to unite behind a common economic cause (the Uruguay Round of GATT) than behind a common military–diplomatic cause (Bosnia), the EU walks a fine line between aggravating the threats so evident in the economic inequality between the EU and its neighbouring states and becoming a protectionist bloc. Inclusion and enlargement may, in short, deepen the security conundrum further.

In the end, as in any democracy, the final say should (and one must hope will) be with the voters of each EU country. They are likely to reject, at least in the foreseeable future, any further moves to tighten CFSP. While it is easy to agree with Louise B. van Tartwijk-Novey that the EU 'needs to proceed rapidly toward the creation of a common foreign policy, solidify security and defence cooperation and agree on effective means to execute them', one is hard pressed to see this happening in the near future.[29] There are, to put it simply, too many divergent and geographically defined threats – Islamic fundamentalism, Russian nationalism, the crisis in former Yugoslavia, the prospects of migration – to provide for a unified vision based on a common 'enemy' as was the case during the Cold War. At the same time, there are too many internally divisive issues – varied national interests that still continue to proclaim the importance of the nation-state and national identity as the common denominator that far outweighs any sense of 'Europeanness' – to provide for unity from within. In this context, one needs to ask whether a completely unified decision-making structure, if one could in theory be implemented under, say, the WEU, would actually benefit the individuals that comprise the European Union. What would be the specific needs that it could satisfy? Can all its opponents simply be branded as nationalists? Is it perhaps not only impossible, but also undesirable from the perspective of individual voters in individual countries, to create a coherent and tight decision-making structure in the areas of foreign and security policy, because the end-result might be that they would, to varying degrees, expose themselves to dangers (such as fundamentalist terrorism from a variety of sources) from which they had previously been reasonably immune?

The historical irony may be that European integration was, in the end, significantly fuelled by the Cold War, a confrontation dominated by two superpowers with 'global' interests. As the Soviet–US confrontation drew to a close, European economic integration continued, but, at the same time, cooperation in the field of foreign and security policy became a complex myriad hampered by differing national interests. This is not to say that a grave threat of a resurgent nationalism sweeping across Europe exists. Rather, the point is that with the unifying threat gone, or at least diminished, democracies have and are bound to react to their specific constituencies' demands that they should not be overburdened with visions that seem to have little to do with the everyday lives of the majority of EU citizens. In other words, it is not that 'old-style' nationalism (as was the case with France *vs.* Germany) is bound to be revived within the current EU countries. Rather, as it seems unnecessary to fear invasion by the Red Army, however unlikely it was even during the Cold War, the majority of people are likely to find local issues more significant than the broad plans handed down from Brussels or Strasbourg or Luxembourg. As long as that remains the case, as long as the policy-makers themselves are unable either to agree on what the acronym CFSP actually means in practice or to explain it to their constituencies, the EU will continue to lack an effective common foreign and security policy.

NOTES

1. The TEU (and/or extracts) has been published in a variety of forms. These quotes are from Articles J.1 and J.4 in Dorman and Treacher (1995: 168–9).
2. Lundestad (1986: 1–21). On the United States, Europe and NATO, see Kaplan (1994). For two differing views on the impact of the Marshall Plan, see Hogan (1987) and Milward (1984).
3. For example, Hanrieder (1989), Duchin (1992: 431–60) and Hershberger (1992: 511–49).
4. On British policy, see Young (1994).
5. See, for example, Urwin (1995: 68–71).
6. A concise overview of these developments can be found in Young (1991: 14–20) and van Oudenaren (1992). On de Gaulle's policies, see Lacoutre (1991).
7. For a thorough outline of the development of EPC prior to the Maastricht Treaty, see Nuttal (1992).
8. On the uneasy Franco-American relationship during the Cold War, see Costigliola (1992).
9. For a collection of documents that outline the reinvigoration of the WEU, see WEU (1988).
10. For an overview of these events, see Garthoff (1994: 375ff).
11. Resurgent nationalism in the Balkans and the war in former Yugoslavia have produced a plethora of literature in recent years. One of the most comprehensive accounts is Rieff (1995).
12. Probably the most balanced account of the Gulf War is Freedman and Karsh (1993). See also Divine (1995: 117–34).
13. On the CSCE in the post-Cold War era, see Lucas (1993). A good overview of the institutional uncertainties in the 1990s is Howorth (1995: 330–8).
14. See Otte (1992: 234–51). Much of the discussion below is based on Dean (1994).

15. See van Tarwjik-Novey (1995: 137–4). For a contemporary discussion, see Williams *et al.* (1993).
16. See *Financial Times*, 22 November 1995, p. 2.
17. TEU, Article J.4.
18. Huntington (1993).
19. The discussion on Algeria and the fear of migration from North Africa is based largely on Roberts (1995) and Dean (1994: 185–99). On the 1995 elections, see, for example, *Financial Times*, 23 November 1995, 5.
20. Such fears reached a particularly high point in France in 1994. See Blunden (1994).
21. One of the best and most comprehensive accounts of the significance of Middle East oil for 'western' economies is Yergin (1992).
22. On the Middle East, see Nonneman (1993).
23. See Dean (1994: 166–7). On German unification see, for example, Garton (Ash 1993: 344 ff).
24. See 'The EU Goes Cold on Enlargement', *The Economist*, 28 October 1995, pp. 55–6.
25. For a generally more hopeful discussion on the prospects of enlargement, see Moisi and Mertes (1995).
26. See Bebler (1992).
27. See Malcolm (1995: 68).
28. See Wolf (1995).
29. See van Tartwijk-Novey (1995: 145).

REFERENCES

Bebler, A. (1992), 'The Neutral and Non-Aligned States in the New European Security Architecture', *European Security*, Vol. 1, No. 2, pp. 132–51.
Blunden, M. (1994), 'Insecurity on Europe's Southern Flank', *Survival*, Vol. 36, Summer, pp. 130–47.
Costigliola, F. (1992), *France and the United States: The Cold Alliance since World War II*, Twayne Publishers, New York.
Dean, J. (1994), *Ending Europe's Wars: The Continuing Search for Peace and Security*, Twentieth Century Fund, New York.
Divine, R.A. (1995), 'Historians and the Gulf War: A Critique', *Diplomatic History*, Vol. 19, Winter, pp. 117–34.
Dorman, A. and Treacher, A. (1985), *European Security: An Introduction to Security Issues in Post-Cold War Europe*, Darsmouth, Aldershot.
Duchin, B.R. (1992), 'The "Agonizing Reappraisal": Eisenhower, Dulles, and the EDC', *Diplomatic History*, Vol. 16, Spring.
Freedman, L. and Karsh, E. (1993), *The Gulf Conflict, 1990–1991: Diplomacy and War in the New World Order*, Faber and Faber, London.
Garton Ash, T. (1993), *In Europe's Name. Germany and the Divided Continent*, London: Vintage, pp. 344ff.

Garthoff, R. (1994), *The Great Transition*, Brookings Institution, Washington, DC.

Hanrieder, W.F. (1989), *Germany, America, Europe*, Yale University Press, New Haven, CT.

Hershberger, J.G. (1992), '"Explosion in the Offing": German Rearmament and American Diplomacy', *Diplomatic History*, Vol. 16, Fall, pp. 511–49.

Hogan, M. (1987), *The Marshall Plan: America, Britain, and the Reconstruction of Western Europe, 1947/52*, Cambridge University Press, Cambridge.

Howorth, J. (1995), 'Towards a European Foreign and Security Policy?' in Jack Hayward and Edward C. Page (eds.), *Governing the New Europe*, Polity Press, Cambridge, pp. 317–45.

Huntington, S.P. (1993), 'The Clash of Civilizations?', *Foreign Affairs*, Vol. 72, No. 3, pp. 22–49.

Kaplan, L. (1994), *NATO and the United States*, Twayne Publishers, New York, 2nd edn.

Lacoutre, J. (1991), *De Gaulle: the Ruler, 1945–1970*, Harvill, New York.

Lucas, M. (ed.) (1993), *The CSCE in the 1990s*, Nomos Verlagsgesellschaft, Baden-Baden.

Lundestad, G. (1986), 'Empire by Invitation? The United States and Western Europe, 1945–1952', *Journal of Peace Research*, Vol. 23, pp. 1–21.

Malcolm, N. (1995), 'The Case against Europe', *Foreign Affairs*, Vol. 74, No. 2, p. 68.

Milward, A. S. (1984), *The Reconstruction of Western Europe, 1945–1951*, London: Methuen.

Moisi, D. and Mertes, M. (1995), *Europe's Map, Europe's Horizon, Foreign Affairs*, Vol. 74, No. 1, pp. 122–34.

Nonneman, G. (ed.) (1993), *The Middle East and Europe: The Search for Stability and Integration*, Federal Trust for Education and Research, with the collaboration of Trans-European Policy Studies Association, London.

Nuttal, S.J. (1992), *European Political Cooperation*, Clarendon, Oxford.

Otte, T.G. (1992), 'Continuity and Change: NATO's Role after the Cold War', *Arms Control*, Vol. 13, September, pp. 234–51.

Rieff, D. (1995), *Slaughterhouse: Bosnia and the Failure of the West*, London: Vintage.

Roberts, H. (1995), 'Algeria's Ruinous Impasse and the Honourable Way Out', *International Affairs*, Vo. 71, pp. 247–67.

Urwin, D.W. (1995), *The Community of Europe*, Longman, London, 2nd edn.

van Oudenaren, John (1992), *Détente in Europe: The Soviet Union and the West since 1953*, Duke University Press, Chapel Hill, NC.

van Tarwjik-Novey, L.B. (1995), *The European House of Cards*, Macmillan, New York.

WEU (1988), *The Reactivation of the WEU: Statements and Communiqués, 1984 to 1987*, Western European Union, London.

Williams, P. *et al.* (1993), 'Atlantis Lost, Paradise Regained? The United

States and Western Europe after the Cold War', *International Affairs*, Vol. 61, pp. 1–17.

Wolf, M. (1995), 'Cooperation or Conflict? The European Union in a Liberal Global Economy', *International Affairs*, Vol. 71, No. 2, pp. 325–37.

Yergin, D. (1992), *The Prize: The Epic Quest for Oil, Money and Power*, Simon & Schuster, New York.

Young, J. (1991), *Cold War Europe 1945–1989*, Edward Arnold, London.

Young, J. (1994), *Britain and European Unity, 1945–1992*, Macmillan, Basingstoke.

7 East–West Trade
Klaus Heidensohn

This chapter is concerned with the development and future of economic relations between the 'old' Europe, i.e. the European Union (EU) and the 'new' Europe, i.e. the transition economies of Central and Eastern Europe (CEE). Unless otherwise stated, CEE or the CEECs (Central and East European countries) should be understood to include the Visegrad countries (the Czech and Slovak Republics [henceforth referred to as ex-CSFR], Hungary and Poland), Bulgaria and Romania. Trade links between 'European' member countries of the former Soviet Union such as, for example, the Baltic States, will not be covered here; nor will we include Albania and the successor states of the (former) Yugoslavia. And although the remaining EFTA (European Free Trade Area) countries (Norway, Switzerland, Iceland and Liechtenstein) are part of Western Europe, this study is limited to the EU. At the outset, it should also be stressed that we do not seek to treat all aspects of East-West economic relations. A comprehensive discussion of the many facets of the economic interpenetration between the EU and CEE (trade, aid, foreign investment, labour movements, etc.) would clearly be beyond the scope of this chapter. We shall restrict our analysis to trade, arguably 'the economic and political cornerstone' (Costello and Laredo 1994: 155) of CEE's transition process to a market system. The focus of our discussion will be on trade in manufactured goods, as these represent the bulk of trade between CEE and the EU (manufactured products account for some 80 per cent of total EU–CEE trade).

We shall deal with three distinctive aspects of East–West trade in Europe. First, we shall discuss the pattern of trade that characterised the economic relations between Central and Eastern Europe and the EU before the CEECs embarked on a process of economic (and political) transformation in the late 1980s. In dealing with this question we shall consider both the pre-Second World War trade patterns and

East–West trade during the Comecon or CMEA (Council for Mutual Economic Assistance) phase. Second, we shall deal with the trade links between the 'old' and the 'new' Europe that have evolved in the years following the collapse of Eastern Europe's trade bloc and the subsequent trade liberalisation measures introduced by the CEECs and the EU. This part of our discussion will cover the evolution of pan-European trade during the transition phase the CEECs have been going through since the late 1980s; an identification of the market access issues that have resulted from the existence of EU barriers to imports from the CEECs; and the Europe Agreements negotiated between the EU and the CEECs with the aim of promoting trade (and harmonious economic relations) between the 'old' and the 'new' Europe. Third, we shall endeavour to predict the nature and extent of future trade links between the EU and the CEECs: Central and Eastern Europe's potential trade; the impact that greater economic interpenetration between the EU and the CEECs is likely to have on the EU economy; and the question of an enlargement of the European Union to the east.

PRE-TRANSFORMATION

Although we do not intend to offer a history of European trade, in dealing with East–West economic relations prior to the demise of the CMEA trade bloc, it is useful to distinguish between the pre-Second World War situation, when the CEECs were market economies, and the post-1945 phase, when the CEECs' trade was characterised by central planning and state-trading.

Pre-Second World War

According to League of Nations data (1942), CEE's trade performance in the pre-Second World War years was not significantly different from Western Europe's. Some of the CEECs, notably Hungary and Czechoslovakia, made major contributions to Europe's world exports. In 1928, the most recent pre-Second World War year for which official statistics exist, Czechoslovakia, for example, was the seventh largest

European exporter; and the exports of Bulgaria and Romania equalled those of Ireland and Finland (League of Nations 1942). Although data problems make comparisons with post-war years difficult, the available evidence would suggest that the CEECs contributed much more significantly to total European exports in 1928 than in 1991. Their shares of Europe's exports were 2–5 times larger in 1928 than in 1991 (Baldwin 1994: 106). The years 1928 and 1991 not only differed in terms of CEE's relative volume of trade; differences can also be found when we consider the direction of trade: the CEECs' shares of exports going to EU countries fell between 1928 and 1991; intra-CEE exports were more important in 1928 than in 1991 (League of Nations 1942; IMF 1992). While the CEECs were, during their state-trading phase, not considered major export markets for West European producers, the situation was quite different in 1928 when CEE provided important export destinations for many West European countries. Exports from Austria, Germany, Ireland and Italy to CEE, for example, amounted to approximately 40, 14, 8 and 7 per cent respectively of these countries' total exports. Czechoslovakia, Hungary and Poland absorbed most of the imports from Western Europe (League of Nations 1942). We should, of course, not expect countries' positions in world trade and the direction of their trade flows to remain unaltered over a 60-year period (the United Kingdom is a case in point). But, although competitive advantages of nations change over time, the economic policies pursued by the Eastern bloc (the former Soviet Union and the CEECs) over the four decades between the end of the Second World War and the dismantling of Comecon in the late 1980s were such that they were bound to have a dramatic impact on the Comecon countries' trade flows. The Eastern bloc's declared trade policy objective was, after all, to restrict its member countries' economic links with market economies.

Comecon Phase

The incorporation of Central and Eastern Europe into the centrally planned and state-trading Eastern bloc at the end of the Second World War significantly affected the CEECs' involvement in world trade. For the political separation of Europe into 'West' and 'East' disrupted natural and previously established trade flows between CEE and Western Europe. The increase in the CEECs' trade with the (former) Soviet Union was largely due to the influence exerted by Comecon which was established in 1949 and embraced the CEECs plus the republics of the (former) Soviet Union. The aim of Comecon was to promote the economic development of the Eastern bloc via co-operation, more intensive trade relations between CMEA countries, notably trade between CEE and the (former) Soviet Union, and joint bulk buying from Western capitalist countries.

Until 1989 bilateral agreements dominated trade between the EU and the CEECs. East–West trade in Europe was, furthermore, influenced by the following factors (Nello 1991: 4):

- centrally fixed prices and foreign trade monopolies, absence of currency convertibility and other features of non-market economies in CEE;
- CEE's shortages of hard currencies and its high foreign indebtedness;
- interconnectedness of political and economic aspects of east-west relations (trade embargoes and arrangements to confine exports of, for example, strategic items to Warsaw Pact countries);
- protectionist measures (anti-dumping measures, quantitative restrictions including voluntary export restraint agreements and safeguard measures adopted by EU countries).

The impact of these factors was such that it severely restricted CEE's (and the former Soviet Union's) trade with the market economies of the EU (and other western industrialised countries). Producers in CEE did not, unlike suppliers in Western Europe, have to make their industries globally competitive. Comparative advantages – the most important determinant of international trade in market-oriented economies – had only a limited influence on their trade flows. There was, furthermore, no discernible benefit to be derived by any CEEC from achieving a trade surplus. 'Transferable' roubles a Comecon country would earn as a net exporter to other CMEA countries could not be used to pay for imports from market economies because they were not fully convertible.

Although meetings between the Comecon Secretariat and the European Commission took place in the early 1970s with the aim of establishing more trade links between the EU and the Soviet Union and Eastern Europe, little progress was made until Mikhail Gorbachev came to power in 1986. Prior to 1986 Comecon had, at the request of the Soviet Union, insisted on acting on behalf of all its members. The EU, whilst willing to work with Comecon, was only prepared to negotiate trade agreements with CMEA countries on an individual basis. Following the signing of a joint declaration by Comecon and EU delegates in June 1988 to agree on mutual recognition of the two organisations, a number of trade agreements were signed between the CEECs and the EU. Although these first-generation trade agreements opened the way for a new era of trade links between the EU and CEE, they could not be expected to bring about significant increases in East-West trade in the short run. They were too limited in scope and were not supported by corollary economic reform measures.

CENTRAL AND EASTERN EUROPE IN TRANSITION

Expansion of East–West Trade

Although Comecon formally existed until 1991, the actual process of transformation in Central and Eastern Europe started in 1989. What impact has this transformation had on trade between the EU and CEE? In order to obtain a picture of the evolution of the CEECs' trade performance after 1989, it seems appropriate to compare the pre-transition phase (1987–9) with the transition phase proper (1990–2).

As can be seen from Table 7.1 and Figures 7.1(a) and 7.1(b), trade between the EU and the CEECs has grown at an exceptionally fast rate since 1989. The expansion of EU–CEE trade is the more remarkable if we consider that it occurred in years of recession in the EU when industrialised economies' growth rates of trade were falling. Between 1987 and 1989 EU imports from CEE grew at a slower rate

Table 7.1 EU–CEE Trade in Manufactured Goods, 1987–92

	1987	1989	% Change	1990	1992	% Change
		EU Imports from CEE, in bn ECU				
Poland	2.05	2.84	39	3.96	5.98	51
ex-CSFR	1.78	2.23	25	2.40	5.10	113
Hungary	1.64	2.18	33	2.55	3.55	39
Visegrad countries	5.47	7.25	33	8.91	14.63	64
Romania	1.45	1.65	14	1.17	1.33	14
Bulgaria	0.35	0.40	14	0.44	0.76	73
CEECs	7.27	9.30	28	10.52	16.72	59
		EU Exports to CEE, in bn ECU				
Poland	2.03	3.30	63	3.72	6.97	87
ex-CSFR	1.90	2.14	13	2.34	5.63	141
Hungary	2.16	2.67	24	2.62	3.75	43
Visegrad countries	6.09	8.11	33	8.68	16.35	88
Romania	0.59	0.64	8	1.02	1.56	53
Bulgaria	1.33	1.32	−1	0.82	0.98	20
CEECs	8.01	10.07	26	10.52	18.89	79
		EU Trade Balance, in bn ECU				
Poland	−0.02	0.46		−0.25	0.98	
ex-CSFR	0.12	−0.09		−0.06	0.53	
Hungary	0.52	0.49		0.08	0.19	
Visegrad countries	0.62	0.86		−0.23	1.70	
Romania	−0.86	−1.01		−0.15	0.22	
Bulgaria	0.98	0.93		0.38	0.30	
CEECs	0.74	0.78		0.00	2.22	

Source: European Commission (1994a: 3).

than total (external) EU imports. In contrast, imports from the CEECs to the EU displayed a well above average growth rate between 1990 and 1992. Extra-EU imports increased, on average, by less than 5 per cent per annum during the transition period, whereas supplies from CEE (and China) for EU markets grew by over 20 per cent (European Commission 1994a: 4). The EU's imports from CEE increased by 59 per cent between 1990 and 1992; during the pre-transition period they rose by only 28 per cent. The Visegrad countries performed particularly well. While the EU's imports from this group of countries grew by 64 per cent during the transition period (with the ex-CSFR emerging as the most dynamic trade partner), imports from ex-CSFR to the EU increased by 113 per cent between 1990 and 1992. Exports from the EU to CEE also grew much faster during

Figure 7.1(a)   EU–CEE Trade in Manufactured Goods, 1987–92: EU Imports from CEE (bn ECU)

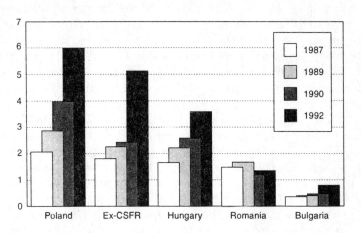

Source: Winters and Wang (1994).

Figure 7.1(b)   EU–CEE Trade in Manufactured Goods, 1987–92: EU Exports to CEE (bn ECU)

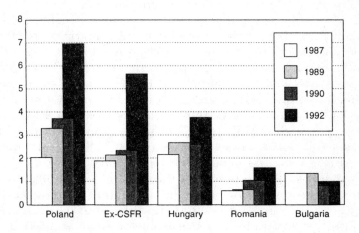

Source: Winters and Wang (1994).

the transition years than in the pre-transition period. While EU exports to the CEECs increased by 26 per cent between 1987 and 1989, the rise amounted to 79 per cent in the transition phase. Once again, the Visegrad countries, as a group, outperformed the other CEE economies. Exports from the EU to this group of countries increased by 88 per cent between 1990 and 1992 with EU exports to the ex-CSFR increasing by as much as 141 per cent during this short period.

Although the data in Table 7.1 and Figures 7.1(a) and 7.1(b) clearly show that the economic and political transformation of CEE was accompanied by an exceptional expansion of trade between the EU and the CEECs, it should be stressed that CEE has remained a relatively insignificant trade partner for the EU countries. In 1992, only 5 per cent of the EU's exports were destined for markets in CEE countries. In the same year the CEECs' share of the EU's imports amounted to a mere 4 per cent (Eurostat 1993). While the CEECs are as yet neither major export destinations nor import sources for the European Union (for a discussion of the EU's principal trade partners see, for example, Heidensohn 1995), the CEECs are highly dependent on trade with the EU. As Table 7.2 and Figure 7.2(a) show, nearly half of total CEE exports were destined for EU markets in 1992 (the corresponding figure for 1989 was about a quarter). While the EU provided 20 per cent of the CEECs' total imports in 1989, this figure had, by 1992, risen to 45 per cent. It is also worth noting that the EU, in trading with the CEECs, ran a considerable surplus (2.14 bn ECU) in 1992. Although the EU tended to be a net exporter to CEE during the CMEA phase, the size of the CEECs' trade deficit with the EU has been much larger since 1989.

It is interesting to note that the EU and CEE not merely trade in products from different industries (inter-industry trade); there is also a considerable degree of intra-industry trade (trade in goods from the same sectors). Between 1988 and 1993 the Grubel–Lloyd (1975) intra-industry index (which measures the degree to which countries are trading similar products) increased, when applied to trade between the 'old' and the 'new' Europe, especially for the ex-CSFR, Bulgaria and Hungary. Furthermore, the levels of

Table 7.2 Percentage Shares of CEE's trade with the EU

	1988	1989	1990	1991	1992
			Exports		
Bulgaria	5.8	6.7	10.4	15.7	30.8
ex-CSFR	24.2	25.7	32.0	40.7	49.5
Hungary	22.5	24.7	34.2	47.6	49.5
Poland	30.3	32.1	46.8	55.6	55.6
Romania	24.0	26.7	31.4	34.2	32.5
CEECs	22.5	24.5	33.5	44.6	48.2
			Imports		
Bulgaria	16.7	16.5	14.8	20.7	32.6
ex-CSFR	17.7	17.8	32.1	34.3	42.0
Hungary	25.2	28.5	31.5	40.4	42.4
Poland	27.2	33.8	42.5	49.9	53.1
Romania	6.2	6.1	19.6	27.4	37.5
CEECs	19.2	20.8	27.8	39.5	44.7

Source: European Commission (1994a: 3).

Figure 7.2(a) Percentage Shares of CEE's Trade with the EU: Exports

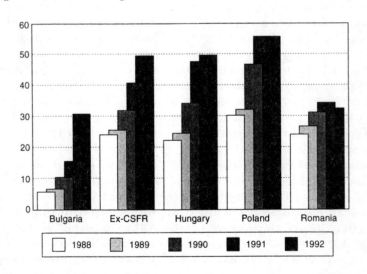

Source: Winters and Wang (1994).

Figure 7.2(b)   Percentage Shares of CEE's Trade with the EU: Imports

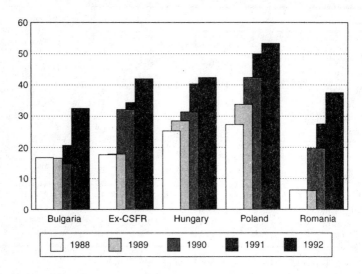

Source: Winters and Wang (1994).

intra-industry trade recorded in 1993 were very similar to
the extent of intra-industry trade between the EU and Spain
in 1980, suggesting that these two 'new' European countries are 'structurally similar to the EU as Spain was in 1980'
(European Commission 1994b: xii). But the CEECs' export
base is fairly narrow in that a relatively small number of
industries account for CEE exports to the European Union.
Table 7.3 and Figure 7.3 illustrate this aspect of the CEECs'
trade links with the EU. While some diversification has,
admittedly, taken place in the transition period (in 1987
the five largest sectors in CEE contributed 63 per cent of
its exports to the EU), a narrow range of products continued to dominate the CEECs' exports to the Union even in
1992 (56 per cent). In fact, the CEECs have, in exporting
to the EU, tended to concentrate and specialise in products for which there has been somewhat restricted access to
EU markets. The five sectors in the CEE economies that, in
1992, predominantly contributed to their exports to the EU
are the following: footwear and clothing (16 per cent); production process metals (13 per cent); food, drink, tobacco

Table 7.3 Percentage Shares in the CEECs' Total Exports to the EU, by sector, 1987 and 1992

Product	1987	1992
Footwear, clothing	14.9	16.4
Production process metals	12.4	12.7
Chemical industry	11.6	9.2
Timber, wooden furniture	11.3	8.8
Food, drink, tobacco	12.3	8.5
Total	62.5	55.6

Source: European Commission (1994a: 4).

Figure 7.3 Percentage Shares in the CEECs' Total Exports to the

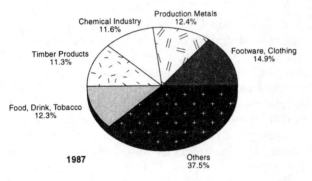

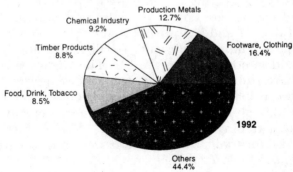

EU, by sector

Source: Winters and Wang (1994).

(9 cent); chemical industry (9 per cent); and timber/wooden furniture (9 per cent).

The demise of Comecon is likely to have played a significant role in bringing about the drastic shift in the composition of the CEECs' export destinations and import sources. For the abolition of Comecon amounted to a dismantling of its system of artificial preferences for mutual trade among CMEA countries:

> trade at administered CMEA prices expressed in non-convertible monetary units was replaced by trade at world prices expressed in convertible currencies, which put an end to the discrimination against non-CMEA markets.
> (European Commission for Europe 1993: 121)

The effects of abolishing Comecon could be compared to the changes in the direction of trade flows one would expect to result from the dissolution of a customs union with trade diversion (welfare losses experienced by a country as a result of its consumers having to buy goods or services from less efficient domestic producers instead of more efficient trade partners) being replaced by trade creation (welfare gains accruing to a country that replaces supply from less efficient domestic producers by more efficient suppliers from trading partners).

In considering recent pan-European trade flows, we must, of course, not ignore possible inter-country differences. As Table 7.1 and Figures 7.1(a) and 7.1(b) illustrate, the CEECs have exhibited different growth rates both in exporting to and importing from the EU. The trade deficits the CEECs have run (only Romania was a net exporter to the EU between 1987 and 1992) have also been of different magnitudes. Although the CEECs have been more dependent on the EU as a trading partner than the EU countries have needed CEE for trade, there are variations in the degree of dependence (Table 7.2 and Figures 7.2(a) and 7.2(b)). And although we identified five sectors that account for more than half of the CEECs' exports to the EU, Hungary, for example, exports electrical rather than wood products; it also relies much more on EU markets for exporting food products than the other CEECs (Table 7.3). The relative importance of EU trade with CEE furthermore varies considerably once we consider individual EU Member States. Germany dominated trade links with the CEECs in the Comecon and pre-transition years and has continued to be CEE's most important EU trade partner since 1989. For the peripheral Mediterranean EU Member States (Greece, Portugal and Spain), on the other hand, trade liberalisation does not appear to have had any noticeable impact on trade with Europe's transition economies (European Commission 1994b: x).

EU Trade Barriers

Although East–West trade has evidently expanded within Europe since 1989, barriers to trade between the EU and CEE have continued to exist. The EU has, admittedly, endeavoured to support the CEECs' transition to market economies by liberalising its trade with the 'new' Europe. But the arrangements the EU countries have made so far in an attempt to bring about a liberalisation of trade flows with CEE have been limited, although fuller trade liberalisation is envisaged to take place in the future when the 'Europe Agreements' will come into force.

What are the principal barriers that have affected the CEECs' exports to the EU countries since 1989? The restrictions on trade the EU has imposed on imports from CEE appear to be due to the following: tariffs; quantitative restrictions and other non-tariff barriers; and government procurement restrictions and technical regulations.

Although the EU has, for many years, granted most-favoured-nation treatment to all countries, a 'pyramid of preferences' has existed: duties for industrial products have been either partially or completely removed for some of its trading partners. Within the hierarchical system of trade preferences the EU had established vis-à-vis different groups of countries – EFTA, ACP (African, Caribbean and Pacific Ocean countries), the Mediterranean Basin and the group of developing countries belonging to UNCTAD (United Nations Conference on Trade and Development), 'the CEECs used to be at the bottom of the preference pyramid, and only recently started to climb to the top' (Schumacher and Moebius 1994: 23).

While the EU has, in an attempt to improve the CEECs' access to its markets, included the CEECs in the group of GSP (General System of Preferences) beneficiaries, by granting relief on duties payable to imports from CEE to EU countries, Schumacher and Moebius (1994: 26) found that only a small number (TV sets, paper processing, and plastics processing) of all the sensitive or 'protected' sectors were significantly affected by these tariff reductions. As a result, some sectors, for example, woven fabrics, knitting industries and clothing (which have hardly benefited from preferential treatment), appear to have faced more rather than less discrimination in exporting to the EU.

Both the EU and individual EU Member States have used non-tariff barriers in trading with external trade partners including the CEECs. These non-tariff barriers have comprised both quantitative restrictions (restraint agreements within the Multi-Fibre Arrangement, other textiles export restraint agreements, various voluntary export restraints, etc.) and other non-tariff barriers (anti-dumping duties and undertakings, import surveillance procedures, rules of origin, safeguard actions, etc.). In 1990, the EU's quantitative restrictions on imports from the CEE were highly concentrated. They affected fewer than 10 industrial sectors including, *inter alia*, steel, artificial fibres, textiles, clothing; other non-tariff barriers affected over 20 sectors, including chemicals, electrical goods, fur goods, leather products, musical instruments, optical instruments and steel (Schumacher and Moebius 1994: 27).

For some CEECs public procurement procedures and regulations governing technical standards have impeded exports to the EU. In 1990, for example, nearly half of Hungary's supplies to the EU were adversely affected by trade barriers resulting from public procurement practices and technical regulations with 5 per cent of Hungarian deliveries to the EU being highly impeded by such trade barriers (Schumacher and Moebius 1994: 33).

The Europe Agreements

In trying to improve CEE's market access conditions, the EU adopted a phased trade liberalisation programme. The EU signed trade, economic and commercial co-operation agreements with Hungary in 1988, Poland in 1989, and Bulgaria, the CSFR and Romania in 1990. GSP status was accorded to Hungary and Poland in 1990, and subsequently to Bulgaria, the CSFR and Romania in 1991. Further trade liberalisation is expected to be brought about by the six Europe Agreements signed between the EU and the CEECs.

The Europe Agreements contain five core features: free movement of goods; movements of workers, establishment and the supply of services; payments, competition and the approximation of laws; economic co-operation; and financial co-operation. The objective of the trade part of these Europe Agreements is to facilitate increased trade between the EU and CEE by establishing a (bilateral) free trade area for industrial goods within a 10-year period. The stages envisaged for the process of trade liberalisation are expected to be as follows:

- tariffs and quantitative restrictions to be abolished for the import of most products from CEE to EU countries;
- the EU to reduce tariffs on imports of specified metal products from the CEECs over a four-year period;
- the exports of 'sensitive' products (chemicals, footwear, furniture, glass, leather goods, steel products and vehicles) from CEE to the EU to be subject to tariffs for a further five years;
- import duties on coal imported into the EU from the CEECs to be removed over a four-year period; quantitative restrictions on the Visegrad countries' exports of coal to be discontinued within one year for all but two EU Member States (Germany and Spain);
- import duties on textiles and clothing from CEE to be phased out within six years; quantitative restrictions on the CEECs' exports of textile and clothing articles to be phased out within five years;
- quantitative restrictions on the CEECs' exports of iron and steel to be abolished when the Europe accords come into force; import duties on these products to be levied for a further six years.

In assessing the extent of the trade liberalisation these association agreements are likely to bring about, it would seem appropriate to consider two important issues: the coverage (effective liberalisation), and the trade restrictions the EU is allowed to apply (contingency protection).

The effective liberalisation of the CEECs' access to EU markets resulting from reduced standard protection (in the form of import duties and quantitative restrictions) would appear to more apparent than real because the products listed under the 'slow' liberalisation schedule such as iron/steel and textiles/clothing are the very goods CEE has been particularly successful in exporting to EU countries. The restrictive nature of the European association accords is in marked contrast to the NAFTA (North American Free Trade Area) agreement, which has given Mexico free access for agricultural commodities (the Europe agreements explicitly excluded the agricultural sector from the trade liberalisation process) to the US and Canadian markets.

The Europe Agreements, while aiming to liberalise trade in non-agricultural products, contain provisions which permit the EU to resort to contingency measures in order to restrict trade between the EU and CEE. The EU is allowed to apply contingent protection measures if import penetration from CEE threatens EU industries. Opportunities for future restrictiveness in East–West trade within Europe exist also through safeguard clauses, origin rules and anti-dumping actions. The Europe Agreements furthermore contain provisions which allow the EU to take unspecified safeguard measures if exports from CEE to EU countries are deemed to result in either

> 'serious injury to domestic producers of like or directly competitive products' or 'serious disturbances . . . or difficulties which could bring about serious deterioration in the economic situation of a region', in which case 'the Community or the relevant associated country may take appropriate measures under the conditions and in accordance with the procedures laid down in Article 27'.
>
> (Article 24 of the [Interim] Europe Agreements)

Both this general safeguard clause and a number of additional specific safeguard regimes for trade in agriculture, textile and clothing negate the trade liberalisation the market access provisions of the Europe Agreements even before these association agreements have become fully operative.

Rules of origin (or local content requirements), although in principle providing less discretionary protection for the EU against imports from CEE, are also likely to inhibit the CEECs' exports to the EU. The 60 per cent local content requirement (imports must not account for more than 40 per cent of the value of an exportable), for example, would seem to be rather strict. And the absence of pan-European cumulation means that, while cumulation of inputs may be possible across some countries, it may be ruled out if applied across other countries (at present it is, for example, possible to have cumulation of inputs among the Visegrad countries, but not between the Visegrad countries and Bulgaria or Romania). This differential treatment of the Visegrad countries and the other CEECs, when origin rules are being applied, means that East–West trade would be restricted because market forces will have less of an impact on trade flows.

The Europe Agreements, while representing an appropriate first step in liberalising the EU's trade with the CEECs, clearly need to be amended to bring about free trade between the 'old' and the 'new' Europe by the beginning of the next millennium. The Agreements should not provide the EU with scope for restricting future trade by resorting, for example, to anti-dumping actions, safeguard clauses and 'consultations'. And the establishment of a pan-European free trade area, embracing the EU and the CEECs, would require the EU to abolish import controls and relax the rules of origin embodied in the Agreements.

FUTURE ECONOMIC INTERPENETRATION BETWEEN THE EU AND CEE

The 'New' Europe's Trade Potential

After more than 40 years of operating as state-trading countries, the CEECs have been involved in world trade as market economies for a comparatively short period of time. While trade flows between the EU and the CEECs have undoubtedly increased in the 1990s, East–West trade is far from being liberalised. It could, therefore, be argued that a gap exists between CEE's actual and potential trade volume with Western Europe.

According to recent research, the CEECs appear to have an enormous trade potential. Most of the studies attempting to quantify the 'new' Europe's trade potential based their analysis of CEE's potential exports on the so-called gravity model, developed by Linnemann (1966) in order to simulate trade flows of economies at an aggregate level. Gravity models assume that trade flows are mainly determined by three factors: the costs of doing business, the exporting country's supply, and the importing country's demand. The costs of doing across-border business are considered to depend on natural trade obstacles (transport costs resulting from the physical distance between suppliers and customers; transaction costs) and artificial trade barriers (costs resulting from the trade policies pursued by the trading countries). Exports are deemed to be a function of a country's gross national product (the larger a country's GNP, the larger its export potential) and of its 'openness' (measured by the share of total output being exported) with the 'openness ratio' being expected to vary inversely with the exporting country's population size. A country's imports are assumed to vary with the country's GNP (the larger the GNP, the higher the imports) and the size of the population (the larger the population, the higher the degree of self-sufficiency and the lower, therefore, the imports). Gravity models, although arguably lacking in coherent economic reasoning, have been widely used because they appear to be capable of yielding robust predictions of trade flows.

Projections derived from gravity models and concerned with pan-European trade flows and based on gravity models tend to make two addtional assumptions. First, it is assumed that pan-European trade flows in the whole of Europe are influenced by the same factors as the trade patterns in western Europe, i.e. they are comparative advantage-based. Second, it is assumed that the same level of protectionism applies to any trade flows under consideration. Given these assumptions, the projections that have been made suggest that the CEECs' trade would be significantly higher than the trade flows actually recorded since 1989. Table 7.4 and Figures 7.4(a) and 7.4(b) summarise the findings on actual/poten-

Table 7.4 CEECs' Trade Potential

	Germany	UK	Japan	USA
Exports to CEECs				
Potential minus actual 1992 exports (in US $ millions)	18 136	7236	3880	17 886
Difference as multiple of actual exports in 1992	2.5	7.7	5.9	17.6
Imports from CEECs				
Potential minus actual 1992 imports (in US $ mio)	16 804	7069	3674	15 454
Difference as multiple of actual imports (in US $ mio) in 1992	3.4	5.9	14.0	12.1

Source: Winters and Wang (1994: 24).

Figure 7.4(a) CEECs' Trade Potential: Exports to CEECs

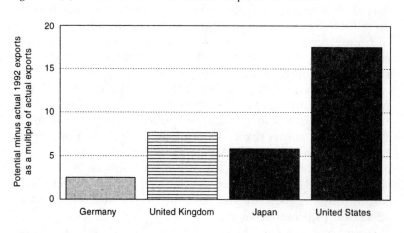

Source: Winters and Wang (1994).

Figure 7.4(b)   CEECs' Trade Potential: Imports from CEECs

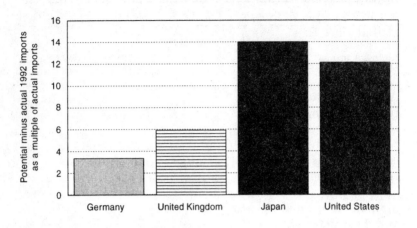

Source: Winters and Wang (1994).

tial exports to and imports from CEE of one major study (Winters and Wang 1994). For the year 1992, potential (minus actual) exports from two EU states (Germany and the United Kingdom) were estimated to be 2.5 (for Germany) and 7.7 (for the United Kingdom) times actual exports (the comparatively low 'multiplier' effect for Germany does not mean that the German economy would not gain very much from the CEECs realising their trade potential: in absolute terms Germany has so far benefited more from the CEECs' trade liberalisation than any other Western industrialised country and the low multiplier is attributable to the already high volume of trade Germany has had with CEE since 1989). The corresponding figures for two other principal world exporters, Japan and the United States, were found to be 5.9 and 17.6 respectively. In considering EU imports from the CEECs, Winters and Wang estimated that potential imports from CEE were 3.4 times actual imports in 1992 for Germany and 5.9 times for the United Kingdom. The corresponding figures for the United States and Japan were 12.1 and 14.0 respectively.

    Estimates of the CEECs' large trade potentials were also produced by van Bergrijk and Oldersma (1990). Using a gravity model covering 49 countries including the CEECs, van Bergrijk and Oldersma (1990) estimated that pan-European trade flows would have been eight times higher in 1985 if CEE had been integrated into the world trading system at that time.

Impact on the European Union

Assuming that trade with CEE will be liberalised in the future, what impact is increased trade liberalisation likely to have on the EU?

EU consumers would undoubtedly benefit from trade liberalisation with the CEECs because more competition would result in lower prices. The possible impact of freer trade on EU producers and industries, on the other hand, is more difficult to predict. According to a study carried out by Faini and Portes (1995), the benefits accruing to EU producers can be expected to be significantly larger than the likely adjustment costs resulting from the removal of trade barriers between the EU and the CEECs. Although making EU markets more accessible to CEE producers means that EU producers would face more severe competition in the European domestic market, there are no findings to support the view that trade liberalisation with CEE would have any more than minor negative effects on the EU economy as a whole. Nor is there any evidence to suggest that more liberalised trade between the EU and the CEECs would cause particular problems for the EU's relatively poorer Mediterranean Member States. Case studies of two countries of the EU's south – Greece and Spain – show that increased trade with the CEECs is unlikely to be detrimental to EU producers in that region. In fact, trade with the CEECs can apparently be expected to generate a considerable export potential for the Greek economy. While exports from Greece to CEE are likely to increase by 190 per cent, imports from the CEECs to Greece are, according to Dimelis and Gatsios (1995), are projected to rise by less (90 per cent). Gual and Martin (1995), whose study focused on Spain, found that trade liberalisation would not lead to a significant expansion of Spanish trade with CEE; they also established that the trade expansion that was likely to result from removing trade barriers would not lead to net job losses in Spain.

Considering that some sectors of the EU economy (steel, textiles and clothing, and chemicals) have emerged as 'sensitive' industries in pan-European trade, will East–West trade liberalisation cause damage to these sectors in the EU? Two of these sensitive industries have been investigated in detail. Corado (1995), who studied textiles and clothing found that, far from harming EU producers, expansion of trade with the CEECs might actually benefit EU industries for two reasons. First, she found that trade liberalisation would be conducive to increasing EU exports of textiles and clothing to CEE in general and of high quality clothing articles in particular. Second, it would render EU producers more competitive vis-à-vis imports from developing countries because it would enable them to take advantage of lower labour costs by transferring very labour-intensive aspects of the production process to CEE. Investigating the EU's steel sector, Winters (1995) concluded that any possible concern about adverse effects of trade liberalisation with the CEECs on the EU's steel industries would appear to be misplaced. Winters' study of the effects of implementing the market access provisions of the Europe Agreements suggests that trade liberalisation would have only negligible consequences for EU steel output, which would, at worst, be reduced by 1.6 per cent. But while the CEECs' steel production would, because of their comparative advantage in producing lower quality steel, grow by up to 18 per cent, the EU should, in the long run, find their exports of higher quality steel to CEE increase quite considerably once the CEECs experienced growing demand for consumer durables.

An Eastern Enlargement of the EU?

The transformation of Central and Eastern Europe has, once again, made the issue of enlargement more topical. Not surprisingly, it has been the CEECs that have been seeking membership of the EU. The break-up of Comecon meant that the 'new' Europe has become politically and economically independent. The CEECs' trade flows with the 'old' Europe have increased; and the former Comecon countries wish to become full members of the EU in order to reap the economic benefits resulting from economic integration.

Integrating a relatively small economy such as CEE and a comparatively large economy such as EU-15 usually results in the small area gaining relatively more than the large area (Baldwin 1994: 161). For the integration of two economies that differ in size tends to generate more opportunities for producers and consumers in the small economy than in the large economy. There should be more scope for specialisation in the small economy than in the large economy; there is likely to be more pressure on competition in the small economy than in the large economy; and the small economy can be expected to have more opportunities to take advantage of economies of scale. We should, nevertheless, bear in mind that an Eastern enlargement of the EU presents a much more difficult issue than the North-East enlargement that took place when Austria, Finland and Sweden became full members on 1 January 1995. Difficulties in enlarging the EU to the East are likely to arise for a number of reasons. First, the ex-Comecon countries (the CEECs, the Baltic states (Estonia, Latvia and Lithuania), the successor states of the former Yugoslavia, and countries that belonged to the ex-USSR) intent on becoming EU members in the future are a very heterogeneous group of economies. Second, an Eastern enlargement would be associated with quite considerable increases in EU expenditure even if only some of the above-mentioned economies became full EU Member States. A recent study estimated that admitting the Visegrad countries would increase the EU budget by as much as 74 per cent (Baldwin 1994: 170). The CEECs could be expected to draw on the EU's structural funds for many years because many of their regions' incomes are likely to fall short of the EU average income for some considerable time. Being more agricultural than most of the EU states, the CEECs would also make significant demands on the EU's agricultural budget. But, although an Eastern enlargement of the EU would result in the EU incurring costs, there would also be gains accruing to the existing members of the EU. The economic power of the EU in the world trading system would be greater; admitting the Visegrad countries alone would increase the EU's population nearly 20 per cent (from 372 to 436 million people); and comparative advantage-type gains from trade would be derived by both the acceding CEECs and the existing EU countries.

That an Eastern enlargement of the EU is going to take place would seem to be fairly certain. But at this stage it is difficult, if not impossible, to predict when a pan-European Union embracing the EU and CEE will be created. For a number of reasons, it seems likely that it will take about two decades for the EU to fulfil the promises of full membership given to the CEECs. The wording of the Association Agreements was such that it has provided the EU with escape clauses. For the 'Conclusions of the Presidency' that were issued after the June 1993 meeting of the EU heads of government in Copenhagen, while in principle committing the EU to admitting the CEECs, also state that

> accession will take place as soon as an associated country is able to assume the obligations of membership by satisfying the economic and political conditions required.

They also stress that

> the Union's capacity to absorb new members, while maintaining the momentum of European integration, is also an important consideration in the general interest of both the Union and the candidate countries.
> (European Commission 1993)

Although both statements are carefully phrased and coined in diplomatic language, their importance should not be ignored. For while it is recognised that long-run economic benefits are, as a result of pan-European liberalisation, likely to accrue to the incumbent EU member countries, the statements make it clear that the EU could object to the CEECs joining as full members. The EU Member States could oppose the CEECs joining as long as they are remain poor. They could object to the CEECs' membership if the ensuing enlargement would be too costly for them, or if measures taken to 'deepen' the EU would have to be delayed because of the enlargement to the east. Finally, it is possible that today's euphoria about an enlarged EU will, as some economic historians have argued, be replaced by a more sceptical attitude towards a federal Europe. The existing EU members may, in future years, be less inclined to favour a further enlargement on the grounds that the EU might

become so large and diverse through increased membership that nationality conflicts and inter-country disparities in development and structures could well lead it to
splinter and break down.

(Aldcroft 1991: 196)

As an interim solution, the CEECs might, therefore, be well
advised to join EFTA. Such a step would mean that the CEECs
would be able to play a more prominent role in the process
of European economic integration. It would also render EFTA,
whose membership was reduced to four at the end of 1994,
more effective. Both the incumbent EFTA countries and the
CEECs would, as Baldwin (1992) found, derive economic
gains from such an eastern enlargement of the European
Free Trade Area.

In the meantime EU-15 has to respond to both the huge
increases in pan-European trade flows and to the growing
trade imbalance between Eastern and Western Europe we
have witnessed since 1989. In exploiting the East-West trade
potential, the EU should recognise that the large increases
in pan-European trade that are deemed feasible do not only
refer to trade in one direction:

If it wishes to expand its exports, or to help the CEECs
to develop, the west must accept their exports. These will
be cheap and, at least for a period, of low quality; but to
exclude them from our markets in order to protect un-
competitive western producers of simple goods, will only
prevent the producers of more sophisticated goods from
gaining the sales that they deserve in the east.

(Winters and Wang 1994: 30)

REFERENCES

Aldcroft, D.H. (1991), 'The Federal Idea in Europe before 1914', in P.
King and A. Bosco (eds.), *A Constitution for Europe*, The Lothian Foun-
dation, London, pp. 187–97.
Baldwin, R.E. (1992), 'An Eastern Enlargement of EFTA: Why the East
Europeans Should Join and the EFTANS Should Want Them', *Occa-
sional Paper* No. 10, Centre for Economic Policy Research, London.

152   *The Future of Europe*

Baldwin, R.E. (1994), *Towards an Integrated Europe*, Centre for Economic Policy Research, London.
Corado, C. (1995), 'The Textiles and Clothing Trade with Central and Eastern Europe: Impact on Members of the EC', in R. Faini and R. Portes (eds.), *European Union Trade with Eastern Europe: Adjustment and Opportunities*, Centre for Economic Policy Research, London.
Costello, D. and Laredo, E.T. (1994); 'Transition through Trade: Do the Europe Agreements go Far Enough? An Assessment of the Market Access Provisions of the Interim Europe Agreements', *European Economy*, Reports and Studies, No. 6, pp. 151–88, European Commission, Brussels.
Dimelis, S. and Gatsios, K. (1995), 'Trade with Central and Eastern Europe: The Case of Greece', in R. Faini and R. Portes (eds.), *European Union Trade with Eastern Europe: Adjustment and Opportunities*, Centre for Economic Policy Research, London.
European Commission (1993), 'Conclusions of the Presidency', Meeting of the EU Heads of Government in Copenhagen, 21–22 June.
European Commission (1994a), 'Trade Liberalisation with Central and Eastern Europe', *European Economy*, Supplement A, Recent Economic Trends, No. 7, July, pp. 1–19, European Commission, Brussels.
European Commission (1994b), 'The Economic Interpenetration between the European Union and Eastern Europe', *European Economy*, Reports and Studies, No. 6, European Commission, Brussels.
European Commission for Europe (1993), 'Recent Trade Performance of the Visegrad Countries', *Economic Bulletin for Europe*, No. 43, pp. 117–40, United Nations, Geneva.
Eurostat (1993), *External Trade and Balance of Payments Statistical Yearbook*, Recapitulation 1958–92 .
Faini, R. and Portes, R. (1995), *European Union Trade with Eastern Europe: Adjustment and Opportunities*, Centre for Economic Policy Research, London.
Grubel, H.G. and Lloyd, P.J. (1975), *Intra-Industry Trade: The Theory and Measurement of International Trade in Differentiated Products*, Macmillan, London.
Gual, J. and Martin, C. (1995), 'Trade and Foreign Direct Investment with Central and Eastern Europe: Its Impact on Spain', in R. Faini and R. Portes (eds.), *European Union Trade with Eastern Europe: Adjustment and Opportunities*, Centre for Economic Policy Research, London.
Heidensohn, K. (1995), *Europe and World Trade*, Pinter, London and New York.
IMF (1992), *Direction of Trade Statistics Yearbook, 1985–1991*, International Monetary Fund, Washington, DC.
League of Nations (1942), *The Network of World Trade*, League of Nations, Geneva.
Linnemann, H. (1966), *An Economic Study of International Trade Flows*, North-Holland Publishing Company, Amsterdam.
Nello, S.S. (1991), *The New Europe: Changing Economic Relations between East and West*, Harvester Wheatsheaf, New York and London.
Schumacher, D. and Moebius, U. (1994), 'Analysis of Community Trade Barriers Facing Central and East European Countries and Impact of

the Europe Agreements', *European Economy*, Reports and Studies, No. 6, The Economic Interpenetration between the European Union and Eastern Europe, pp. 17–76, European Commission, Brussels.

van Bergrijk, P. and Oldersma, H. (1990), 'Détente, Market-oriented Reform and German Unification: Potential Consequences for the World Trade System', *Kyklos*, Vol. 43, No. 4, pp. 566–609.

Winters, L.A. (1995), 'Liberalization of the European Steel Trade', in R. Faini and R. Portes (eds.), *European Union Trade with Eastern Europe: Adjustment and Opportunities*, Centre for Economic Policy Research, London.

Winters, L.A. and Wang, Z.K. (1994), *'Eastern Europe's International Trade*, Manchester University Press, Manchester and New York.

8 Monetary Integration in the EU: Issues and Prospects. Or, Will You Be Paying for the Millenium Party in ECU?

Valerio Lintner

INTRODUCTION

Monetary integration, and in particular the prospect of a monetary union among all or most EU members in the not too distant future, is probably the most significant internal economic issue confronting Europe and the process of European integration in this latter part of the twentieth century. Its outcome will undoubtedly be an important indicator of the strength, the direction and the immediate prospects of the whole European integration project, and as such it will both reflect and help to determine the economic, political and social shape of the continent into the next twenty-first century.

However, monetary union by the turn of the century, which had appeared a feasible proposition before the 1992 Exchange Rate Mechanism (ERM) crisis and before the Maastricht ratification process, has now become deeply controversial and uncertain. Indeed, at the time of writing (1995) it seems certain that we will be paying for the millennium party in national currencies rather than any new Euro-money. Nowhere has the controversy been more evident than in the United Kingdom, where the prospect of European Monetary Union (EMU) under the aegis of the EU, and of British participation in such a venture, is dominating British politics and economics as we approach the turn of the century. We have already seen the party of government deeply divided by such a prospect, and we can only guess at the crises and the gyrations that are in store over the next few years, as the United Kingdom contemplates coming to terms (or not, as the case may be) with what many regard as its new and objective position in the world.

This chapter sets out to examine the EMU debate predominantly from an economic viewpoint, while accepting the fact that the issues and the possible outcomes in this area are fundamentally conditioned by the political implications and realities that it throws up. The paper will thus survey the theory of monetary integration, outlining the economic implications of such a development for Britain and for the rest of Europe. It will then briefly examine the attempts that have been made to work towards monetary union in the EU. Emphasis will be placed on the critical analysis of the Maastricht Treaty as an appropriate model for achieving monetary union in Europe. Finally, prospects for the future will be discussed.

THEORETICAL ASPECTS OF EMU

It seems fair to say that the popular conception of EMU is focused predominantly on the replacement of national currencies by a single European currency: the ECU, the Jean Monnet, the Crown, the Gazza, or whatever nomenclature finally emerges. The recent furore in the United Kingdom surrounding the rumour that the Queen's head might disappear from the new single currency and the recent concern in Germany over the loss of the Deutschmark provide evidence of this. However, from an economic point of view, one should note that the single currency in itself is in some ways the icing on the cake. The really important features of EMU consist, rather, of the policy consequences that it entails, and in particular, the co-ordination and joint determination of certain aspects of economic policy which must accompany a monetary union.

This is not to diminish the importance of the single currency itself: it would represent *inter alia* an important symbol of the EU monetary union,[1] it would save on transaction costs and it might make the internal market function better by increasing the 'transparency of prices', allowing economic agents to make more rational decisions concerning issues such as consumption and investment. It would also allow Europe to benefit from advantages such as seigniorage which are inherent in possessing what would undoubtedly be a major world currency.[2] Nevertheless, it should be noted that in principle one could achieve broadly similar economic effects without a single currency, simply by having irrevocably fixed exchange rates and total convertibility of currencies within the context of a complete common market.[3]

The precise nature and extent of the joint policy-making that is required in a monetary union is an interesting issue and a matter of some debate. In the recent economic and ideological climate, the emphasis has been on the joint determination of policies that impact on inflation. It is indeed important to have roughly similar rates of inflation among participants in a monetary union, for widely differing rates of inflation are likely to result in significant economic costs in higher inflation countries. In essence, members of a monetary union who experience relatively higher rates of inflation lose competitiveness vis-à-vis other participants, and may experience balance of payments difficulties as a result.[4] In the absence of monetary union, countries have the option of restoring competitiveness by means of devaluation, as Britain has done over the last half-century,[5] but with a single currency this is, of course, impossible. The result is likely to be that the burden of adjustment will fall on more painful areas, such as the level of employment, investment, real incomes and growth. The alternative is the export of economic activity from high-inflation areas to ones with lower inflation, and the relative economic decline of weaker parts of the EU, at least in the short run.[6]

The present accepted wisdom is that inflation is fundamentally a monetary phenomenon, and the emphasis has thus been on monetary policy as a means of controlling it:[7] hence the measures designed to co-ordinate national monetary policies, to transfer important aspects of monetary policy to the supranational level, and the emphasis on interest rates and public borrowing as convergence criteria in the Maastricht Treaty (see below). However, a balanced view would suggest that factors other than monetary aggregates are also likely to impact on inflation. Accordingly, in the long run it will probably be necessary to adopt a supranational dimension to fiscal policies and to certain macroeconomic and structural policies in the context of EMU. In addition, it should be noted that the co-determination of these non-monetary policies may be necessary to promote convergence in other real variables, such as levels of unemployment, regional disparities and the like, since, despite what many economists appear to believe, inflation is by no means the sole dimension of the economic convergence required to limit the costs of EMU.

The fact that EMU necessitates the conduct of important aspects of economic policy at the EU level gives rise to the first potential disadvantage of monetary integration: losses in national economic sovereignty, which in this context may be defined as the power, in practice, of European nation-states to determine and successfully implement their first preferences in economic policies in isolation of events and policy preferences elsewhere.[8] On the face of it, the joint determination of economic policy which comes with EMU would indeed appear to involve the surrender of substantial economic sovereignty. If economic convergence does require a substantial degree of co-operation and joint policy-making at the supranational level, then it is most unlikely that every country's preferences will be accommodated all of the time.

The economic sovereignty losses that may result from EMU fall into two categories. First, countries lose control over the objectives of economic policy. There is a body of economic theory, pioneered by Fleming (1971) and Corden (1972), which examines these welfare costs in terms of countries having to accept second-best preferences in the Phillips trade-off between inflation and unemployment.[9] For example, a country involved in a monetary union cannot pursue a policy designed to reduce unemployment when its partners are involved in pursuing policies designed primarily to reduce the level of inflation. If the country wants to pursue its preferred policy stance, it must first win the political battle over the objectives of economic policy. The distribution of these losses will be determined by the nature of joint decision-making in the EU. If the process is a consensual one, based on some concept of averaging of preferences, then the costs will be more or less equally shared. If there is a 'leadership' outcome, then the leader (Germany, in the case of the EU) suffers none of the losses, which are then borne exclusively by other participants.[10] All this throws up the issue of the democratic accountability of economic policy-making, which is discussed below.

Once common objectives for economic policy have been determined, there is the issue that individual countries lose individual control over the tools of policy. Policy has to be implemented in close co-operation with other countries, or, more probably, jointly implemented by supranational bodies such as the European Monetary Institute (EMI), the European System of Central Banks (ESCB) or the European Central Bank (ECB). Such authorities will need to pursue a common monetary policy for the EU, with central determination of variables such as the money supply and the rate of interest (assuming this were possible). There is clearly a good deal of scope here for sovereignty costs. It may be, for example, that a macroeconomic stance that is appropriate for the EU as a whole is not at all appropriate for individual regions. Or, as we have arguably seen in the wake of German unification, that the most powerful country in the union imposes a policy stance that is appropriate to its own needs but not to those of the union as a whole.

The real question here, and the issue at the very centre of the whole monetary union debate, concerns the extent to which these apparent losses of national economic sovereignty would in fact be a reality in the case of EMU. Does national economic sovereignty really exist in contemporary Europe, or is it an illusion? Put another way, to what extent could individual European nation-states hope to exercise their own individual macro- and other economic policies outside the EU? The answer to these questions is very significant, for if countries currently do enjoy substantial independent control of their economies, then sovereignty losses of the type discussed above will indeed have to be borne. If, on the other hand, national economic sovereignty is limited, then sovereignty losses will be similarly limited – one cannot lose what one has not got in the first place. This issue is controversial, it is not empirically verifiable, and it is like to depend on a number of relatively complex factors.[11]

Nevertheless, there are general observations that one can make. On the whole, recent history is not very encouraging for what one may loosely refer to as the Eurosceptic or nationalist stance, which suggests that individual European countries do have the option of determining their own independent policies. The experiences of the last UK Labour government and of the Mitterrand administration in France from 1981 to 1983[12] suggest that 'alternative' policies that go against the grain may be precluded by interdependence. At the same time, the futile attempts by the UK government to control the money supply in the mid-1980s and the recent ERM crisis provide examples which would suggest that there are limits to the power even of mainstream governments to exercise control over their own economies in an interdependent and deregulated world with large amounts of internationally mobile capital. This leads the author to believe that, in macroeconomic policy at least, there are limits to the extent of real national economic sovereignty.[13]

Perhaps the strongest evidence in favour of this view is provided by examining a little more closely the issue of capital mobility and how it can affect economic policy. The world economy is currently characterised by extremely powerful capital markets that control very large amounts of highly internationally mobile funds. The power of these markets has increased markedly over the last decade as a result of a number of factors, ranging from an increased volume of petrodollars[14] and the privatisation of pensions and other social provision, to deregulation and the communications revolution. If we take the case of portfolio investments, it is clear that the unhindered mobility of capital can now effectively subvert national economic policy, as we saw at the time of the United Kingdom's ignominious exit from the ERM in 1992. The role of speculation in this process is often highlighted, but it should be noted that other forms of market adjustment can have similar effects. It is a sobering fact, for example, that the investments of the UK financial services industry alone are roughly equivalent to the United Kingdom's GDP, and that thus a mere precautionary 5 per cent shift of these holdings out of sterling would effectively neutralise the whole of the United Kingdom's foreign exchange reserves – the frontline means of intervention in

support of the currency. Even in the absence of speculation, prudent portfolio adjustment alone can thus affect the
government's ability to control the economy.[15]

Proponents of the alternative view (referred to above as
Eurosceptic or nationalist) point to the UK devaluation and
its consequent early emergence from recession. Whether this
recovery has been a strong one, and whether it can be sustained, seems to be in some doubt at the time of writing.
Only time will tell the extent to which each view is justified.[16]

A further cost of EMU is likely to involve its distributional
impact. The distribution of any economic gains that result
from the EU is likely to be uneven, and the costs of structural change that are likely to result from a monetary union may be concentrated in some regions of the union. There
are two grounds for believing this. First, the impact costs of
entry into the EU (for example the impact on unemployment and social provision of attempts to meet the present
Maastricht convergence criteria)[17] is likely to be borne disproportionately by weaker EU countries and regions. Secondly, EMU would remove another important barrier to the
operation of free markets within the EU. From a neoclassical perspective, free markets in general, and in particular
the free movement of capital within an area, should increase
economic welfare by facilitating a more efficient allocation
of resources, whilst at the same time promoting the equalisation of factor earnings between participating countries and
regions, thus leading to convergence in the monetary union.
However, free markets can, from another perspective, be
seen as leading to the exacerbation of national and regional
differences in real income and welfare, with more prosperous
areas benefiting at the expense of less well-off countries and
regions (see Symes, this volume, chapter 10).

What of the benefits of EMU? Monetary union would
certainly reduce uncertainty in trade and reduce transaction costs in the European economy, and we have discussed
above how the single currency itself would confer certain
specific advantages. However, the real potential advantages
that EMU might offer concern improvements that may result in the effectiveness of economic policy-making. There
are two dimensions to this argument. First, it might be
maintained that EMU will permit participating countries to

adopt 'best practice' (i.e. German practice) in the conduct of policy, and that consequently the overall conduct of policy in Europe might be rendered more efficient. This presupposes, of course, a belief that the German approach to economic management, based on tight control of inflation by means of monetary policy controlled by a central bank which is independent of the political process, is appropriate and acceptable.

Secondly, one might hold that the joint conduct of economic policy is likely to increase the effectiveness of such policy by restoring to European nation-states some of the control of their own economies that has been removed by ever-increasing interdependence in a world currently characterised by the power of deregulated capital and foreign exchange markets. This is closely linked to the national economic sovereignty arguments discussed above, the initial assumption being that there are indeed limits to the powers of individual small and medium-sized European economies to control their own economic affairs in isolation, and that sovereignty can thus be enhanced by a process of pooling.

The pertinent question here is clearly whether EMU can indeed enhance control over the forces of capital, and thus enhance sovereignty by such pooling. My conclusions are a guarded yes, for it must surely be the case that a united front on the part of up to 15 (or more) of the richest countries in the world have the potential to enhance democratic control over capital markets, speculation and even multinational enterprises (MNEs). A subsidiary question concerns the extent to which EMU itself might enhance capital mobility and thus further erode control over capital markets. Here my views are more guarded. EMU is bound to have an effect of capital mobility, but the EU effect on capital mobility is probably limited in its importance: the mobility of capital has increased dramatically, mainly as a result of developments outside the EU's direct control.

Thus it will be seen that the economic theory of monetary integration can shed some light on the meaning and likely effects of EMU. None the less, as ever, the evaluation of many of the issues it throws up ultimately depends on one's own view of how modern market economies function. Much is therefore left unresolved, and it is probably fair to say that the final outcome is likely to be determined by the political process.

THE ROAD TO EMU

We now turn to an examination of the EU's attempts to move towards EMU – how we arrived where we are, so to speak. These can be divided conveniently into three phases: the Werner Plan of the late 1960s and early 1970s; the EMS; and the Maastricht Treaty and its aftermath. The issue of monetary integration first appeared on the European agenda at the Hague summit in 1969, partly as a strategy to restore stability in Western Europe after the political events of May 1968. The debate at the time centred on the extent to which Europe was in fact an 'optimum currency area',[18] and on the best strategy for constructing a monetary union. On the latter issue, there were two points of view, which came to be referred to as the 'economist' approach and the 'monetarist' position.[19] The former position was mainly supported by the Dutch and the Germans in the Schiller Plan, and it favoured a gradualist approach to EMU, involving the promotion of harmonisation and convergence in order to prepare the ground for the single currency. The latter view was canvassed by the Commission, France and Belgium in the Barre Plan, and it advocated a 'shock theory' approach to EMU, involving the introduction of fixed exchange rates as a *fait accompli*, leaving countries to adjust to these expost. Some of the recent debate on EMU demonstrates that this issue is still far from resolved.

The outcome was predictably a compromise between the two views. It took the form of the Werner Plan of 1970, most of which was adopted by the Council of Ministers in March 1971 and which came into effect in March 1972. This provided for efforts to harmonise economic policies, but it also created the 'snake in the tunnel' system of fixed exchange rates. The 'snake' consisted of fixed exchange rates between the ten participants[20] within bands of ±2.25 per cent. The 'tunnel' involved fixing the parity of the snake currencies against the US dollar and other world currencies within the 4.5 per cent bands established in the

Smithsonian Agreements of December 1971. The overall objective was 'monetary union by 1980'. As we know, the plan failed, following the disarray in the international monetary system in the early 1970s. In the final analysis, European nation-states were fundamentally unwilling to subordinate their own national interests to those of the integration process. Britain left the snake in June 1972, Italy departed in February 1973, France in January 1974, and the EMU project collapsed.

The impetus towards monetary integration was revived in 1977 by Roy Jenkins during his tenure as President of the Commission, and the EMS was set up at the Bremen and Copenhagen Councils of 1978, coming into operation in March 1979. The EMS basically consists of two features: the European Currency Unit (ECU), which is the European 'currency in waiting' and is the fulcrum of the ERM. It is based on a 'weighted basket' of all the currencies involved; and the ERM, which attempts to fix exchange rates between the participating countries and between these currencies and the ECU. The initial bands were ±2.25 per cent (±6 per cent for weaker currencies such as the Lira and Sterling).[21] There is thus a 'snake', but this time no 'tunnel', since the European currencies involved can float vis-à-vis other world currencies. The mechanism for maintaining exchange rates within the system exchange consists of agreements for supportive central bank intervention in foreign exchange markets, a (limited) reserve pooling obligation and a (largely unused) divergence indicator. This is backed up by some measures to promote policy convergence and by a very limited redistributive mechanism.

The launch of the EMS was greeted with considerable scepticism, and predictably it encountered early instabilities. However, it managed to weather the turbulence of the early 1980s and eventually became a considerable success. First, it promoted exchange stability in Western Europe. There were only 11 realignments (12 if one includes the exit of Sterling and the Lira in late 1992) altogether, and none at all between January 1987 and the exit of Sterling, while currencies outside the ERM experienced considerably greater changes in the external value of their currencies. It also contributed to lower and increasingly convergent rates of inflation in Europe, although it must be said that price stability was also facilitated by the neo-liberal consensus on economic policy which existed during this period. Finally, the ECU managed to establish an increasing role for itself as a private sector currency during the 1980s.[22]

However, the EMS was weakened by the United Kingdom's refusal to join the ERM (although Sterling was always part of the ECU basket) until 'the time was right' in October 1990,[23] and arguably by over-reliance on German leadership. Nevertheless, it paved the way for what was to follow. The very success of the EMS provided the stimulus in the late 1980s for a debate on the way forward. The Commission's response was to set up the Delors Committee, which produced the Delors Report in April 1989, calling for a full monetary union to be set up in three stages. This led to two Inter-Governmental Conferences (IGCs)[24] and then the Maastricht Treaty. This has now been ratified in EU Member States after an often tortuous and controversial process. The Maastricht Treaty, of course, deals with more than just monetary union, for it constitutes a wide-ranging reform of the Community and a significant step forward for European integration on a number of fronts. Its principal feature is the Treaty on European Union, but there are also 17 assorted protocols (additional agreements not signed by all members) as well as 33 Declarations (guidelines on the interpretation and implementation of the Treaty, which however are not legally binding).[25]

The Treaty of European Union amends the Treaty of Rome and contains five features:

1. A European Union, based on the EC and its institutions, with a common inter-governmental foreign and security policy, a common home affairs and justice policy, again conducted on an inter-governmental basis, and a number of common policies in areas such as education, training, youth, public health, the labour market, industrial affairs, communications, research and development, regional affairs, environmental policy and development policy.
2. Subsidiarity, which was introduced into the Treaty largely to allay British fears that too much power might be transferred to the EU level.[26]

3. A Committee of the Regions, with solely advisory powers.[27]
4. EMU, which is of course our main concern in this context.
5. European citizenship, which is considered elsewhere in this volume.

All this is to be supplemented by some limited institutional reform marginally increasing the powers of the European Parliament, some provisions for tackling fraud and ensuring financial rectitude (the Court of Auditors becomes a full EU institution), and an enhancement of the powers of the European Court of Justice to improve the implementation of EU legislation. Finally, there is the Social Chapter, a separate Protocol to which the United Kingdom has not adhered. The United Kingdom and Denmark also have the right to 'opt out' of the provisions for EMU.

The specific Maastricht proposals and timetable for EMU are shown below. The first of the three stages are undertaken under existing Community powers, while the final two stages require an amendment to the Treaty of Rome:

1. Stage one consists of the completion of the single market, increased co-ordination and co-operation in economic and monetary fields, strengthening the EMS, an extended role for the ECU and an enhanced role for the Committee of Governors of EU members' central banks. This stage began in July 1990 and should have been completed by January 1993.
2. Stage two essentially involves the groundwork for the single currency: all members are to be included in the narrow band of the ERM, the European Monetary Institute (EMI) is to be set up to promote the coordination necessary for EMU. This stage began in January 1994.
3. Stage three is then complete monetary union, with the introduction of the ECU as the single currency for Europe.

A specific agenda has been prepared for this, with deadlines and convergence criteria that are to be met. The timetable is as follows:

1. By December 1996, if the EC Council of Finance Ministers decides by a qualified majority that a 'critical mass'
   of seven states (six if the United Kingdom opts out) have
   met the convergence criteria, then a date is to be set for
   introducing the ECU in relevant states. Failing that:
2. By December 1997, the start of an automatic process leading to complete monetary union among a minimum of
   five states by January 1999. Additionally,
3. 1998 is to herald the start of the creation of the European Central Bank (ECB), which takes over from the EMI
   (this is seen as the independent issuer of currency), and
   of the European System of Central Banks (ESCB) (which
   is seen as the independent conductor of monetary policy
   and foreign exchange operations). If these institutions
   are not yet in place, then national central banks are to
   become independent at this time.

The Maastricht convergence criteria are as follows:

1. States must have a maximum budget deficit of 3 per cent
   of GDP per annum.
2. Countries must have a maximum total public sector debt
   of 60 per cent of GDP.
3. There are to be no realignments within the ERM.
4. Countries are to have a rate of inflation a maximum of
   1.5 per cent above the average rate in the three lowest
   inflation EU countries in the year before the decision
   (1996 or 1998). This qualification rate (4.7 per cen when
   the Treaty was signed) must be judged as 'sustainable'.
5. Long-term (government bond) interest rates should be
   a maximum of 2 per cent above the average of those in
   the three lowest rate countries.

Table 8.1 illustrates the situation regarding these convergence criteria in 1993, just after the Treaty was signed, and
gives an indication of the likelihood of various EU states
meeting the different criteria by 1999. It will be noted that
nine of the current EU-15 countries are considered to be
in a position to meet the criteria for EMU by 1999, including the United Kingdom.[28] The least likely to meet the criteria and thus qualify for EMU are, not surprisingly, Greece,

Table 8.1 Current Position on and Prospects for Meeting the Maastricht Convergence Criteria

Member State	Inflation in 1993, %	Pass Test by 1999?	Public Deficit 1993, % of GDP	Pass Test by 1999?	Long-term Interest Rate 1993, %	Pass test by 1999?	Public Debt 1993, % of GDP	Pass Test by 1999?	Feasible to Join EMU by 1999?
Belgium	2.8	√	7.4	≈	7.3	√	138	x	√
Denmark	1.4	√	4.4	√	8.9	√	79	√	√
Germany	4.3	x	4.2	√	6.3	x	50	√	x
Greece	13.7	x	15.5	x	23.9	≈	114	x	≈
Spain	4.7	≈	7.2	≈	10.2	√	56	√	√
France	2.3	√	5.9	√	6.8	√	45	√	√
Ireland	2.3	√	3.0	√	7.7	√	93	≈	√
Italy	4.4	≈	10.0	x	11.3	x	116	x	x
Luxembourg	3.6	√	2.5	√	6.9	√	10	√	√
Netherlands	2.1	√	4.0	√	6.7	√	83	√	√
Portugal	6.7	x	8.9	x	12.4	x	70	√	≈
United Kingdom	3.4	≈	7.6	√	7.9	√	53	√	√
EU average	3.8		6.4		8.1		66		
Target	< 1.5% above 3 best		3.0%		< 2% above 3 best		60%		
Austria	3.7	√	2.9	√	6.6	√	57	√	√
Finland	2.2	≈	9.1	x	10.0	≈	60	√	≈
Norway	2.3	√	3.2	√	6.9	√	47	√	√
Sweden	4.5	≈	14.7	≈	8.8	√	67	≈	≈

Notes: √ Should achieve the criterion relatively easily.
≈ Will have difficulties meeting the criterion and may not manage to do so.
x Unlikely to meet the criterion.

Source: European Parliament (1994).

Italy, Spain and Portugal, and, perhaps more surprisingly, Finland and Sweden.

CONCLUSIONS

Events since the signing of the Maastricht Treaty have not exactly gone to plan. To begin with, the ratification of the Treaty proved to be fraught with problems, especially in France and the United Kingdom. Then the ERM has been placed under considerable strain by turbulence in the currency markets, which, as we have seen, exert a fundamental influence in today's world. Thus we have seen the exit of Sterling and the Lira in late 1992, the subsequent pressures on the Franc, and the widening of the ERM bands to ±15 per cent at a time when all currencies should have been in the original narrow band.

This is probably the result of a number of underlying factors, some to do with the fundamental deficiencies of the Maastricht model of EMU, others to do with the parameters within which the EMU process has had to take shape. First among these is the prevailing economic climate. Since the signing of the Maastricht Treaty, Europe has been in recession, no doubt exacerbated by the deflationary effects of German monetary policy after reunification. It would have been substantially easier for member countries to bear the social and employment costs of financial convergence under Maastricht in a climate of economic growth.[29] Secondly, the costs of meeting the convergence criteria (especially in the peripheral states) have been increased by the residual diversity in real variables which persists among potential members of EMU, despite the convergence that has occurred recently. This is compounded by the absence of any substantial redistributive mechanism within the Maastricht Treaty, even in the context of EMU's probable regressive effects.

In addition, the convergence criteria have had a deflationary effect on the European economy. They also reflect a neo-liberal ideological bias and are thus narrow in their coverage, being based excessively on financial variables to the detriment of real variables such as the level of employment. Finally, the Maastricht proposals, and in particular the provisions for a European Central Bank based on the German Bundesbank, have highlighted the EU's 'democratic deficit'. Doubts have been raised concerning how economic policy might be made democratically accountable with a Central Bank that is removed from the political process, and in the context of a European Parliament with few powers, and also about the wisdom of freezing current views on economic priorities into the constitution of the new European Central Bank. These weaknesses and problems, allied to the political factors such as the ideological objections of groups such as the so-called 'Eurosceptics' in the British Conservative Party and the election of the Gaullist Jacques Chirac in France, have resulted in a substantial backlash against further integration in general and EMU in particular.

The future of EMU is therefore clearly uncertain. However, a rump of the most economically advanced countries in the EU seem to be both ready and willing to proceed within something like the framework set out in the Maastricht Treaty. The European Commission, meanwhile, has been busy preparing the transition to the single currency. Table 8.2 illustrates the Commission's proposals for its introduction in three phases.

The Green Paper (on which Table 8.2 is based) allows for some slippage in the Maastricht timetable, but assumes that the overall objective can be sustained on the basis of the original criteria and model. The European Monetary Institute (EMI) has also proceeded with its business on roughly similar lines, although it too envisages slippages in the timetable. The important decisions on the way forward are likely to be taken at the IGC planned for 1996, which is generally expected to come with some kind of 'Maastricht II' or 'son of Maastricht'.

There are a number of possible outcomes, including a two-speed or even a 'variable geometry'[30] Europe. The view taken here is that the current Maastricht model of EMU is fundamentally flawed (see above), and that it is unlikely to lead to EMU on anything like a wide scale over the next 5 – 10 years, but that in the longer term EMU is both desirable and a distinct possibility.

The EMU debate has to seen in the wider context of the future of European integration in general. It seems clear

Table 8.2 Introduction of a Single Currency: Sequence of Events

PHASE A *Launch of EMU*	PHASE B *Start of EMU*	PHASE C *Single currency fully introduced*
Start of the phase:	*Start of the phase:*	*Start of the phase:*
• List of participating Member States • Date of start of EMU announced (or confirmed) • Deadline for the final changeover to the single currency • Setting up of the ESCB and the ECB • Start of production of notes and coins	• Fixing of conversion rates • ECU becomes a currency in its own right • Monetary and exchange rate policy in ECU • Inter-bank, monetary, capital and exchange markets in ECU • New government debt issued in ECU • Corresponding wholesale payment systems in ECU	• ECU notes and coins introduced • Banks have completed the changeover (retail business payment systems) • Notes and coins denominated in national currency are withdrawn • Public and private operators complete the changeover • Only the ECU is used
Throughout the phase:	*Throughout the phase:*	
• Stepping up of preparations and implementations of measures that will, if possible, have been adopted beforehand • Legal framework • National steering structure • Banking and financial community changeover plan	• Banks and financial institutions continue the changeover • Public and private operators other than banks proceed with the changeover circumstances permitting	
1 year maximum	*3 years maximum*	*Several weeks*

Source: EC Commission (1995).

that the globalisation of world economic relations and, in particular, the vast increase in the international mobility of capital have ushered in an era in which the ability of European citizens to exercise control over the economic aspects of their lives through the democratic process now requires certain economic policies to be conducted at a level above that of the nation state.

There are still many unanswered questions, however, about which economic policies should be pursued at which level of government. The study of fiscal federalism[31] attempts to address such questions. It needs to be extended and applied to the current situation in Europe. The principle of subsidiarity provides a good starting point, for potentially it offers a means of sustaining democratic accountability.[32] Then another question arises concerning the size of the EU and its relationship with other major international actors such as the United States, Japan and the Newly Industrialised Countries (NICs). Is the EU really the appropriate level for supranational policy-making? And finally, assuming that the EU can replace the nation-state as the agent for some types of policy-making, how can democratic control over its actions be established? These are the questions that are likely to condition the long-term future of monetary union in Europe.

Against this background it seems advisable for any Maastricht II to introduce a number of changes. First, a reformed ERM, which offers greater exchange rate flexibility until there is greater convergence among its members. One possibility would be to charge the EMI with actively managing exchange rates, insisting on realignment when objective criteria dictate it. Another possibility might be an ERM less reliant on the Deutschmark as its fulcrum. Yet another might be to address the destabilising effect of capital movements, perhaps by taxing speculative transfers and regulating capital and financial derivatives markets. Secondly, the Maastricht EMU clauses might be reformed to promote institutional and structural convergence in areas such as education, labour markets, and research and development; to render the financial criteria less rigid and deflationary; to include real variables among the convergence criteria;[33] and to develop a greater redistributive dimension. The latter could be achieved by giving greater weight to structural policies, but also by bringing regional transfers back on to the agenda. Finally, any new Maastricht needs to address the issue of the democratic accountability of EU institutions.

NOTES

1. A 'European monetary identity'.
2. Perhaps the most important role that the single currency would play, however, would be to render the monetary arrangements permanent – with fixed exchange rates there will always be a temptation in times of economic crisis to opt for the 'quick fix' of devaluation. If national exchange rates do not exist, then they clearly cannot be changed.
3. That is an area in which one has the so-called 'level playing field', i.e. the four classic freedoms of movement: the free movement of goods, services, labour and capital.
4. Since the price of their products will be rising more rapidly than those of their competitors, and thus their imports will, all other things being equal, increase while their exports fall.
5. Although there are grounds for believing that devaluation is merely 'fool's gold', since the advantages it confers on economies tend to be temporary, as we have seen in the United Kingdom in the postwar period, and as we are beginning to observe in the aftermath of the 1992 ejection of Sterling from the ERM.
6. This may be part of a larger process of economic polarisation through a process of what Myrdal (1956) refers to as 'cumulative causation'.
7. Under pure 'monetarism' the money supply provided the 'anchor' for policy, the main variable to be targeted. Since it was discovered in the early 1980s that the money supply is difficult to define, let alone control, in open and interdependent economies, the emphasis has been on targeting exchange rates. This in itself helps to explain some of the renewed interest in monetary integration since the mid-1980s.
8. For a detailed analysis of the relationship between national sovereignty and economic integration, see Lintner, in Brouwer *et al.* (1984).
9. Whatever form this trade-off takes, and indeed whether it exists at all, the expectations augmented approach would imply that common rates of inflation can be achieved without serious long-term employment effects.
10. It should be noted that there is a view that Germany would in effect be the only country to suffer this type of sovereignty loss in a Maastricht-type EMU, since it currently holds an almost complete leadership position, which would then be diluted.
11. See Lintner (1994).

12. François Mitterrand was elected in 1981 with a mandate to follow a form of what in the United Kingdom would have been called an 'alternative economic strategy', based on active Keynesian demand management to reduce unemployment and on an interventionist industrial policy. This was at a time when the rest of Europe was implementing restrictive monetary policies, and the United Kingdom and the United States were busy experimenting with pure monetarism. French imports duly increased without a commensurate increase in exports, and the whole policy had to be abandoned.

13. This may be less the case in other areas such as certain microeconomic policies; see Lintner, in Brouwer *et al.* (1994)

14. The balance of payments surpluses of the oil-producing countries that have been recycled into Western capital markets.

15. Direct investment can have obvious and equally serious longer-term effects on sovereignty: for example, if multinational enterprises (MNEs) dislike a tax regime, controls over borrowing, or labour market regulation, they can subvert these or exact punitive costs by locating elsewhere.

16. And presumably even then history will be interpreted in different ways.

17. See European Parliament (1994).

18. An area in which it is possible and beneficial to have fixed exchange rates, see Mundell (1961).

19. Before the term became associated with Milton Friedman.

20. The original EEC 6 plus Britain, Denmark and Ireland, who were in the process of joining the then Community.

21. These bands were widened after the ERM crisis of 1992 to their current ±15 per cent, which some would argue are so wide as to negate the very principle of a fixed exchange rate system.

22. For a more detailed examination of the EMS, see, for example, Lintner and Mazey (1991).

23. Arguably the worst time imaginable, in the context of German unification and the coming recession.

24. One of which was on the subject of political union, which had not originally been on the agenda.

25. For an excellent interpretation of the Maastricht Treaty, see Church and Phinnemore (1994).

26. This it could be argued may also pave the way for regionalism and the marginalisation of the nation state in the (very) long run.

27. See Brouwer, Lintner and Newman (1994).

28. This says much about the underlying conduct and direction of UK macroeconomic policy, which has been significantly influenced by the Maastricht criteria, despite all the Eurosceptic bluster.

29. In fact, there is a view that the process of European integration advances in cycles, roughly in line with the economic cycle.

30. Countries being left to an extent free to opt in and out of various EU developments.

31. See Oates (1972).

32. However, if one adopts this idea, then there may not be an objec-

tive case in terms of efficiency and democracy for action at the national level in the long term: thus subsidiarity may well mark the beginning of the end of the nation-state in Europe.
33. These might include productivity, unemployment, growth rates, regional imbalances and even poverty levels.

REFERENCES

Brouwer, F., Lintner, V., and Newman, M. (eds) (1994), *Economic Policy and the European Union*, Federal Trust, London.

Church, C. H. and Phinnemore, D. (1994), *The European Union and European Community*, Harvester Wheatsheaf, Hemel Hempstead.

Corden, W. M. (1972) 'Monetary Integration', *Princeton Essays in International Finance*, No. 73, Princeton, NJ.

European Commission (1995), *One Currency for Europe*, Green Paper on the Practical Arrangements for the Introduction of the Single Currency, Brussels.

European Parliament (1994), *The Social Consequences of Economic and Monetary Union*, Working Paper, Social Affairs Series, Luxembourg.

Fleming, M. (1971), 'On Exchange Rate Unification', *Economic Journal*, No. 81, pp. 467–88.

Lintner, V. and Mazey, S. (1991), *The European Community: Economic and Political Aspects*, McGraw-Hill, Maidenhead.

Mundell, R. A. (1961), 'A Theory of Optimum Currency Areas', *American Economic Review*, No. 51, pp. 657–65.

Myrdal, G. (1956), *Economic Theory and Underdeveloped Regions*, Duckworth, London.

Oates, W. (1972), *Fiscal Federalism*, Harcourt, Brace, Jovanovitch, New York.

9 The European Road to the Information Superhighway
Carl Levy

INTRODUCTION

Since the early 1990s the arrival of an Information Super-highway has gripped the imaginations of the citizens, politicians and industrialists of Europe. But the concept of a 'wired society' is not new: similar prophecies were voiced in the 1970s and early 1980s before the failures of the French Minitel and British Prestel experiments due to the lack of consumer demand for the pre-digital analogue coaxial versions of the superhighway (Dutton 1995). Compression and digitisation promise to open the way for the merging of telephony, televison and computers with the bandwidth capacity to support full real-time multi-media applications (voice, text and video) on an Integrated Broadband Network (IBN). The digitisation of voice, image and data has undermined the discrete regulatory regimes that have governed the European telecommunications and television industries. We are witnessing a global rush to position nations, regions and industrial interests at the forefront of the next great consumer revolution.

Progress towards an Information Superhighway has been accompanied by the liberalisation of the telecommunications industry. The initial drive was caused by the divestiture of AT&T in the United States, the privatisation of BT in the United Kingdom and the demand by transnational corporations for VANS (value-added-network services) carried through private or leased lines, stimulated by new digitised intelligent telecommunications networks reliant on computer switches.[1] The incremental liberalisation of telecommunications championed by the European Commission did not mean the complete abandonment of older industrial champion approaches. Jacques Delors proposed a Keynesian pump-priming of the fibre-optic infrastructure in order to generate employment during the depths of the early 1990s recession. This transposed the public service remits of the old PTTs (Post, Telegraph and Telecommunications Organisation) to a trans-European level and found its justification in similar plans for government intervention by the Clinton/ Gore administration (Freeman and Soete 1994: 147–56). Fears of European technological obsolesence had advanced the cause of *dirigiste* DGs in the 1980s and inspired the RACE (Research and Development in Advanced Communications Technologies for Europe), ESPRIT (European Strategic Programme for Research and Development in Information Technology) and the intergovernmental EUREKA (the European Research Co-ordination Agency, especially its JESSI [Joint European Silicon Structures Initiative]) programmes. But they had not bridged the technology gap between Europe and the Americans and Japanese.[2] Just as in the earlier, unhappy case of HDTV (High Definition Television), the European Community felt that it would be necessary to capture the standards gateway both in digital and mobile telephone technology. The histories behind the introduction of a *dirigiste* ISDN (Integrated Services Digital Network) and a more successful consumer-friendly GSM (General Standard for Mobile Communications) illustrate the evolution of European industrial policy in the 1990s from that of promoting European champions to partaking in Global champions, but they also point to the restructuring of public policy in Member States from the advocacy of positive state intervention in the economy to the model of the pro-market regulatory state (Grande 1994; Thatcher 1995). The harmonisation of telecommunications markets and technological specifications associated with the digital revolution in Europe has thus forced all the old PTTs to be transformed into privatised industries or commercial organisations separated from direct state control.

PTTs in the EU have been transformed into PTOs (Public Telecommunications Organisation) through a largely European Commission-inspired process.[3] Throughout the EU former PTTs have all followed a series of stages in this process: separation of postal services and telecomunications organisations (except for the Netherlands which privatised them together); commercialisation; partial privatisation; and liberalisation. The first three stages have been much easier to implement than the last, which is still being contested, even though Member States have agreed to the general programme of open competition (Scott 1995: 48). They have either partially or completely privatised their PTOs into private shareholder TOs (Telecommunications Organisations), while the separation of control and ownership has meant that all states have established independent forms of regulation to ensure that these former natural monopolies do not abuse their newly won commercial freedom. With the arrival of the SEM (Single European Market), the Commission and the European Court of Justice have become increasingly the agencies of pan-European telecommunications regulation. However, this raises fundamental questions about the degree to which the creation of an ad hoc or *de jure* European FCC (on the model of the American Federal Communications Commission) will be tolerated by Member States jealous of their sovereignty. The principle of subsidiarity has been invoked by suspicious Member States. Will the crux of pan-European regulation be located at the national or at the EU level?

The interaction of nation-state and EU levels of regulation reflects the very process through which liberalisation occurred. The need to meet the Maastricht criteria in order to qualify for EMU (Economic and Monetary Union) has increased the attractiveness of Member States' privatising their public telecommunications organisations. (This is notably the case in Italy and Belgium who both wish to join EMU but have massive budget deficits.) The Commission's programme meshed nicely with events elsewhere in the EU. The French Right's desire in the 1980s to change the *statut* of France Télécom in order to facilitate its commercialisation, and the rapid preparation for the privatisation of Deutsche Telekom caused by the challenge of re-equiping the former East German Länder with modernised telecommunications, are just two examples (Thatcher 1995: 246–51). But fears of technological obsolence has been the key theme in the liberalisation process. Commission policy-makers have employed *dirigiste* arguments when proposing the harmonisation of technical standards within a Single European Market or funding for R&D programmes. However, in reality the main thrust of policy-making has accelerated the liberalisation of voice telephony and telecommunications infrastructure markets (Wyatt-Walter 1995).

In this chapter I shall examine five aspects of European policy concerning the Information Superhighway. The fear of European technological obsolescence has been one of the key themes in the process of liberalisation of the telecommunications industry. I shall first examine Europe's position in the global IT economy. Secondly, this chapter will present an overview of the European Commission's programme of liberalisation. Thirdly, this policy of liberalisation will be linked to an evaluation of industrial policy and the fostering of the Information Superhighway in the EU. Fourthly, the role of the EU as regulator of the new political economy of telecommunications will be evaluated. Finally, I will discuss the future of regulation at the EU level and the challenges to the public service remit as well as the impacts upon social welfare caused by arrival of an information society.

THE GLOBAL IT MARKET

In the 1990s the EU still lags behind its two chief competitors. The then European Community's IT deficit with the rest of the world was $5.6 billion in 1980, but by 1991 it had risen to $21 billion (Sharp 1993: 218). Much of the consumer electronics, software and semi-conductor industries were either Japanese- or American-controlled, and the entertainment industries, whose own software was destined to fill the hundreds of channels due on digital television, CD-ROMs and other multi-media applications were largely American-inspired or owned. However, in one field, telephone equipment (mobile handsets, switches, public exchanges and transmission equipment, etc.), European firms had some advantages. Siemens (Germany), Alcatel (France) and Ericsson (Sweden) are respectable players in the fields of switches and transmission equipment, and the success of Nokia (Finland) and Ericsson in mobile telephony should also be mentioned. The Scandinavians, along with Motorola, control 70 per cent of the world handset market (*Financial Times*, 3 October 1995: 12). In this respect the promotion of the European-based GSM standards has been a notable success for RACE and the ETSI (European Telecommunications Standards Institute). Mobile handset ownership in Europe stands at 16 million and is set to grow to at least 40 million by 2000 (Stehmann 1995: 165).

However, the global outlook for Europe is mixed. There is great potential for growth. The EU telecommunications market is worth ECU 84 billion per annum in services and ECU 26 billion annum in equipment: the service sector is growing at 8 per cent a year and the equipment sector at 4 per cent a year (Federal Trust 1995: 40). Indeed, a fully functional Single European Market could be worth 20 per cent of the world market (Stehmann 1995: 148). Nevertheless, market fragmentation and wide disparity in the density of telecommunication usage means that 'the total market size of telecommunications services in Europe amounts to only one-half of the size in the USA, despite the fact that there are more inhabitants in the EU' (Stehmann 1995: 149). More crucially, the United States has a much greater IT consumer economy to support the telecommunications industries of scale and scope required to construct the Information Superhighway. There are 10 PCs per 100 inhabitants in the EU, but in the United States the ratio stands at 34 per 100 (Federal Trust 1995: 43). By 2000 the software market in Europe could be worth $35 billion (*Financial Times*, 15 June 1995: IV), while the market for interactive multimedia could be valued at ECU 25 billion in 2004 (*Financial Times*, 21 June 1995: 3). However, European software houses such as the French Cap Sogeti Gemini or Sligos, the British Sema Group or Logica, and the Italian Finisiel are no threat to the market-dominant Microsoft or the new generation Internet software houses (Netscape, etc.). Moreover, in 1992 European semiconductor producers controlled only 35 per cent of their indigenous market. This compares to 80 per cent Japanese and 70 per cent American domination of their respective domestic markets, while the large European producers (Siemens, Philips and SGS-Thomson) managed to control a mere 10 per cent of the entire world market (Wyatt-Walter 1995:

429). Therefore, it seems highly unlikely that the effort to create a fully-fledged IBN network in Europe will dislodge the domination of the Americans and Japanese in key sectors of the IT industry.

Traditional industrial policy has not been the chief catalyst in the development of the Information Superhighway. Rather, the popularity of the project has been immeasurably aided by the explosive growth of the Internet. The Internet, however, is not the same thing as the Information Superhighway. Originally created in the late 1960s as a network of American university research computers funded by the National Science Foundation to facilitate communications between projects (Arpanet), when the US government withdrew its subsidy in 1989 the Internet was run on an inexpensive commercial basis since the larger trunk lines linking the main servers were very cheap due to the deregulation of US telecommunications market. These leased lines charged at bulk traffic rates. Therefore, costs decreased as the Internet became more popular (Gates 1995: 98–100). The increase in popularity due to the rapidly increased power of PCs and greatly improved digital compression technology was assisted by cheaper and more efficient modems allowing for a mass market to connect to the Internet or other on-line services. User-friendly network software (browsers) and the great appeal of the graphical World Wide Web has caused the Internet to double every six months. At the time of writing there were 50 million users worldwide and it is predicted that by 2000 500 million users will be networked worldwide (Emmott 1995: 6). The emergence of the American-originated Internet was thus a curious product of government subsidy and market forces. Unlike the earlier European wired society experiments, it has reached a critical mass through technological innovations and the awakening of consumer interest. The Internet is the greatest event in the IT industry since the introduction of the PC by IBM in 1981. However, since the 'local loop', the final section of copper cable connecting domestic telephones to the main fibre optic cable in the street, lacks the bandwidth capacity to carry video, voice and data, the full Information Superhighway is still some 5–10 years away. Indeed, wireless competing mobile and satellite digital compression technologies could conceivably make the cabled Information Superhighway redundant. Therefore, the 'Information Superhighway' is used here as shorthand, as a bundle of new technologies – the latest mobile technologies PCNs (Personal Communication Networks), LEOs (Low-Earth-Orbiting Satellites), terrestrial digital television transmission, fibre-strengthened forms of coaxial cable and ADSL (asynchronous digital subscriber loop, which however is not interactive) – that complement and compete with fibre-optic cable. All these technologies are merely modes of transporting digitised information: the key technology is digital compression the full potential of which has still not been exhausted (Emmott 1995: 4–5; Stehmann 1995: 21–30).

THE LIBERALISATION OF EUROPEAN TELECOMMUNICATIONS: AN OVERVIEW[4]

The European Commission's *Towards a Dynamic European Economy* (Green Paper on the development of the common market for telecommunications services and equipment, COM (87)290) focused on the liberalisation of telecommunications services and equipment in the context of the Single European Market. Its agenda became the basis for most of the European legislation put in place in the early and mid-1990s. However, in the years immediately before the publication of the Green Paper (1982–6), the Commission generated interest in pan-European telecommunications using arguments concerning the technical standardisation of digital specifications, particularly ISDN, linking it to developments in the Commission's R&D programmes. ISDN, which was suppposed to be the technical basis of an integrated European digitised communications network largely dominated by PTOs, has instead been placed within the context of a liberalised and increasingly privatised European telecommunications industry. This rolling process of liberalisation has been shaped by four interconnected phenomena discussed by Thatcher (1995). First, the 'Commission has been able to formulate a coherent approach at Community level'. Thus it has used the logic of the single market 'to ensure that competition is 'fair' and that certain standards of supply are maintained' (p. 264). Secondly, the Commission's position was reinforced employing Articles of the Treaty of Rome, interpreted by the European Court of Justice to restrict the scope of member states 'to offer special regulatory protection to selected undertakings'. Thus, Article 85 prohibits concerted action which might distort competition and 'horizontal agreements' between PTOs or TOs to fix prices, to limit hub competition or the routing of calls. Thirdly, Article 86 was used in the early 1990s to limit the restriction of competition in the non-reserved market (everything except voice telephony which comprises 80–90 per cent of PTO and TO income) through the use of cross-subsidies and restricted access of competitors to their networks. Fourthly, Article 90 allowed the member states to grant exclusive rights to entities operating a service of public interest (a universal network and universal service), but the Commission's right to ensure that PTOs did not infringe upon non-reserved services was affirmed in a landmark decision issued by the European Court in 1991.[5]

The Green Paper also led to the separation of regulatory from operational functions in order to prevent the abuse of power by the dominant TO or TCO. The process of liberalisation after 1987 used a three-fold model of the telecommunications market (equipment/telecommunication services/network services).[6] A Directive in 1988 freed the terminals equipment market (88/301/EEC). The Open Network Provision – Directive (90/387/EEC) provided the legal basis for all users to gain access to telecommunications networks throughout the Community. The aim was to introduce in stages measures to assure that transparent conditions allowed for access to technical interfaces and usages so that competitors would not be subject to discrimination. This meant that 'special and exclusive rights' were removed from Member States in respect to VANS and data services (90/388/EEC). Leased lines were opened to free competition and resale through a Directive (92/247/EEC). On 22 July 1993, the Council of Ministers agreed that the all-important voice telephony market be opened by 1 January 1998 with optional derogations for Luxembourg (2000) and Greece, Ireland, Portugal and Spain (2003).

In other fields the EU has also increased the pace of liberalisation. A Green Paper (*Towards the Personal Communica-*

tions Environment (Com(94) 145)) was issued in 1994 to develop an EU system of technical harmonisation and universal coverage via market freedom. Pioneered by the success of GSM, the goal is to create a Universal Mobile Telecommunications System (UMTS) using the interconnection of GSM, DCS-1800 (Digital Cellular Standard) and DECT (Digital, European Cordless, Telecommunications), serviced by low-orbiting satellites. Since the vast majority of mobile calls are routed through the TOs' PSTNs (Public Switched Telecommunications Network), this necessitates that they offer fairly priced interconnection charges. This will require that mobile operators have the full freedom to develop and operate their networks and be unrestricted in offering a combined service via fixed and mobile networks. By the autumn of 1995 the Commission had forced competition in every Member State, with new mobile operators in Ireland, Belgium, the Netherlands, Italy and Spain (*Financial Times*, 27 November 1995: II).

The liberalisation of the satellite market is directly linked to the evolution of the pan-European market in digital mobile communications, since only 3 per cent of the terrestrial telephone traffic uses this mode for intra-European telephony. However, a UMTS will have to rely on interactive two-way VSATs (Very Small Aperture Terminals), which are increasingly employed by larger European and multinational firms. The most important legislation has been a Directive (94/46/EEC) which liberalised satellite communication based on the same principles as the liberalisation of terrestrial telecommunication. Liberalisation has been concentrated in the allowance of private corporate networks. Finally, the European Commission adopted legislation which lifted restrictions in effect in certain member states for the transmission of teleshopping and telebanking. However, member states can still prohibit telephony until 1 January 1998 (*Financial Times*, 12 October 1995: 2).

By 1998 most of the liberalisation process inaugurated in the late 1980s will have been completed. At first the process of liberalisation was based on service-based competition: the liberalisation of terminals, value-added networks and voice services. Each wave of liberalisation undermined the logic of maintaining previously reserved services. Prevention of the cross-subsidisation of VANS by the PTOs using revenues from the reserved voice telephone sector motivated much Commission action, but even the entry of other players into voice telephony would still force them to be reliant on the former PTOs for lines and switching. They could control gateway access and technology and thereby easily sabotage competition. The next step was facility-based competition with the allowance of separate owners of infrastructure (Preiskel and Higham 1995). After 1 January 1998 most of the EU will see competition to establish alternative infrastructures to transmit telecommunications (these new players being cable companies (Haag and Schoof 1994), utilities, railways and large firms with previously private networks). After liberalisation, former PTOs could use the entire EU market as the basis for competition in services and infrastructure. In other words, if we consider the EU as a single integrated market, the new ground-rules will have similar effects as the divestiture in the United States of AT&T and other legislation which followed. The former PTOs might perform the equivalent role to the American RBOCs (Regional Bell Operating Companies), whilst newcomers would be the equivalent of Sprint or MCI, which have competed with AT&T for long-distance telephone calls in the United States (Stehmann 1995: 291–6). This has implications for the future and shape of the Information Superhighway in Europe.

EUROPEAN UNION INDUSTRIAL POLICY: INTRODUCTION

A fully functional Information Superhighway in the EU will be very expensive, but its final price is still open to debate. We can now assume that some of these costs will be lowered due to infrastructure competition between new and older players involved in terrestrial telephony, while bridging the gap between the 'local loop' and the street-based main fibre-optic cable could be solved through a variety of technologies (microwave, radiowave and hybrid cables). It is also possible that satellite technology and a new generation of digital mobile telephony might allow much digital transmission to avoid the terrestrial system. Furthermore, the appearance of terrestrial digital television and satellite transmitted digital television will create hundreds of new television channels and allow the possibility of interactive communication through set-top boxes. This in turn would liberate valuable bandwidths which could be auctioned by Member States to allow the expansion of PCNs in a future generation of digital mobile telephony. However, it remains the case that the terrestrial fibre-optic superhighway will be the backbone of the information society. Although the idea of dozens of satellites beaming digital information to laptops throughout the EU seems like a sensible alternative, the project will be extremely costly in its own right: the Motorola-led Iridium project has recently had to reduce the number of satellites it intends to launch (*Financial Times*, 27 November 1995: I). It is also questionable whether the billions now wagered on satellite-transmitted digital television will find an audience. But the amazing success of the Internet now makes the commercial possibilties of a fibre-optic IBN seem more likely.

THE CREATION OF AN INFORMATION SUPERHIGHWAY

According to a recently commissioned report produced by KPMG on behalf of the European Commission, the full price of cabling the EU would be ECU 333 billion. If we assume that the entire process might take 20 years (as is estimated for the United States), then the EU would have to spend ECU 16.7 billion per annum. This is equivalent to 40 or even 50 per cent of the total annual capital expenditures of the EUs PTOs (*Federal Trust* 1995: 92–5).

But public funds from Member States were not forthcoming in a period of strict budget constraints imposed upon them by the aftershocks of the deepest recession since 1945 and the criteria needed to move towards Stage Three of EMU. The limitations on funding were revealed in the responses to Jacques Delors' White Paper on *Growth, Competitiveness, Employment: The Challenges and Ways Forward into the 21st Century* (CEC:COM (93) 700), in which Delors suggested that the EU would rejoin the economic growth path by improving competitiveness, particularly through the use of TENs (Trans-European Networks) in the areas of information and communication. But funds expended by the EU itself would be raised largely through long-term Union Bonds. However, Member States did not support this approach. In any case, Martin Bangemann, the European Commissioner for telecommunications and industrial policy, produced a report in the wake of Delors', which stressed another route and this has become extremely influential in the EU. His group's report was submitted to the European Council in Corfu in June 1994 (*Europe and the Global Information Society*, Report of the High-Level Group on the Information Society). Policy-makers on the Bangemann Committee were convinced that cash-rich PTOs could be enticed into investing, and that a far better way of boosting take-up of services was to abolish monopolies and allow competition to exert a strong downward pressure on prices. The privatisation of the PTOs would also release them from pressures of state control and liberate investment potential, although no one suggested that receipts pocketed by Member States should be transferred to the information superhighway project.

The Bangemann Report presents the EU as an enabler and a catalyst (Schoof and Watson Brown 1995: 329). The spread of an intelligent fibre-optic networks will be facilitated through the liberalised telecommunications market, which the Commission has shaped in the past decade. Indeed the process is already underway: Deutsche Telekom is deploying fibre-optic cable and had 1.2 million residential lines in place by the end of 1995 (Federal Trust 1995: 94); private competitors (Veba) also plan a smaller system in the Ruhr (*Financial Times*, 6 June 1995: 26); France Télécom plans to have a full fibre-optic network in place by 2000 (Federal Trust 1995: 94) and Telecom Italia plans to cable 10 million residences by 1998 (*Financial Times*, 3 October 1995: 6). Hermes Europe RailTel, Europe's 11 main rail companies, plans to run trackside fibre optics, offering to lease the system to TOs and other smaller operators. Hermes will be in alliance with Alcatel, AT&T, Ericsson, Nokia, Northern Telecom and Siemens. The estimated cost of this project linking major cities will be £393 million and should be completed in 1998 to coincide with full liberalisation (Clifford 1995: 24). It has also been estimated that 34 per cent of all European homes have been passed by coaxial cable (through CATV) and this could be strengthened with fibre to upgrade to near-IBN standard (Haag and Schoof 1994; Federal Trust 1995: 94).

The Bangemann Report introduced the concept of a Common Information Area (CIA) (Turner 1995). But if the CIA is to be a market-led process, the financial contribution of the EU will be rather modest. The Commission has estimated that a properly functioning CIA by the turn of the century would require ECU 150 billion. Particular focus should be centred on interconnected advanced networks (a high-speed communications network and the consolidation of ISDN – cost ECU 35 billion), general electronic services (electronic access to information, electronic mail and electronic images: interactive video services – cost ECU 12 billion) and telematic applications (teleworking, links between administrations, teletraining and telemedicine – cost ECU 14 billion). But the EU itself will spend only a total of ECU 422 million on financing telecommunications networks between 1994 and 1999 (Turner 1995: 502–4). The lobby group of Europe's software companies, SIX (Services Information Expertise Advisory Group), has suggested that the EU could act as a pump-primer, using funds already allocated from the Framework Programmes to establish an EU database on environmental information and support the pan-European Social Security Net (SoSeNet) (*Financial Times,* 12 December 1994: 13). The EU has already helped to establish a Trans-European Network for public administration through computer linkages between over 40 public administrations in 12 Member States (Zotschew 1995). But given the vast sums needed to create the CIA and the rather modest amounts pledged, the EU's role can only be one of 'smoothing the path of private finance by, for example, offering money for feasibility studies, largely as part of the trans-European networks (TENs) initiative' (Turner 1995: 503).

THE EUROPEAN UNION AS REGULATORY STATE

The EU exercises a more significant role in European digital industrial policy as a regulator and standard-setter. The future of regulation will be discussed in the final section of this chapter. However, in the past decade the EC/EU has played a major role in the reshaping of the corporate structures of the telecommunications industries. Liberalisation has opened European telecommunications markets to the pressures of global competition, but first I shall examine the rush in Europe to establish a new universal digital standard. A global digital standard such as ISDN seemed important in a sector where Miscrosoft's MS-DOS and Windows software has achieved near proprietary status. Much of the corporate collaboration in Eureka or the Community's R&D programmes over the past decade, as well as the ongoing search for European and global coporate alliances of super-carriers, hardware and software manufacturers and multimedia firms has been caused by the expensive quest to achieve an advantage in new forms of gateway digital technology (Fuchs 1992, 1994; Hawkins 1992, 1995).

Thus, while the neo-liberal DGs in the Commission were gradually prising open various European telecommunications market, since the late 1980s the Community (working through the European Telecommunications Standards Institute) has promoted the ISDN standard. ISDN is the technical gateway which allows the transmission of voice, data, facsimile, telemetry and slow-motion video. The Commission's conception of ISDN was based on the three principles of digitisation, increased capacity of transmission and the integration of networks (Stehmann 1995: 19). And although the commitment to ISDN was reiterated in the liberal Bangemann Report, it has not been uncontroversial. The Americans believe that Euro-ISDN is not a technically neutral but a hegemonic proprietary technology (Noam 1992: 363). That is to say, the technical specifications behind Euro-ISDN will, they argue, lead to a top-down centralisation of networks dominated by the Europeans (Stehmann 1995: 20). Furthermore, the capacity of ISDN is in excess of the requirements of the average residential user. The universalisation of the cost of its installation might disportiately benefit larger companies rather than the residential user. In effect, the residential user would subsidise the adoption of the ISDN standard (Mansell 1993: 80). Furthermore, as Mansell argues, Euro-ISDN could be used by the super-carriers to exercise an indirect monopoly because the technology requires the most sophisticated form of intelligent telecommunications network (Mansell 1993: 69–109). The gradual liberalisation of the telecommunications network, outlined above, was partly motivated by a desire to end disguised forms of cross-subsidisation of VANS services through revenue earned by PTOs due to their monopoly of voice telephony. But even after the future liberalisation of voice telephony and infrastructure provision, the super-carriers could still seize an unfair advantage in the market by creating proprietary gateways in the intelligent digital network using Euro-ISDN. On the other hand, the American approach of allowing competing ISDN standards might retard the development of the IBN because of the lack of inter-operability of competing network infrastructure providers.

In fact, rapid technological progress may have made these disputes redundant. The emergence of the Internet 'halfway house', and competing systems of digital transmission to complete the local loop, probably means that the threat of 'hegemonic' ISDN will not materialise. ISDN is not adequate to transmit video-on-demand without the use of ATM (Asynchronous Transfer Mode) technology which is still at an experimental stage. The demand for multi-media entertainment might be a chief source of finance of the IBN. But in the most advanced cable environment in the world – the United Kingdom – Oftel has refused to allow BT to transmit video-on-demand through its network before 2001. In any case, the great success of CD-ROMs (*Financial Times*, 3 October 1995: 28) and the forthcoming satellite and terrestrially-based forms of digital televison equipped with set-top boxes (see below), may satisfy the public's thirst for digitised entertainment. So far, ISDN has been commercially successful by attracting larger firms, notably in the United Kingdom, France and Germany (where Deutsche Telekom has significantly lowered the cost of installation). In these cases it has been used to good effect for the rapid transfer of files in Large Area Networks (LANS) (*Financial Times*, 3

October 1995: 28). It therefore seems likely that the adoption of ISDN on a wide scale will first appear in the commercial districts of Europe's largest cities. So far the most significant effect of the Commission's Euro-ISDN campaign has not been the triumph of a hegemonic centralised seamless IBN but the very liberalisation of the EU's telecommunications industry.

If the anarchic Internet or World Wide Web might be the evolutionary path to the Information Superhighway, the development of the protocols and standards governing its future development will play an increasingly important role. The explosive growth of the Internet is partially based on the common standard of TCP/IP (Transmission Control/Internet Protocol) established when it was still largely used by the American university research community. But the digitisation of television and telephony has meant that the commercial interests behind network technology, computer platforms, multi-media services and, most importantly, software are converging on the Internet and struggling either to monopolise or open potential proprietary gateway standards. The recent flurry of activity surrounding Microsoft and the next generation of Internet software giants illustrates how attempts by Microsoft and other on-line commercial services to establish proprietary standards through the control of gateway software have been contested by the next generation of browser software (*Financial Times*, 8 December 1995: 37). This relates largely to an American-dominated software industry, but it also demonstrates the need to establish standards in Europe which allow for open interfaces in the future.

In this case, it has been suggested that future standardisation should be restricted to 'certain tools', so long as they do not stifle continual innovation (Federal Trust 1995: 82). The chief area of interest is APIs (Application Programming Interfaces). Further standardisation in audio-visual coding and EDI (Electronic Data Interchange) is necessary but the computer platforms themselves should be left open to unrestricted competition. The most important gateway between PCs or information appliances are the application platforms created by servers and databases. Inter-operability between different database technologies must be maintained. In the future it will be commonplace for software agents and search engines to locate relevant information, but there is still a need for standardised directories on the Internet (*Financial Times*, 29 December 1995: 11). The ETSI has established a high-level taskforce to investigate whether or not the standards-making process and the standards themselves are appropriate for the needs of Europe. This taskforce is examining the extent to which existing networks – PSTN, GSM and ISDN – can be tapped to help design the appropriate APIs. In this regard, the EU's R&D Fourth Framework Programmes (ACT [Advanced Communications, Services and Technologies], Esprit and Telematics) could provide a useful testbed for future standardisation in the same fruitful way GSM evolved from the first RACE programme. The informal nature of the Internet means that established institutions of standardisation – the ETSI, CENELEC (Comité Européen de Normalisation Electrotechnique = European Committee for Electrotechnical Standardisation), or the ITU (International Telecommunications Union) – will have to work with ad hoc fora of users, manufacturers, telecommunciations operators, and service providers to arrive at de facto and de jure decisions for the enhancement of UNIs (User Network Interface).

Another standards issue concerns the successfully established GSM. As noted previously, the success of GSM has allowed the European digital mobile telephone industry to flourish. More than 86 countries have recognised the standard, but the Americans are developing a new digital standard – CDMA (Code Division Multiple Access) – which may be capable of accommodating ten times the number of telephone calls on the same bandwith. If the Iridium project is successful (see above), GSM may be under pressure. However, the consensus is that it will remain the standard for mobile telephony into the first decade of the twenty-first century (*Financial Times*, 3 October 1995: 12).

Although the Europeans were wrongfooted in their earlier failed attempts to establish the proprietary standard for HDTV, they have learned from their mistakes. By the year 2000, satellite and terrestrial digital television will be a significant force in Europe. Astra and Eutelsat will have massive capacity through a series of satellites launches planned

to take place between 1995 and 1997. The new private television interests of the 1980s – Sky, Canal Plus, RTL, etc. –
are well placed to take advantage of this market, while the
BBC is planning the world's first terrestrial digital television
service. Within a few years the Europeans have leapfrogged
the Americans. As Cawson notes: 'Europe is at the forefront
of digital television technologies. Its single frequency transmission technology, developed within the RACE programme
and now being launched as Digital Audio Broadcasting services
is ahead of anything in the US and Japan' (Cawson 1994:
64). This has been achieved by the Commission's abandonment of the HD-MAC analogue programme in 1993 and
the promotion of the intergovernmental Digital Video
Group (originally advanced by the British and Germans).
Under Martin Bangemann, DG III has shifted the direction of European Commission policy from creating an HDTV
European champion by subsidising industrial projects
aimed at seizing the high ground in the struggle for a
new generation of proprietary standards to 'the competition policy issues of how to regulate the new digital technology to prevent unfair discrimination against new market
entrants by the established channels' (Cawson and Holmes,
1995: 661).

The main focus has been the set-top boxes, that is, computers that facilitate inter-active capacity and are used to
decode digitised television signals permitting telebanking,
home learning, video-on-demand as well providing a valuable computerised database of customers which could be
sold on to advertisers. DG XIII (Directorate-General for
Innovation and Telecommunications) is working with the
DVB (Digital Video Broadcasting) Committee on Conditional
Access to reach a consensus on a common interface to prevent firstcomers from stifling new service providers (Cawson
and Holmes 1995: 662). After much haggling with the European Parliament, the Council of Ministers agreed to an
amended European Directive opening the field of set-top
fabrication to the all manufacturers under 'fair, reasonable
and non-discriminatory terms which would not "foreclose
common interface"' (Graham 1995a, 45). But by the end
of 1995 various industrial groups and public broadcasters
within the DVB were racing to create a common European

standard. Multimedia Betreibsgesellschaft (MMGB-Deutsche Telekom, Veba, Bertelsmann, ARD and ZDF of Germany, France's Canal Plus, Luxembourg's CLT with linkages to the Kirch-Gruppe's interests in Germany, Italy and Spain) claimed to have reached the standard. Concurrently, a UK group including the BBC, ITV and BT were also working on their own set-top box (*Financial Times*, 12 December 1995: 2). The Commission, through the links via DG XIII, will be influential in mediating the race for gateway technology. However, the competition officials found in DG IV will probably be the final arbiters. The role of the Commission is rather similar to its activities in the liberalisation of telecommunications: the subversive logic of the digitial revolution and Single European Market have seen the technocratic arguments used in the failed HDTV experiments unknowingly ushering in their opposite. If the Commission as honest broker and meso-corporatist has facilitated the formation of the group of European broadcasters, manufacturers, telcoms operators and regulators that comprises the DVB, 'the emergence of this new technology shows how blurred the traditional lines are between aspects of regulatory and industrial policy' (Cawson and Holmes 1995: 667).

GLOBAL ALLIANCES

This takes us to our final, if closely related, method in which regulatory policy has been shaped in the 1990s. The privatised or soon to be privatised super-carriers are forming global alliances (Curwen 1995: 342–3). These are:

1. The unnamed alliance of AT&T (WorldPartners) with Unisource (Netherlands (KPN)), Spain (Telefónica), Sweden (Telia), and Swiss Telecom (1994).
2. Concert: BT and MCI (1994).
3. Phoenix (now known as Global One): Atlas (Deutsche Telekom and France Télécom) and Sprint (1995). (Atlas is also linked with Olivetti which in turn has a joint partnership in Italy with Bell Atlantic (Infostrada) to rival Telecom Italia) (*Financial Times*, 16 November 1995: 3).

The last linkage demonstrates how the Commission has been intimately involved in these corporate shake-ups. The Commission's Competition Commissioner, Van Miert, was initially reluctant to approve the Atlas joint partnership before the French and Germans carried out further liberalisation of their provision of alternative networks, while Washington was reluctant to agree to the joint partnership with Sprint if liberalisation was not accelerated. The French and the Germans wanted both alliances approved in order to offer services to the multinationals and replace income which will be lost after the 1998 liberalisation opens voice telephony to competition. In this case Van Miert and the Americans applied joint pressure to force the Germans and French to allow alternative networks by July 1996, whilst their high-speed data services, which have a near stranglehold on the continental European market, will not be allowed to participate in the joint venture until full liberalisation is achieved in 1998 (*Financial Times*, 2 October 1995: 3, 17 October 1995: 3). Furthermore, the French have proposed to sell 49 per cent of the shares in their telecoms giant in 1996 to reinforce their liberal credentials for the benefit of Brussels and Washington (*Financial Times*, 4 December 1995: 3).

By the mid-1990s the European Commission had abandoned its role of promoting European industrial champions. Instead, it had adopted the role of liberaliser, honest broker and catalyst (Fuchs 1994: 189–90). Van Miert's actions during the controversies over the Phoenix and Atlas alliances were not unique. Earlier, Bangemann had encourged the association of large corporate telecommunications users, EVUA (European Virtual Network Users Association), to put pressure on the Member States to increase the speed of liberalisation (*Financial Times*, 17 October 1994: II; Schneider *et al.* 1993). Thus the Information Superhighway would not be built through locking European industries into set and fast technological solutions, but through the facilitation of limited consensual standardisation and broad global corporate partnerships. The aim is to encourage the privatised and liberalised European super-carriers to use the critical mass of the Single European Market in order to replace their dependence on formerly monopolised national markets (Arlandis 1993; Thatcher 1995). It is still too early to tell if this strategy will be successful, or if it will even result in a seamless European Information Superhighway, but the foremost issue for the future is the challenge of regulation at the European level.

THE FUTURE OF REGULATION: PUBLIC SERVICE, EQUITY AND SOCIAL WELFARE

By 1995 liberalisation had only affected the non-reserved sectors of the telecommunications industry: open competition in voice telephony and infrastructure in 1998 will be a quantum leap forward. The cumulative effect of liberalisation and digitisation will undermine the linkage between former PTTs and the guarantee of universal service. Since they have been commercialised and/or privatised and their markets open to European and foreign competition, the former PTTs will be relieved of the duty of providing universal service, if not, new entrants will gain an unfair advantage in as much as it would allow them to cream off the lucrative sophisticated business or administrative clientele. It was therefore recognised in the second part of the Commission's Green Paper on the *Liberalization of Telecommunications Infrastructure and Cable Television Networks* (Part II, COM(94) 682 (25 January 1995)), that although universal service must be preserved, it was no longer the duty of the former PTTs to carry out this remit (Prieskel and Higham 1995: 385–7).

The reshaping of universal service is only one of many new regulatory challenges that will confront the Commission and the European Court of Justice. How will the wave of mergers and alliances between European and Global supercarriers or telecommunications giants and multi-media entertainment firms be vetted in the future? How can the Commission be certain that member states' implementation of Directives will not be used to favour former PTTs? How can the Commission prevent former monopolists exercising a stranglehold on sectors of the multi-media market through control of gatekeeper technologies? And most importantly, how will the Commission assure that inter-operability is achieved after 1998? Competition after 1998 will only be

assured if former monopoly owners allow easy interconnection for new entrants. And if the EU wishes to achieve an
Information Superhighway using the piecemeal evolutionary Internet approach (a network of networks) rather than
top-down planning, then it will be imperative to monitor
competition for the 'local loop' where the former PPTs still
exercise a near-monopoly. As we have seen, cable, microwave and radiowave could be effective alternatives to the
dominant carriers. But even in the United Kingdom, where
cable telephony has been permitted since 1991, BT still controls over 90 per cent of the residential market (*Financial
Times*, 3 October 1995: 17).

In many respects regulation will remain at the national
level. The crucial control of tariff policies and licensing would
be left in the hands of the regulatory authorities in the
Member States. The Commission has proposed a light-handed
European regulatory regime based on the principle that licences granted should follow EU framework legislation which
would allow all operators the right to offer voice telephony
and other services throughout the EU via the mutual recognition of standards. Therefore, a nationally issued licence
would serve as an EU 'passport' to offer services in the market
of any Member State (Preiskel and Higham 1995: 387). It
would be the task of the newly created national regulatory
authorities to ensure that cross-subsidies by dominant carriers were not stifling competition, and that the granting of
licences was a transparent and non-discriminatory exercise
(*Financial Times*, 16 November 1995: 2). The Commission
was unable to endorse the Bangemann Report's call for a
pan-European regulator when Member States (Belgium,
France, Greece, Ireland and Spain) had already complained
that it was moving too swiftly and undemocratically towards
the 1998 deadline (*Financial Times*, 28 November 1995: 1).
Although various commentators have argued for a European
Federal Communications Commission (most crucially so as
to assure fair interconnection of all participants (Mansell
1995)), the Council of Ministers is determined to keep a
clearly defined pan-European regulatory remit out of the
hands of Brussels. Therefore, the Commission will persist
in setting the regulatory agenda and the pace of the growth
of the network using Articles 85 and 86 of the EEC Treaty,

and with caution, Article 90 (which permits it to circumvent the Council of Ministers). Furthermore, the Commission's policy-making community will remain balkanised between a variety of Directorates-General (DG III – Internal Market; DG IV Competition; DG X-Audio – Visual, Information, Communication and Culture; DG XII – Science, Research and Technology; DG XIII – Telecommunication, Information Industries and Innovation; DG XVI – Regional Policy) (Goldfinger 1995). Finally, for the foreseeable future, the liberals rather than the industrial interventionists in the Commission will have the upper hand.

If a pan-European regulator is an unlikely prospect in the near future, the institutions of the EU (particularly the Commission) still retain important regulatory tasks. The main issues will be: the mutual recognition by Member States' regulatory authorities of a minimum requirement for, and method of, funding for universal service; the effects of the Common Information Area on the (LFRs) Less Favoured Regions and the regulation of converging technologies and monitoring the attenuation of media pluralism through the multi-media/telecommunications pan-European or global oligopolies.

A consensus is emerging concerning the first issue. Nationally-based universal service funds, financed through licence fees, taxation on operators and profits from long-distance and international services have received widespread support in the EU (Federal Trust 1995: 100–3; Preiskel and Higham 1995: 385–7; Stehmann 1995: 160–1). Support for poorer residential users and regions could be targeted to ease the distortion of cross-subsidisation. But these important tasks would be left to national regulators who set tariffs and issue licences. Advocates of liberalisation have also argued that the ending of exclusive rights might achieve the very universalisation of service which had been the justification for monopoly rights. Pointing to the early universalisation of telephony in a competitive Swedish market, or the recent lowering of the costs of access in the United States, they argue that the ending of exclusive rights might achieve what the PTOs had failed to accomplish in the poorer regions of Europe (Berben and Clements 1995: 276). But this might be an over-optimistic interpretation of liberalisation.

The STAR (Special Telecommunications Action for Regional Development) and the Telematic programmes have been designed to connect LFRs with basic services, but it has also been argued that PCNs or the IBN will not occur in these disadvantaged regions if the growth of an Information Superhighway is market-driven. Moreover, in the past decade the poorer members of the EU have spent considerable sums of scarce public funds to upgrade services so as to maintain the modest number of advanced services aimed at corporate customers found in their capital cities. With full liberalisation, it is possible that former PTOs of larger Member States, or a virtual users' network of global companies, could 'cherry pick' the most lucrative business from a the local operator. Even with the use of Structural Funds, the arrival of the IBN will be delayed and the LFRs will be further disadvantaged in the Common Information Area (Preston 1995).

Suggestions in the Bangemann Report that tele-cottages might be a conduit through which LFRs could be revived must also be examined carefully. Highly skilled teleworkers living and working in LFRs would have little effect on the overall local economy if they did not generate a locally-based information skills labour market. In any case, much of teleworking is still composed of semi-skilled part-time women workers with little job security and no hope of career advancement (Huws 1994; Bibby 1995).

Moreover, the controversy over the degree of penetration of universal service begs the question of its quality. It is not at all clear what a minimum level of service would mean. Some commentators have argued that Member States should agree the maximum set of new services to be included in universal service (Mansell 1993: 225). Since it is clear that universal access to full IBN services is some time off in the LFRs and economically impossible for the urban poor in areas within reach of fibre-optic capacity, it has been suggested that IBN services should be made available in libraries, schools and other public institutions. It has also been argued that if national regulators do not accelerate liberalisation, Europe will experience a two-tier provision, with former monopolists retaining 'local loop' residential markets while virtual private networks of large companies lease lines or create new capacity for high performance ISDN networks (Stehmann 1995: 305). Of course, many of these arguments were predicated on access to full IBN services delivered through a top-down Information Superhighway. It may be the case that the Internet route, and further innovation in digital compression technologies, will considerably lower costs and widen accessibility. But even today, libraries are accessible to all: social capital usually decides how individuals use these public goods, and this conundrum will not be wished away as certain free-market advocates of the Internet seem to believe.

However, the most strategic regulatory issues concern technological convergence and the concentration of telecommunications and multi-media interests. Many of the regulatory issues caused by technological convergence have been treated as questions of technical standards and resolved through the ETSI, other international standards bodies or ad hoc fora. But convergence has also amalgamated two different and self-contained cultures of telecommunications and television regulation, whose continued separation is becoming untenable due to digitisation.[7]

Several examples illustrate this process. Recently, the Council of Ministers reaffirmed the long-standing policy that, where practicable, 51 per cent of all content shown on European television should be of European origin (*Financial Times*, 21 November 1995: 3). Whilst the loophole mitigated the effect of this Directive, the arrival of video-on-demand through IBN, or near video-on-demand through digital satellite television, will make this quota totally irrelevant. Is not video-on-demand the digital equivalent of renting a video at a shop where quotas do not exist (Schoof and Watson Brown 1995: 332)? On the other hand, telecommunications regulation has never been concerned with questions of content. With the arrival of the Internet, there is an increasing need to protect minors, monitor racist electronic bulletin boards, clarify the position of advertising, protect intellectual property rights and guarantee privacy (Russell 1995: 55–6). The Commission has only recently started to investigate these issues, which in fact might persuade Member States to abandon some of their rights so that a pan-European regulator could control these problems. But without perfect

harmonisation and implementation of framework EU legislation, one might see the creation of 'information havens';
and if regulation is not consistent across different varieties
of digital transmission, service providers might migrate to a
less regulated form of provision. In any case, this is certainly not easily solved through regulation: the Internet is
global and Europe's Common Information Area may appear
increasingly meaningless.

Such pressures also affect the approach to the regulation
of the concentration of telecommunications and multi-media
interests. Recently, the Single Market Commissioner, Mario
Monti, returned to a 1994 plan to regulate concentration
(*Financial Times*, 13 November 1995: 2).[8] Germany and Britain both opposed the earlier attempt as an infringement
on their rights of subsidiarity, but the presence of massive
interests such as BT and Deutsche Telekom was certainly
another reason why they did not want to be hemmed in by
legislation. According to Monti's new plan, regulation would
be measured by the company's audience share and the identification of the real controllers behind multi-media investments. While the Member States discuss this proposal, the
Commission has used older methods to regulate the multi-
media market. The Competition Commissioner, Van Miert,
has been effective at preventing, or delaying, three different
joint multi-media projects of Deutsche Telekom and Kirch;
Burda, Luxembourg financial interests and Microsoft Network;
and the new project of America Online, Bertelsmann, Deutsche
Telekom and Springer (*Financial Times*, 7 December 1995:
2). These joint ventures, the Commission argued, would have
created cartels capable of dominating the multi-media market
before full liberalisation came into effect. But this line of
reasoning has caused a certain amount of disquiet among
those who argue that Europe needs alliances of scale and
scope to stay in the global market. It has also been argued
that this type of line-of-business restriction, employing Article
8(3) of the EEC Treaty and Council Resolution (EEC: 4064/
89) to vet mergers and alliances, should be waived when
the purpose is pan-European business (Schoof and Watson
Brown 1995: 333–4). It is certainly the case that Concert
(BT and MCI) was approved because the entire world was
considered its market (Schoof and Watson Brown 1995: 328).

Future regulation will be neither easy nor straightforward. In the future, digital communications and multi-media companies will no longer be divided into historically separate hardware and software computer, telecommunications and televison industries (Noam 1991: 337–8). Digital communications might be conceptually divided between conveyers and providers of transmission, content providers who package programmes or data, and providers of creativity. What effect this will have on the shape and reach of pan-European regulation is hard to say. In my conclusion the implications for European political culture and democracy will be essayed.

CONCLUSION

The initial impetus towards an Information Superhighway derived from a renewed attempt to pick European industrial champions. If there is a functioning industrial policy now in the EU, it is one that seeks to encourage European participation in Global champions. But concurrently, the promotion of TENs has suggested that the network might become the method through which EU policy, and its democratic accountability, will be legitimised for the European citizen. But if the Internet forms part of such a network, there is nothing particularly European about it. It is possible to envisage communications on the Internet between European schools and universities deepening the sense of Europe within the political culture of the Member States, or the use of a type of electronic democracy to create closer links between the European Parliament, Member States' parliaments and the European electorate.[9] In any case, what we have witnessed is the effective usage of global networking by the Commission to implement its vision of the Information Superhighway.

In what ways do the themes discussed in this chapter reflect on the nature of the European project? The EU being neither a state nor intergovernmental entity has invented a new art of government associated with the 'relaunching' of the EC in the 1980s and linked to the acceptance of a market-driven form of integration. As Andrew Barry has written (1994), harmonisation and networking are the policy styles and methods best suited to this neo-liberal project. The Commission followed this strategy in its programme to liberalise the telecommunications industry of Europe and encourage the development of a Common Information Area. It remains to be seen, however, whether the strategic behaviour of Member States, former PTTs and other global players will capture digital gateways in the intelligent networks to the advantage of pan-European and global oligopolies and subvert the first principles of an open and competitive market (Graham 1995b: 37). How this will affect the evolution of a European political culture is difficult to say. The Common Information Area in a future of global real-time instantaneous transfer of data may have limited relevance. And if some experts are correct, the arrival of global digitised money (e-money) may in retrospect make the current ructions over a single European currency appear as a quaint, obscure episode in this continent's history.

NOTES

1. For the historical background see Noam (1992); Grande (1994); and Steinfield *et al.*(1994).
2. For the various technological programmes, see Sandholtz (1992) and Petersen (1993). For a sober evaluation of their impact, see Sharp (1993) and Sharp and Pavitt (1993).
3. There is a rich and interesting literature on the role of the Commission, see Dang-Nguyen *et al.* (1993); Fuchs (1994); Curwen (1995); and Stehmann (1995).
4. For an overview of the process of liberalization, see Curwen (1995) and Stehmann (1995: 147–77).
5. For a general survey of EU law and its effects on the liberalisation process, see Ellger (1995) and Stehmann (1995: 150–4).
6. For full details of the legislation described in the following two paragraphs, see Curwen (1995).
7. For the regulation of European television, see Davis and Levy (1992); Collins (1994); Kaitatzi-Whitlock (1994); and Cawson and Holmes (1995).
8. For the Commission's previous interventions on this question see, CEC, *Pluralism and Media Concentration in the Internal Market: An Assessment of the Neeed for Community Action*, Green Paper, COM (92) 480 (23 December 1992).
9. On electronic democracy, see Venturelli (1993); van de Donk *et al.* (1995).

REFERENCES

Arlandis, J. (1993), 'Trading Telecommunications. Challenges to European Regulation Policies', *Telecommunications Policy*, Vol. 17, April, pp. 171–85.

Barry, A. (1994), 'Harmonization and the Act of European Government', in Chris Rootes and Howard Davis (eds.), *A New Europe? Social Change and Political Transformation*, UCL, London, pp. 39–54.

Barry, A. (forthcoming), 'The European Networks', *New Formations*.

Berben, C. and Clements, B. (1995), 'The European Framework for Competition in Telecommunications. The Benefits for Peripheral Countries', *Telecommunications Policy*, Vol. 19, No. 4, pp. 273–83.

Bibby, A. (1995), *Teleworking: Thirteen Journeys to the Future of Work*, Calouste Gulbenkian Foundation, London.

Cawson, A. (1994), 'Keeping the Lead in New-Age TV', *European Brief*, December, pp. 63–4.

Cawson, A. and Holmes, P. (1995), 'Technology Policy and Competition Issues in the Transition to Advanced Television Services in Europe', *Journal of European Public Policy*, Vol. 2, No. 4, pp. 650–71.

Clifford, J. (1995), 'Battle Lines of the Telecom Invaders', *European Brief*, July/August, p. 24.

Collins, R. (1994), *Broadcasting and Audio-Visual Policy in the European Single Market*, John Libbey, London.

Curwen, P. (1995), 'Telecommunications Policy in the European Union: Developing the Information Superhighway', *Journal of Common Market Studies*, Vol. 33, No. 3, pp. 331–60.

Dang-Nguyen, G., Schneider, V. and Werle, R. (1993), 'Networks in European policy-making: Europeification of Telecommunications Policy', in Svein S. Andersen and Kjell A. Eliassen (eds.), *Making Policy in Europe. The Europeification of National Policy-making*, Sage, London, pp. 93–114.

Davis, H. and Levy, C. (1992), 'The Regulation and Deregulation of Television: a British/West European Comparison', *Economy and Society*, Vol. 21, No. 4, pp. 453–82.

Dutton, W. (1995), 'Driving into the Future of Communications?', in Stephen Emmott (ed.), *Information Superhighways. Multimedia Users and Futures*, Academic Press, London, pp. 79–102.

Ellger, R. (1995), 'Telecommunications in Europe: Law and Policy of the European Commission in a Key Industrial Sector', in William James Adams (ed.), *Singular Europe. Economy and Polity of the European Community after 1992*, University of Michigan Press, Ann Arbor, pp. 203–50.

Emmott, S. (1995), 'Introduction', in S.J. Emmott, *Information Superhighways*, Academic Press, London, pp. 3–13.

Federal Trust (1995), *Network Europe and the Information Society*, The Federal Trust, London.

Fuchs, G. (1992), 'ISDN – The Telecommunication Highways for Europe after 1992?', *Telecommunications Policy*, 16, November, pp. 635–45.

Fuchs, G. (1994), 'Policy-making in a System of Multi-level Governance – The Commissio-n of the European Community and the Restructuring of the Telecommunications Sector', *Journal of European Public Policy*, 1, 2, pp. 177–94.

Freeman, C. and Soete, L. (1994), *Work for All or Mass Unemployment? Computerised Technical Change in the Twenty-First Century*, Pinter, London.

Gates, B. (1995), *The Road Ahead*, Viking, London.

Goldfinger, C. (1995), 'The Hare being Chased by the Tortoise', *European Brief*, October, pp. 54–5.

Graham, A. (1995a), 'Exchange Rates and Gatekeepers', in Tim Congdon, Andrew Graham, Damian Green and Bill Robinson, *The Cross Media Revolution. Ownership and Control*, John Libbey, London, pp. 38–49.

Graham, A. (1995b), 'Public Policy and the Information Superhighway: The Scope for Strategic Intervention, Co-ordination and Top-slicing', in Richard Collins and James Purnell (eds.), *Managing the Information Society*, IPPR, London, pp. 30–44.

Grande, E. (1994), 'The New Role of the State in Telecommunications: An International Comparison', *West European Politics*, Vol. 17, No. 1, pp. 138–57.

Haag, M. and Schoof, H. (1994), 'Telecommunications and the TV Infrastructure in the European Union: Current Policies and Future issues', *Telecommunications Policy*, Vol. 18, No. 5, pp. 367–77.

Hawkins, R.W. (1992), 'The Doctrine of Regionalism. A New Dimension for International Standardization in Telecommunications', *Telecommunications Policy*, Vol. 16, No. 4, pp. 339–53.

Hawkins, R.W. (1995), 'Introduction: Addressing the *Problématique* of Standards and Standardization', in Richard W. Hawkins, Robin Mansell and J. Skea (eds.), *Standards, Innovation and Competitiveness. The Policies and Economics of Standardization in Natural and Technical Environments*, Edward Elgar, Aldershot, pp. 1–6.

Huws, U. (1994), Follow-up to the White Paper. Teleworking. Report to the European Commission's Employment Task Force (Directorate General V), European Commission, Directorate General V, Brussels (September).

Kaitatzi-Whitlock (1994), 'European HDTV Strategy: Muddling Through or Muddling Up?', *European Journal of Communications*, Vol. 9, pp. 173–92.

Mansell, R. (1993), *The New Telecommunications. A Political Economy of Network Evolution*, Sage, London.

Mansell, R. (1995), 'The Missing Element in Superhighway Europe', *European Brief*, February/March, pp. 47–8.

Noam, E. (1991), *Television in Europe*, Oxford University Press, New York.

Noam, E. (1992), *Telecommunciations in Europe*, Oxford University Press, New York.

Peterson, J. (1993), *High Technology and the Competition State. An Analysis of the Eureka Initiative*, Routledge, London.

Preiskel, R. and Higham, N. (1995), 'Liberalization of Telecommunications Infrastructure and Cable Telecoms Networks. The European Commission's Green Paper', *Telecommunications Policy*, Vol. 19, No. 5, pp. 381–90.

Preston, P. (1995), 'Competition in the Telecommunications Infrastructure.

Implications for the Peripheral Regions and Smaller Countries of Europe', *Telecommunications Policy*, Vol. 19, No. 4, pp. 253–71.

Russell, M. (1995), 'When Technology Moves Faster than the Law', *European Brief*, October, pp. 55–6.

Sandholtz, W. (1992), *High-Tech Europe: The Politics of International Cooperation*, University of California Press, Berkeley.

Schneider, V., Dang-Nguyen, G. and Werkle, R. (1993), 'Corporate Actor Networks in European Policy-making: Harmonizing Telecommunications Policy', *Journal of Common Market Studies*, 32, 4, pp. 477–98.

Schoof, H. and Watson Brown, A. (1995), ' Information Highways and Media Policies in the European Union', *Telecommunications Policy*, Vol. 19, No. 4, pp. 325–38.

Scott, C. (1995), 'Liberalisation is not a Free-for-all', *European Brief*, June, pp. 47–8.

Sharp, M. (1993), 'The Community and the New Technologies', in Juliet Lodge (ed.), *The European Community and the Challenge of the Future*, London, 2nd edn., pp. 200–26.

Sharp, M. and Pavitt, K. (1993), 'Technology Policy in the 1990s: Old Trends and New Realities', *Journal of Common Market Studies*, Vol. 31, No. 2, pp. 130–51.

Stehmann, O. (1995), *Network Competition for European Telecommunications*, Oxford University Press, Oxford.

Steinfield, C., Bauer, J.M. and Caby, L. (eds.) (1994), *Telecommunications in Transition. Politics, Science and Technologies in the European Community*, Sage, London.

Thatcher, M. (1995), 'Regulating Reform and Internationalization in Telecommunications', in Jack Hayward (ed.), *Industrial Enterprise and European Integration. From National to International Champions in Western Europe*, Oxford University Press, Oxford, 1995, pp. 239–72.

Turner, C. (1995), 'Trans-European Networks and the Common Information Area. The development of a European strategy', *Telecommunications Policy*, Vol. 19, No. 6, pp. 501–8.

van de Donk, W.B.H.J., Snellen, I.Th.M. and Tops, P.W. (eds.) (1995), *Orwell in Athens: A Perspective on Informationization and Democracy*, IOS Press, Amsterdam.

Venturelli, S.S. (1993), 'The Imagined Transnational Public-sphere in the European Community's Broadcast Philosophy: Implications for Democracy', *European Journal of Communications*, Vol. 8, pp. 491–518.

Wyatt-Walter, A. (1995), 'Globalization, Corporate Identity and European Technology Policy', *Journal of European Public Policy*, Vol. 2, No. 3, pp. 427–46.

Zotschew, S. (1995), 'Exchange Programmes', *European Brief*, June, pp. 57–8.

10 Economic and Social Convergence in Europe: A More Equal Future?

Valerie Symes

INTRODUCTION

In the Preamble to the Treaty of Rome of 1957 the signatories were 'anxious to strengthen the unity of their economies and to ensure reduction of the differences existing between the various regions, and the backwardness of the less favoured regions'. Economic cohesion was an explicit commitment in Article 130A of the Single European Act some 30 years and six extra Member States later, reinforced by the Maastricht Treaty in 1991, where the Community was charged not only with pursuing economic growth, but also with the promotion of a high level of social protection and environmental improvement throughout the Member States. The Delors Report 1987 warned that 'if sufficient consideration were not given to regional imbalances, the economic union would be faced with grave economic and political risks'. There is no question of the commitment of the EU to greater economic and social equality for its inhabitants, but there are several questions which must be asked: What is meant by convergence or cohesion? Are the official indicators of divergence a good basis for measuring inequalities? Is there a conflict between the economic policies of the EU, in the form of the Single European Market and the push towards monetary union and a single currency, and the aim of convergence? How adequate are the European Commission's policies on regional convergence and cohesion in narrowing the gaps? What in reality, would be needed to bring about a more equal income for Europeans? This chapter will attempt to answer these questions and assess the likelihood of a more equal Europe in the years to come.

ECONOMIC AND SOCIAL CONVERGENCE IN THE EUROPEAN UNION: PROBLEMS OF DEFINITION

In order to narrow differentials in economic and social welfare over time, it is necessary to know what is meant by economic and social welfare, to try to measure current differentials, and to have a coherent and effective policy that will bring this about. There are also, of course, the questions of what would be an acceptable level of divergence socially and politically, and the timespan in which convergence should take place. The Single European Act of 1987 is vague on all these subjects. A study for the European Parliament by the NIESR (1991) defined cohesion as 'the degree to which disparities in social and economic welfare between regions or groups are politically or socially tolerable' and considered that, although income per head and unemployment levels were the indicators most widely used, they were inadequate measures of social cohesion. Emphasis on economic indicators may risk disguising problems of social welfare, especially in large urban areas. More appropriate measures could include educational levels, provision of health facilities, the level of social protection available, life expectancy and housing conditions. There is also concern that the use of economic indicators, and the push for economic growth this entails, may result in unsustainable development which degrades the environment and results in lower levels of welfare for some regions (Scott 1995). This concern has to some extent been recognised in policy since 1993 (see below).

Using the official indicators of GDP per head and unemployment, the criteria for EU aid to regions, there was some convergence in disparities until 1974, the only real problem in terms of income and unemployment levels within the then current Member States being in southern Italy and later Ireland, after its accession. Leonardi (1995), using Purchasing Power Standards (PPS) per inhabitant for the period 1970–90, and employing data from only the nine Member States, showed that differentials between the ten most developed regions and the ten least developed over the 20-year period had narrowed. In 1970 the average income per head in the top ten was three times that of the poorest, but in 1990 it had narrowed to 2.3 times. On this basis of slow change it would take a long time for significant real convergence to take place. The poorest regions were also all in Italy, where the national government had been pouring resources into the Mezzogiorno since the 1960s, with most of the available EC regional funding (though not on the same scale) going to these areas until the mid-1980s.

The enlargement of the Community to include Greece, Spain and Portugal inevitably entailed a widening of GDP differentials per capita. In the period 1989–91 West Germany had an income per head $2\frac{1}{2}$ times that of Greece. The gap was even wider at the regional level, with Hamburg having six times the GDP per head of Alantejo (Portugal). Change in GDP per inhabitant for 1980 and 1990 of Member States is shown in Table 10.1.

It appears that three of the poorest Member States (Spain, Portugal and Ireland) improved their position marginally through faster growth rates, while the relative position of Greece worsened quite significantly. Disparities in the period 1980–8, analysed at NUTs level 2 regional level, a breakdown of large European regions (Level 1) into more coherent economic areas, showed that average per capita income for the 25 weakest regions fell from 57 to 56 per cent of average EU income, while in the 25 strongest regions it rose from 135 to 137 per cent of the average (CEC 1991). The range in income per head at the regional level was from a low of 39.9 per cent of average income per head in Vareio Aigaio (Greece) to 183 per cent of the average in Groningen (Netherlands).

Taking higher than average unemployment rates for 1990, the main official indicator of social divergence, the 25 regions with the highest levels of unemployment ranged from Cueta y Melilla (Spain) with 351.6 per cent of average EU unemployment rate, to Languedec-Roussillon at 148 per cent. All had below average per capita incomes. The picture is not as clear at the regional level when looking at the regions with the lowest unemployment levels – supposedly those with the lowest social divergence. Here 9 of the 25 regions with the lowest levels of unemployment also have a lower than average GDP per head, 5 of them with less than 75 per cent of the average – Algarve, Centro and Norte (Portugal) and Ionia Nisia and Crete (Greece). It would be hard

Table 10.1 GDP per inhabitant at PPS[a] (EUR-12 = 100)

	1980	1990
Belgium	104.5	103.0
Denmark	109.0	107.2
Germany[b]	113.8	113.4
Greece	58.2	53.0
Spain	73.4	76.3
France	111.9	108.6
Ireland	64.5	67.3
Italy	102.5	105.2
Luxembourg	115.6	128.7
Netherlands	111.0	103.9
Portugal	54.2	55.4
United Kingdom	101.1	103.7

Notes: a. Purchasing Power Standards.
  b. Excludes Eastern Länder.

Source: CEC (1991).

to argue that low unemployment in these cases meant a higher than average level of social welfare, since many of the indicators of social well-being, such as housing, health and educational facilities, cannot be afforded on grounds of low income within the Member States concerned.

At national level variations from average EU unemployment rates are again not strongly linked to income (see Table 10.2). While two of the four poorest countries, Ireland and Spain, suffer rates well above the EU average, Greece and Portugal have unemployment rates well below average. France also has above-average unemployment but had the third highest GDP per head in 1994.

Although the social distress caused by unemployment is always considerable, in states which have sufficient income to make fiscal transfers in the form of social protection and other public services, the unemployed do not lose as much, in terms of social inequality, as in states with low GNP, where fiscal transfers are necessarily smaller and more limited. Other social indicators that could be used to measure social divergence, such as the provision of education and training, guaranteed minimum income levels, doctors and hospital beds per head of population, and protection of income in old age are shown in Table 10.3.

Table 10.2 Unemployment Rates in Member States, 1994

	% unemployed
EU-15	11.1
Belgium	10.1
Denmark	10.3
Germany (West and East)	8.4
Greece	6.9
Spain	24.3
France	12.6
Ireland	15.2
Italy	11.3
Luxembourg	3.5
Netherlands	7.0
Portugal	7.0
United Kingdom	9.3
Austria	4.0
Finland	18.4
Sweden	9.8

Source: CEC (1995b).

Table 10.3 Indicators of Social Welfare in Member States, 1991/2

	% of 16–18-year-olds in Education and Training 1992	Guaranteed Income per Month for a Couple 1992 (In ECUs)	Doctors per 1000 Inhabitants 1991	Hospital Beds per 1000 Inhabitants 1991	Average Benefit for over 65s in PPS EU-12=100 1992
Belgium	90	600	3.2	N/A	103.9
Denmark	81	745	N/A	5.4	87.9
Germany	94	433–94[a]	3.1	8.3	109.5
Greece	N/A	–	3.1	4.5	52.7
Spain	66	226	3.9	N/A	61.1
France	89	474	2.7	8.5	117.2
Ireland	72	497	1.5	6.2	44.9
Italy	NA	251–439[a]	1.9	6.8	135.6
Luxembourg	66	872	2.5	11.5	172.0
Netherlands	91	761	N/A	11.4	116.8
Portugal	51	–	2.9	4.3	36.8
United Kingdom	71	391	1.6	5.6	79.6

Note: a. Germany and Italy have variable levels of guaranteed income because the amount is determined by regional governments.
Source: Col. 1 Eurostat Rapid Report (1994): Cols 2 and 5 Eurostat Rapid Report (1994): Cols 3 and 4 Eurostat Regions Statistical Yearbook (1994).

More than 90 per cent of young people over the statutory school-leaving age are in education or training in Belgium, Germany and the Netherlands. In Spain, Portugal and Ireland the figure is below 75 per cent, but this also is the case in the United Kingdom, one of the middle-income states. Guaranteed income is highest in the richer states, Belgium, Luxembourg, Netherlands and Denmark, but considerably lower in France and Germany, where it is of a similar level to Ireland. Greece, Portugal, Spain and Italy have no national scheme of guaranteed income for single people, and Greece and Portugal have no official aid for couples, but rely on local administration and charities to provide minimum aid. Health provision shows that more hospital beds are provided by wealthier than by poorer countries, but the same is not true for the number of doctors per head of population, with Spain having the highest and the United Kingdom the lowest. State benefits to the elderly are highest in Luxembourg, Italy, France and the Netherlands, but less than 62 per cent of the EU average in the four poorest countries (Portugal, Spain, Greece and Ireland). Although there is a great degree of divergence in social provision and services, largely in line with GDP of Member States, between 1980 and 1992 there was a 62.8 per cent increase in spending on social protection per head for the six lowest income states, approximately twice the increase for the six highest income states.

Overall, official indicators and other social indicators of economic and social divergence are greater between Member States than for regions within Member States. In the last decade there has been very little narrowing of the differentials in income and the gap between the poorest, Greece, and the richest has increased.

Before examining the question of how convergence of regional incomes could come about and what is currently being done to promote it, the effect of developments in economic policy in the past few years – namely the Single European Market (SEM) and European Monetary Union (EMU) – will be discussed in relation to their potential effects on regional disparities.

THE SEM, EMU AND REGIONAL CONVERGENCE

The Single European Market (SEM), which came into being in January 1993, was the final stage in removing barriers to trade and allowing totally free movement of labour
and capital within the (SEM). All forms of protectionism
and subsidy operated by Member States to promote their
own domestic industries, and to bolster competitiveness ar-
tificially, were no longer allowed under rules of free competition – the 'level playing field' of Europe. In theory, the
freeing of markets and increased competitiveness brings with
it opportunities for maximising income within the EU. Competitive industries with high levels of productivity would
expand, economies of scale emerge and consequent lower
production costs would boost world competitiveness for
Europe's most efficient industries. The downside is that less
efficient industries would cease to be protected and would
lose out to the more efficient. In theory also, low-cost labour
could seek employment in high-growth areas, thus reducing inequalities between regions; or alternatively, industries
could seek out areas with low labour costs for new projects,
thus increasing their competitiveness, while reducing unemployment and increasing income in these areas. The spatial
distribution of competitive industry and the income it gen-
erates could result in greater convergence of regional incomes, or at least a reduction of high unemployment levels
through inter-regional migration. In practice, as many studies have argued, this will not be the long-term effect of the
SEM. Scale economies are more likely to accrue to existing
large firms concentrated in the richer core regions. The
core regions, and particularly their metropolitan areas, are
the financial and administrative centres and also the hub of
road, rail and telecommunications services. Industries in these
areas benefit, therefore, from all those external economies.
Poorer regions are not well endowed in this respect and
are also geographically peripheral. As we have seen, the poorer
regions also have lower educational standards, and although
labour may be both plentiful and cheaper, it may be inap-
propriate in serving the needs of sophisticated, high-growth,
competitive sectors such as financial services (PA Cambridge
Economic Consultants 1990). The agglomeration benefits

to be had by firms in the core regions far outweigh the theoretical advantages of poorer regions. Hence the process of economic integration will further weaken the economies of the poorer Member States, and strengthen the more prosperous. The general consensus (Armstrong 1995; CEC 1991; Dignan 1995; European Parliament 1991) is that the process of economic integration itself results in increasing disparities between regions.

Monetary union has been on the European agenda for many years. The Werner Report of 1971, in discussing the preconditions for monetary union, remarked that persistent regional disparities could undermine attainment of EMU, and provided a case for promoting convergence of regional income levels. This was at a time when there were only six Member States and disparities were minimal compared to the current situation. It was not, however, until the Maastricht Treaty of 1991 that a set of nominal convergence criteria, as a prerequisite for membership of a single currency area, was introduced. Targets were set for the convergence of inflation rates, interest rates and the level of public deficits in relation to GDP. Table 10.4 shows the position on these criteria in 1993. In terms of past inflation rates, public deficits and interest rates, Greece and Portugal are furthest from achieving nominal convergence. Spain is considerably out of line in inflation and interest rates, Ireland in interest rates. Whilst not the only Member States to need considerable changes in fiscal and monetary policy to bring about nominal convergence, they face the greatest problems. (See also Table 8.1.) The wealthier countries, with the exception of Italy, are nearer to fulfilling the criteria and have less need for corrective policies. In order to meet the targets the most stringent anti-inflationary policies are required in the poorest countries with consequent negative effects in terms of growth of GDP and employment. The benefits of a single currency are mainly in the reduction in transaction costs, which will vary according to the proportion of national output going to other Member States. These costs vary from 0.15 to 1.00 per cent of GDP, with the poorer regions getting least ben-efit, as it is the richer regions that are the major exporting regions. It seems likely that moves towards a single currency will result in most of its benefits

Table 10.4 Convergence Criteria for Monetary Union – Indicators for Member States

	Public Deficit/Surplus as % of GDP, 1993 (target 3%)	% Rise in Consumer Price Rates Index, 1985–93	Short-term Interest Rates 1993
EU-12	–	39	–
Belgium	–5.1	21	8.7
Denmark	–4.6	28	7.4
Germany	–3.3	20	7.5
Greece	–17.4 (1990)	253	23.5
Spain	–6.7	61	12.3
France	–4.5	26	8.8
Ireland	–1.2	27	14.9
Italy	–9.2	54	10.2
Luxembourg	–0.4	20	8.7
Netherlands	–3.7	15	7.1
Portugal	–12.5	120	13.3
United Kingdom	–7.8	49	6.0
Austria	–3.0	24	7.2
Finland	–12.7	40	7.7
Sweden	–14.8	58	9.1

Source: Eurostat Yearbook (1995).

and least of the costs falling on already wealthy areas. The harsh conditions imposed on Member States with inflation and debt problems have not only short-term consequences in terms of income and employment, but also reduce these countries' ability to achieve the structural changes that are necessary to promote long-term growth. One further consequence for poorer regions that emerges once a single currency is a reality is the inability to use an exchange rate policy to compensate for lower competitiveness. This will permanently lock less competitive states into a cycle of disadvantage, if no action is taken to improve growth competitiveness in these areas. As the report from the European Parliament (1991) points out, 'the outlook is bleak for many less prosperous regions from the adverse effects of SEM and EMU.'

The alternative for weaker Member States is that the worst effects of EMU can be avoided by going for 'slow-track' membership of a single currency whilst stronger members take the 'fast track'. This will allow them a longer period to fulfil nominal convergence criteria and absorb the shock to the domestic economy at a slower rate. The effects of the SEM are, however, inescapable. One further point on the Maastricht Treaty – the effects of the Social Charter, signed by all the economically weaker Member States, involves obligations to workers in terms of minimum remuneration, and working hours and conditions, as well as to raising living standards and social protection for the elderly. The latter involves greater public expenditure in a situation where public deficits are to be controlled; the former in higher labour costs. There is some evidence that increased social and economic protection of workers has already resulted in increased official unemployment in Spain, as well as the growth of an informal, low-income labour market (Symes 1995). The Maastricht criteria may have negative effects on employment and welfare in poorer states and widen social inequalities within Europe.

HOW TO ACHIEVE ECONOMIC AND SOCIAL CONVERGENCE

Neoclassical trade theory views disparities in income as the result of variations in resource endowments. At a simplistic level, as stated above, the SEM, by freeing markets, could lead to convergence of income, when capital and labour flows lead to factor price equalisation. Alternatively, regions specialising in capital-intensive goods will specialise in this sector and exchange products with low-wage regions specialising in labour-intensive goods; thus trade substitutes for factor mobility. As we have seen, reality does not appear to be like this. Economies are more complex, and high productivity based on high skills and technological innovation gives some regions 'resource endowments' that are reinforced, not reduced, by free markets.

A different theoretical stance is that leading regions, in accordance with Myrdal's development model, have self-reinforcing advantages. In this model of cumulative causation the rate of productivity growth depends positively on the rate of growth of regional output, and the growth of regional output depends on a region's competitiveness in export markets. This in turn depends on productivity growth. Hence growth is circular and self-sustaining. It is essentially a demand-oriented model, and any divergence from trend growth of demand will affect regional growth. Experience of the last two decades in Europe shows that the level of demand and the return on capital are determined by the level of investment and that there has to be growth in demand greater than 2.3 per cent per annum to sustain a positive investment level.

Clearly lagging regions and Member States suffer from less attractive resource endowments, and recent economic policies of the EU (discussed above) have resulted in national policies that severely restrict demand in poorer states, to conform to the Maastricht convergence criteria. This has had a detrimental effect on investment. Support for regional convergence policy at the EU level should, therefore, attempt to overcome the structural and investment gaps between regions in order to generate faster growth, at the very least, since it either cannot (in the case of the SEM) or is unlikely (in the case of EMU) to change the basic direction of major economic policy, which continues to aggravate regional disparities. How in principle is this best done?

In Europe the most basic prerequisite is to bring the infrastructure levels in communications, transport and energy of the most lagging regions up to a level where the poor regions are no longer permanently disadvantaged – something that is, vital to private sector development. Research has also shown that regions with higher levels of investment in human capital, research and development, and technological innovation have a faster rate of productivity growth.

Investment in human capital varies considerably both between and within Member States. Within Spain, for example closing the gap in post-statutory secondary education between the richest and poorest regions would require a 30 per cent increase in educational places. To bring Spain as a whole up to the same level as Germany, the Netherlands and Denmark would require a huge level of extra investment in education and youth training, and an increase in places of over 95 per cent. Pompili (1995) found a good correlation between GDP per head and secondary schooling, and some correlation between the presence of graduates in a region and GDP per head within European regions. Regional policy, therefore, should aim to close the gap in educational and skill levels within Europe.

Goddard *et al.* (1987) and Higgins *et al.* (1987), in studies of the effect of R&D expenditure and the rate of introduction of new technology, found very positive relationships between R&D, innovation and growth. While innovation is not dependent on a region's own R&D, in practice information and technology transfer works better in regions with high R&D investment. Higher investment in R&D tends to improve access to innovation and also attracts well-qualified workers.

In 1989, three-quarters of all R&D expenditure in the EU was concentrated in Germany, France and the United Kingdom. Within Member States there was less R&D expenditure and employment in poorer regions – for instance, 70 per cent of expenditure in Spain was concentrated in Madrid and Catalonia, and in Portugal 72 per cent in Lisbon. In a survey of European firms on product or process innovation, an important factor in increasing competitiveness, nine out of ten firms had undertaken innovation within the previous five years, but in the lagging regions the figure was only eight out of ten. Concentration of R&D and innovation in core regions is an important factor in explaining regional disparities in income and productivity. In order for poorer regions to catch up with the more prosperous regions, higher rates of R&D investment are required in lagging Member States and regions than in the core.

Not all lagging regions require the same types of aid, as Pompili (1995) pointed out. Lagging urban regions already have relatively high numbers of graduates, access to R&D and adequate basic infrastructure, while at the other extreme, what he terms the 'marginal regions' – most of Greece and Portugal – basic infrastructure, R&D, levels of secondary education and presence of graduates are all below the EU average. Regional policy, therefore, should be flexible enough to take into account different needs rather than proposing blanket solutions. The aim of encouraging investment in prerequisites for growth is to attract a larger share of fast-growing private sector economic activity. But of what kind? Large-scale firms are the most competitive, but the effect of multinational enterprises (MNEs) does not always bring as much benefit to a local economy as a smaller indigenous firm in terms of retained income and extra employment (Young *et al.* 1995). Regional policy might, therefore, do well to encourage medium-sized domestic firms in lagging areas.

It is against this background that existing regional policy in Europe will be discussed both in terms of its direction and the scale of expenditure needed to bring about real, as opposed to the nominal convergence, required for EMU.

REGIONAL POLICY IN THE EUROPEAN UNION

In the period up until 1989, when EU policy on the regions changed significantly, resources devoted to the problems of convergence were minimal. For instance, for the period 1975–7 they represented only 0.04 per cent of the combined GDP of Member States (Armstrong 1994), and formed only a very small percentage of total EC funding. Over half the community budget was directed towards the Common Agricultural Policy (CAP), most of which went towards supporting guaranteed prices. As the McDougall Report (1977) and, more recently, Ardy (1988) pointed out, this funding went disproportionately to wealthier countries and regions and was regressive in nature. Member States did, of course, operate their own regional policies, largely based on the provision of business incentives for relocation and to some extent on infrastructure improvements. During the 1980s expenditure on regional incentives by Member States fell in Belgium, France, Netherlands, the United Kingdom and Denmark, and although they rose in Portugal and Greece, the amount involved was low. Only in Italy and Spain were there really significant increases in expenditure on regional development. The decrease in regional incentives in Northern Europe was not so much a reflection of a reduced problem as an inability to implement incentives to the private sector, which would contravene the rules of competitiveness.

The instability of regional policy in Northern countries, and the lack of resources in Southern Europe (with the exception of Italy) together with the paucity of funding for regions by the EC, did little to reduce disparities effectively during the 1980s. The Single European Act 1987 led to the reform of the EC's Structural Funds to improve economic and social cohesion. Co-ordination of the efforts the EC's various funding agencies, which had previously operated on a piecemeal basis, was incorporated into the reforms of Community Structural Funds (CSFs) that took place in 1989. Regions were designated, for aid purposes, into Objective 1 (lagging regions) which included the whole of Greece, Portugal and Ireland, large areas of Spain, Northern Ireland, southern Italy and Sardinia, and the French overseas departments and Corsica; Objective 2 (areas of industrial decline); and Objective 5a (low-income agricultural areas). Resources to cover all forms of development – infrastructure, training, reclamation of land and other aids to economic development – were doubled with an allocation of 63 billion ECU for the period 1989–93. Objective 1 regions, those with the lowest GDP per head, were to receive 80 per cent of available funding, and Objective 2 regions most of the rest. Actual funding was dependent on the Commission receiving 'suitable' proposals from Member States, and on Member States being prepared to contribute matching funds to the proposed projects. A prerequisite for application for funds was that projects suggested should be additional to any expenditure on regional development that Members States previously intended to spend. The concept of 'additional' was almost impossible to assess, and the shifting of Member States' resources to Commission-funded projects undoubtedly occurred. The more serious problem, though, was that of matching funds, which was a burden on the fiscal capacity of the poorer Member States. This may well explain why some low-income countries failed to take up their share of indicative funding. In this first period of new funding for regions the lack of criteria for judging the effectiveness of schemes and the concentration of spending on a rather narrow range of infrastructure and human resource development, not necessarily the most needed forms of aid in given regional contexts, can be criticised.

In the Maastricht Treaty, extra funding became available through the Cohesion Fund to all countries with a GDP per head of less than 90 per cent of the EU average. Changes were also made to the CSF system. The amount to be allocated through the CSFs in the period 1994–9 more than doubled in real terms. Regions were redefined, so that all the Eastern Länder in Germany, plus three industrial areas – Merseyside in the United Kingdom, the border region of north-eastern France and Hainault in Belgium – and the Highlands and Islands of Scotland were given Objective 1 status. Priority in funding was given to IDPs (Integrated Development Programmes), which spanned a number of small regions with similar development problems, such as Programme for Integration of the Mediterranean (PIM), rather than granting aid on the basis of narrowly defined regional projects. Member States were required to produce regional plans in partnership with regional and local authorities, to try to ensure greater effectiveness of single policy initiatives within a prescribed, long-term development strategy. New rules were introduced to reinforce the concept of 'additional' by requiring Member States to maintain public expenditure in the regions concerned at the same level as in the period 1989–93.

The requirement for matching funds on projects in Objective 1 areas was reduced, with a maximum EU contribution of 85 per cent, thus easing the burden on the poorer countries. A further requirement for receiving CSFs or loans from the European Investment Bank (EIB) was that projects had to satisfy conditions laid down by EC legislation on the environment taking into account the Environmental Impact Assessment Directive. Grants were also to be made available to help young people set up a business; and also to set up business development centres in order to facilitate technology transfer in disadvantaged regions. Both these measures are a very small step towards redressing the balance of advantage in new firm formation and technology innovation in the more prosperous areas. The total amounts available through the CSFs and the Cohesion Fund are shown in Table 10.5.

While the sums involved may appear large, the total available for increasing cohesion and convergence was 0.3 per cent of EU GDP in 1993, compared with 0.6 per cent to the CAP. The scale of funding in relation to the problem is tiny, and consequently severely limits what can be achieved.

Table 10.5 Community Structural Funds and Cohesion Fund, 1994–9 (ECU billion in real terms)

	CSFs	Objective 1	Cohesion Fund
1994	20.1	13.2	1.8
1995	21.5	14.3	2.0
1996	22.7	15.3	2.3
1997	24.1	16.4	2.5
1998	25.7	17.8	2.6
1999	27.4	19.4	2.6

Source: Eurostat.

Leonardi (1995) suggests that EC grants have made a real contribution to economic and social cohesion and were one of the major factors in fuelling an acceleration in the rate of cohesion. He cites the cases of Ireland, Greece and Portugal. While there is some evidence that this is true in Ireland, in the period in which Greece has been a member of the EC there has been a fall in the GDP per inhabitant, and little change in Portugal (see Table 10.1). More recently in the 1990s the effects of the SEM and EMU have had negative consequences, which have outweighed any minor effects of regional policy on the poorest areas, as discussed above. The 'surge of these countries [the low-income Member States] towards convergence', predicted by Leonardi, seems even less likely to occur in the current economic climate. No attempt was made in the 1989 or 1993 reforms to identify how large a budget would be needed to achieve a significant effect on regional disparities. Funding appears to be based on 'whatever can be done, will be done', but the ability to redistribute via the Commission is constrained by the political willingness of Member States (particularly net contributors) to provide funding, not on any assessment of real needs to meet stated aims. But before looking at the scale of change that is needed to achieve convergence, some further points on existing policy should be made.

The first is linked to political willingness. There is no doubt that the 'new' regions in Germany, Belgium, France and the UK designated as Objective 1 in the 1993 reforms have an income per capita well below the European average. They are, however, situated in countries with per capita incomes

either above or at the average. It is well within the capacity
of the Member States concerned to operate a system of internal transfers to bring about the necessary development,
with little or no effect on their national GDP. Substantial
subsidies from European taxpayers are being given in order
to maintain, and ultimately increase, GDP in already prosperous countries. Effectively, a system of the poor subsidising
the rich, or at least the rich subsidising themselves rather
than the poor, is being operated through the new designation of 'lagging regions'. Although the designation is technically correct under the CSF framework, in fact, it contradicts
the underlying aim of regional policy. It raises two questions: (1) Should a region be considered 'poor' if it is part
of a Member State with a high per capita level of income,
or be defined as a region, when it is in fact a large urban
area, such as Merseyside? (2) What are the responsibilities
of Member States to their own domestic divergences, compared to their responsibilities to other Member States, and
how should the EU define its own role in relation to Member States on this question?

On the question of using the criteria of GDP per head
and unemployment rates as a basis for assessing regional
need, the EU can be criticised for failing to address the
issue of social convergence. Although per capita income may
measure overall economic welfare, it does not address problems of distribution and marginalises social welfare needs
such as education, healthcare and public services. Widening
the criteria for eligibility for CSFs, to include disparities in,
for example, education and healthcare, could assist in addressing social cohesion. While this is now possible with the
Cohesion Fund, the scale of potential aid is minimal (see
Table 10.5). Although transfers of this kind in the social
field yield little in terms of economic return in the short
run, they cushion the negative effects arising from the SEM
and EMU, and in the long run Europe as a whole may benefit
from the greater willingness of less competitive states to suffer
the short-term consequences and remain within the EU.

Let us turn now to what would be required in terms of
growth for a greater degree of convergence to take place,
in 1977 it was estimated that a transfer of 2 per cent of EC
GDP was required to reduce disparities between the six richest

Table 10.6 Requirements for Regional Convergence

% Change in GDP per capita		% Growth Rate above EU Average for Time Period		
From	To	10 years	15 years	20 years
50	70	3.5	2.25	1.75
50	99	6.00+	4.00+	3.00
70	90	2.5	1.75	1.25

Source: CEC (1991).

and three poorest Member States by 40 per cent in 10 years. In a more recent report (CEC 1991), it was estimated that, to raise GDP per capita from 50 per cent of average to 99 per cent of average, required a growth rate of 6 per cent per annum above EU average growth over 10 years, or 3 per cent over 20 years (see Table 10.6). To bring about this convergence would involve a transfer of 6–7 per cent of EU GDP, whereas the total EU budget is at present 1 per cent of GDP.

Taking the past annual growth rates of the four lowest income Member States (Greece, Portugal, Ireland and Spain) for the period 1986–90 the average was 4.2 per cent, whilst that of the other eight Member States was 3.0 per cent. The EU average was 3.1 per cent. Growth rates for the four would need to accelerate considerably to show any noticeable convergence within 10 years, and would have to be well above historical growth rates to bring about some convergence within 20 years.

The total inadequacy of current policy on convergence, in terms of the scale of resources available for aid, is strikingly apparent. The measures used are moving in the right direction in differentiating measures more appropriate to different contexts; including environmental requirements; and making some, albeit weak, attempt to encourage research and innovation in lagging regions. The educational gap is not addressed. Human resource development is addressing the problem of unemployment and short-term job training, not secondary and university education which has a real long-term impact on growth. Social convergence, by using unemployment as the main indicator of divergence, is dealt with inadequately. The emphasis on upgrading skills does little to create jobs in areas of high unemployment, and areas of low unemployment are by no means all regions with high levels of social provision, yet they get little funding to encourage better social conditions and achieve greater social convergence.

CONCLUSIONS

It seems highly unlikely that in the current economic conditions and current policy there will be much noticeable convergence in the next decade. The Commission, in its own analysis, admits that, even with an increase in EU support in resources used for human capital investment, infrastructure and the real capital stock of firms, the process of convergence will take a long time. It is clear that funding to 1999 is inadequate. Is it likely that the funding could increase by sevenfold to make an impact which could show real convergence in one or two decades? One of the problems with any action at the EU level is that it has to be politically and socially acceptable to the majority of Member States and European citizens. The lagging regions of Europe represent only some 20 per cent of the population. They are, in a sense, constrained by what the majority and the wealthier members are prepared to pay for convergence. There is no question that convergence is an aim of the EU. This has been signed up to on many occasions. It is the political will to make it a reality that is lacking. Member States are concerned primarily with the needs of their own electorates. Hence, for example, we see a redistribution of regional funding to Eastern Germany, which is no doubt necessary to prevent social and political unrest arising from economic change within an expanded Germany, but is not economically necessary within an already rich nation.

More is needed than that the EU should redefine what is meant by a 'region'. There needs to be clarification of the relationship between the EU and the Member States and a definition of responsibilities. Within the coming decade it is possible that there will be further expansion in the number of Member States to include some or all of the Visegrad states. This will mean an increase in low-income regions in the EU, although the majority of Europeans will still live in the richer core regions. If existing areas of disadvantage are not to suffer from an increase in membership, resources used for regional convergence will need to increase above current levels. Some regions may, in fact, find themselves disadvantaged by no longer coming within the required low-income bracket for regional aid and thus suffer instability in their development.

What is needed is not just more funding, but for the EU to set targets on economic and social convergence that are realisable within a given period. Funding should be adjusted to meet these targets. There is little point in ends being stated without the means to achieve them. Whether or not this happens is largely a matter of political will. If it does not happen, the 'fast-track' Europe will continue to benefit from cumulative competitive advantage in European and world markets, while the 'slow-track' Europe will improve only very slowly in terms of economic and social welfare, resulting not in the stated aims of convergence but in a widening of disparities in the long run.

REFERENCES

Ardy, B. (1988), 'The National Incidence of the European Community Budget', *Journal of Common Market Studies*, Vol. 26, No. 4, pp. 401–29.
Armstrong, Harvey W. (1995), 'The Regional Policy of the European Union', *Economic and Business Education*, Vol. 2.7, pp. 111–17.
Bachtler, J. and Michie, R. (1993), 'The Restructuring of Regional Policy in the European Community', *Regional Studies*, Vol. 27.8, pp. 719–25.
Barrel, R. (1992), *Economic Convergence and Monetary Union in Europe*, Sage, London.
Begg, I. and Mayes, D. (1992), 'Cohesion as a Precondition for Monetary Union in Europe', in Barrel (1992).
CEC (Commission of the European Communities) (1991), *The Regions in the 1990s*, Directorate General for Regional Policy, CEC, Brussels.
CEC (1992), *Social Europe: First Report on the Application of the Community Charter of the Fundamental Social Rights of Workers*, CEC, Luxembourg.
CEC (1994), *Eurostat*, Rapid Reports 5 and 6.
CEC (1995a), *Regions Statistical Yearbook 1994*, CEC, Luxembourg.
CEC (1995b), *Employment in Europe*, Directorate General V, CEC, Luxembourg.

Curwen, P. (1992), 'The Economics of Social Responsibility in the EC', *Economics*, Vol. 28.4, pp. 156–62.

Dignan, T. (1995), 'Regional Disparities and Regional Policy in the European Union', *Oxford Review of Economic Policy*, Vol. 11, No. 2, pp. 64–95.

Dunford, M. (1994), 'Regional Disparities in the European Community: Evidence from the Regio Databank', *Regional Studies*, Vol. 27.8, pp. 727–43.

European Parliament (Directorate General for Research) (1991), *A New Strategy for Social and Economic Cohesion after 1992*, Study by NIESR, London.

Goddard, J.B. *et al.* (1987), *Research and Technological Development in the Less Favoured Regions of the Community*, Stride Project, CEC, Luxembourg.

Gripaios, P. and Mangles, T. (1995), 'An Analysis of European super Regions', *Regional Studies*, Vol. 28.7, pp. 745–50.

Higgins, B. *et al.* (1987), *Stride: Science and Technology for Regional Innovation and Development in Europe*, CEC, Luxembourg.

Jones, B. and Keating, M. (1995), *The European Union and the Regions*, Clarendon Press, Oxford.

Leonardi, R. (1995), *Convergence, Cohesion and Integration in the EU*, Macmillan, London.

McDonald, F. and Dearden, S. (1992), *European Economic Integration*, Longman, London.

PA Economie Consultants (1990), *The Regional Consequences of the Completion of the Internal Market for Financial Services*, CEC, Luxembourg.

Pompili, T. (1995), 'Structure and Performance of Less Developed Regions in the EC', *Regional Studies*, Vol. 28.7, pp. 679–93.

Scott, J. (1995), *Development Dilemmas in the European Community: Rethinking Regional Development Policy*, Open University Press, Buckingham.

Symes, V. (1995), *Unemployment in Europe*, Routledge, London.

Thomsen, S. and Woolcock, S. (1993), *Direct Investment and European Integration*, Pinter, London.

Tsoukalis, L. (1993), *The New European Economy*, Oxford University Press, Oxford.

Young, S., Hood, H. and Peters, E. (1995), 'Multinational Enterprises and Regional Economic Development', *Regional Studies*, Vol. 28.7, pp. 657–77.

Yuill, D. *et al.* (1993), *European Regional Incentives*, Bowker Sauer, London.

11 Unemployment in Europe: A Continuing Crisis

Valerie Symes

INTRODUCTION

At the opening of the Inter-governmental Conference (IGC) in March 1996, prime ministers of the EU-15 identified unemployment as the most serious problem facing Europe in the next decade. More than 18 million people were unemployed, that is more than 11 per cent of the total workforce. The employed workforce fell by about 4 per cent between 1991 and 1994 in the EU as a whole,[1] the largest fall in a similar period since the Second World War. Since 1983, unemployment in Europe has been higher than in the United States, and much higher than in Japan, two economies with similar levels of economic development. There is, of course, a great variation in unemployment rates between Member States, ranging from below 5 per cent in Luxembourg and Austria to over 20 per cent in Spain. The most surprising development in the past year or so has been that Europe's most fail-safe national economy, Germany, the model of a low-inflation, low-unemployment economy, has seen a rapid rise in unemployment to 11 per cent in 1996, a factor that is not wholly to be explained by the problems of reunification.

In this chapter, the problems faced by the EU and its members will be examined first. Explanations of the divergence of rates between Europe, the United States and Japan will be followed by an analysis of the various reasons put forward to account for the rising trend in overall unemployment in the EU – a subject of much controversy in the emphasis placed on various possible factors, reflected both in national policies and in the contradictory policies of the Directorates of the Commission. Although the major policy directions are, in essence, attacking the problem from a microeconomic stance, it is clear that this is doing little to create the millions of jobs that are required to reduce European unemployment. The future for the unemployed requires a more sophisticated economic strategy.

UNEMPLOYMENT AND EMPLOYMENT IN THE EUROPEAN UNION

There has been an upward trend in the rate of unemployment since the first oil crisis of 1974, 1985 to 1990 being the only years during the past two decades when the rate fell. During this period, 10 million new jobs were created, with Germany, Spain and the United Kingdom each having a net increase of around 2 million. In the recession of the early 1990s, some 6 million jobs were lost: 1.7 million in Italy, 1.6 million in Germany (of which 1 million were in the former East Germany), 900 000 in the United Kingdom and 800 000 in Finland and Sweden combined.

After the recession of the early 1980s, it took over three years for unemployment to fall significantly and the view of the Commission is that 'the number [of unemployed] seems unlikely to decline very rapidly in the near future'.[2] The official figure of just over 18 million unemployed in early 1995 underestimates the number who would work if employment were available. The number in the labour force increased in the late 1980s as more jobs became available and contracted in the recession after 1990. The lack of job opportunities was accompanied by a withdrawal of men from the labour market, and a reduction of potential participation of 3 million young workers. Most of the latter were accounted for by increased numbers in education and training, which should result in better long-term employment prospects. Although many of the men who ceased to seek employment were over 55 years of age and taking early retirement, a large proportion were prime-age workers, particularly in the United Kingdom, Italy and Ireland.

The 1990s generally has seen increasing activity rates of women and an increase in female employment, while the number of male workers in employment has fallen. Overall,

Table 11.1 Employment, Unemployment and Activity Rates in the EU-15, 1985–94

	1985	*1990*	*1994*
Employment (millions)			
Men	83.3	87.1	85.8
Women	51.4	57.5	60.4
Total	134.7	144.6	146.2
Part-time (% of all in employment)	12.5	13.5	15.3
Fixed-term contracts %	9.1	10.3	11.0
Unemployment (%)			
Men	8.7	6.1	10.0
Women	11.6	9.7	12.8
Total Work force	9.8	7.6	11.1
Total No. (millions)	14.7	11.8	18.5
Youth (under 25s)	21.8	15.4	21.2
Activity rate (% of working age seeking or in work)			
Men	80.0	79.1	76.0
Women	50.7	54.5	56.0
Total (all working age)	65.3	66.8	66.1

Source: CEC (1995).

between 1991 and 1994, there was a contraction in the labour force of 0.7 per cent. The number of men in the labour force fell by 2.1 per cent at the same time as the number of women in work or seeking work increased by 1.4 per cent. In the past decade, virtually all the growth in the labour force in Europe can be accounted for by the increased participation of women.

The other significant change in the labour market was an increase in workers on fixed-term contracts and in part-time employment (see Table 11.1).

The change in the employment patterns of men and women came about initially from structural change as well as social change in Europe. The main job losses in the period up to 1985 were in manufacturing industry, where most of the jobs were held by men. Although manufacturing jobs increased by some 6 per cent between 1987 and 1990, and most of these jobs were taken by men, women took over twice as many of the newly created jobs – mainly in the service sector of the expanding economy in the late 1980s. Many of the new jobs created were in part-time employment, and in the United Kingdom nearly all new jobs were part-time. Nevertheless, despite an increase in participation and in filling many more of the new jobs than men, the unemployment rate for women is significantly higher than for men in the EU as a whole, although lower in the United Kingdom, Finland and Sweden.

The most worrying element of unemployment is the very high and persistent level of youth unemployment. Despite the large increase in numbers in education and training after statutory school-leaving age, over 21 per cent were unemployed in the EU as a whole in 1994, and in Spain the figure was 45 per cent. This will inevitably result in long-term economic and social problems as a high percentage of prime-age workers in the future will have had little or no work experience.

The scale of unemployment does vary a great deal between countries and also between regions of the same country, as does the potential for generating new jobs (see Chapter 10). Table 11.2 shows the unemployment rates in Member States for 1985, 1990 and 1994.

All fifteen countries, with the exception of Denmark, experienced a considerable reduction in the rate of unemployment between 1985 and 1990, and all had increases in unemployment between 1990 and 1995, with Finland, Sweden, Spain and Germany experiencing a faster rate of increase than the other Member States. The differences in average rates of unemployment between Member States have tended to widen significantly during the recession of the 1990s. In the period 1985–90, when economic growth and job creation were high, the countries with the highest rates of unemployment experienced the largest decline and there was some convergence in unemployment rates. By 1994, the disparities between Member States with the lowest and highest rates were greater than they had been in 1985.[3] In ten Member States, unemployment was higher in 1994 than it had been in 1985, at the time of the previous recession. In the Netherlands, it was lower (which was ascribed by DGV to a reduction in working hours and shift to part-time employment by DGV); in the United Kingdom and Ireland, it

Table 11.2 Unemployment Rates in Member States, 1985–94 (% of workforce unemployed)

	1985	1990	1994
Belgium	10.3	6.7	10.1
Denmark	7.1	7.7	10.3
Germany	7.2	4.8	8.4*
Greece	7.0	6.4	8.9
Spain	21.7	16.2	24.1
France	10.2	9.0	12.6
Ireland	16.9	13.4	15.2
Italy	8.1	8.3	11.3
Luxembourg	2.9	1.7	3.5
Netherlands	8.4	6.2	7.0
Austria	4.4	3.6	4.0
Portugal	8.7	4.6	7.0
Finland	6.3	3.4	18.4
Sweden	3.0	1.8	9.8
United Kingdom	11.5	7.1	9.3
EU-15	9.8	7.6	11.1

* Including East Germany.
Source: Employment in Europe (1995) CEC.

was below the level in 1985, possibly as a result of emerging from the recession somewhat earlier than the other countries, and in the United Kingdom's case with the extended benefit from depreciation of sterling in late 1992 still working in its favour. It was expected that there would be growth of around 3 per cent per annum in 1995 and 1996, with substantial increases in investment and an increase of employment of around 1 per cent per year, or three million new jobs (CEC 1995). Unemployment was, therefore, forecast to fall in all Member States between 1994 and 1996. The reality was somewhat less agreeable. Growth was low, and unemployment has risen in Austria (to 7.3 per cent) Belgium (to 13.7 per cent), Germany (to 11.1 per cent), and Italy (to 12.6 per cent).

In Italy, the rise in unemployment was surprising, as it was accompanied by the fastest growth rate of all the major EU states, at 3.7 per cent. Spain, the United Kingdom, Sweden and Denmark did, however, experience a fall in unemployment between 1994 and 1996 to 22.8 per cent, 7.9 per cent, 7.7 per cent, 9.8 per cent respectively.[4]

Table 11.3 Long-term Unemployment in Member Staes,* 1994

	% of Total Unemployed for more than 1 year	Unemployment Rate(%)
Belgium	58.3	10.1
Denmark	32.0	10.3
Germany	43.9	8.4
Greece	50.5	8.9
Spain	52.6	24.1
France	37.3	12.6
Ireland	57.8	15.2
Italy	60.9	11.3
Luxembourg	33.3	3.5
Netherlands	43.5	7.0
Portugal	41.2	7.0
Sweden	12.3	9.8
United Kingdom	45.4	9.3
EU average	47.0	11.1

Note: * No figures are available for Austria or Finland.
Source: CEC (1995).

One of the most persistent features of the unemployment in Europe is the large number of unemployed workers who have been without work for over a year – the long-term un-employed (LTU). Nearly half of the 18 million out of work were in this position in 1994. Long-term unemployment does not appear to have any consistent relationship with the overall unemployment rates within Member States.

Sweden, with moderate unemployment, had a very low proportion of LTU; Belgium, the Netherlands and the United Kingdom, all with lower than average unemployment, had relatively high rates of LTU – over 50 per cent for women in Belgium, and for men in the Netherlands and the United Kingdom. On the other hand, France, with above-average unemployment, had one of the lower rates of LTU. The low percentage of LTU in Sweden could be explained by the relatively recent experience of high unemployment, or by more effective active policy for the long-term unemployed, which may also account for France's lower than average rate.

While the creation of new jobs will reduce the rate of unemployment (bearing in mind, however, that new entrants to the labour market may take some of these jobs), it will not do much to reduce the LTU rate. The long-term unemployed are generally at the back of the queue for employment. Jackman (1992) and Budd *et al.* (1986) found that the probability of finding work if you had been on the unemployment register longer than 15 months was less than a third of the probability for those unemployed for less than 3 months. Prolonged unemployment has a psychological effect on workers' morale, motivation and expectations, which results in a lowering of job search, and is also made more difficult by a lack of money to spend on job search activity. Workers, also, are unable to update or maintain their work skills, and cannot signal their quality to employers, who are unable to refer to recent work experience. Employers tend to discriminate against the long-term unemployed and prefer to select from the more recently unemployed, who are more attuned to work culture. Nearly 9 million people have been without work for over a year, and the proportion of very long-term unemployed who have not had a job for over two years, is increasing as unemployment continues to increase in many Member States. The solution to this problem clearly does not lie with economic recovery and an increase in employment alone, of which more later.

But what of job creation? How is Europe to create the millions of new jobs needed to alleviate the severe economic and social costs of unemployment? Is economic growth the answer?

GROWTH AND EMPLOYMENT IN EUROPE

Put very simply, one of Europe's major problems in trying to reduce unemployment is the low employment content of economic growth. This is the major reason why unemployment rates in the EU have been consistently higher than in the United States and Japan during the 1980s and early 1990s.

While growth in the EU was not very different from that in the United States in the period 1981–9, the employment content of growth was over three times as high in the United States. Japan, on the other hand, had much higher GDP growth than Europe and was able to generate more jobs as a result, but also had a slightly higher job content of growth.

Table 11.4 Changes in Real GDP/GNP and Employment Growth 1981–9 and 1992 (%)

	GDP/GNP 1981–9	1992	Employment 1981–9	1992	Unemployment 1981–9	1992
United States	2.9	2.1	2.0	1.1	7.3	7.1
Japan	4.2	1.8	1.2	1.1	2.6	2.2
EU	2.5	1.5	0.6	–0.3	9.9	9.4

Source: OECD Employment Outlook (1992).

The recent recession, however, has seen an absolute decline in productivity (output per worker) in Japan. In both 1993 and 1994, when GDP hardly changed at all, employment increased marginally; in other words, productivity had been sacrificed to the preservation of jobs. Japan chose full employment rather than increased efficiency. The contrast between what has been happening in Europe on the one hand, and the United States and Japan on the other, is especially marked in non-manufacturing sectors. Productivity in manufacturing has increased as fast in the United States and Japan as in Europe. There has, however, been a much greater expansion in employment in the former countries in sectors where competitiveness is less critical, i.e. in the non-traded sectors (CEC 1995a). In the United States millions of new low-paid jobs were created, largely in low-skill service sectors.

Table 11.5 shows the long-term trends in employment in the EU by private and public sector. After the effects of the oil price shock on the European economy private sector employment decreased markedly between 1975 and 1983, but employment in the public sector increased by 3.8 million jobs, thus almost compensating for losses in the private sector.

Both public and private sector employment increased in the second half of the 1980s, but with less of an increase in public sector employment than had been seen in the late 1970s. Since 1992 the overall job losses have been in both the public and private sectors. Private sector losses in the recession have not been compensated for by public sector gains, thus the effect of the recession has been drastic as

Table 11.5 Job Creation in the EU, 1976–95 (millions of jobs)

	1976–80	*1981–83*	*1984–91*	*1992–94*	*1995*[a]
EU-13[b]	2.8	–3.1	10.0	–4.4	1.1
Private sector	0.0	–4.1	17.4	–3.4	1.2
Public sector	2.8	1.0	2.6	–1.0	–0.1

Notes: a. November 1995 forecasts.
    b. Excludes Portugal and Greece.
Source: CEC (1996).

far as unemployment is concerned. The loss of over one million public sector jobs is not unrelated to the Maastricht convergence criteria, which require a reduction in public sector deficits (see Chapters 8 and 10). In a somewhat sanguine analysis (CEC 1996) the Commission stated: 'job losses in certain sectors with fast productivity growth may indirectly help generate employment in other sectors of the economy via a reduction in the relative price of products ... which helps raise the purchasing power of consumers boosting overall demand.' This appears a strange logic, since it would involve a loss of overall purchasing power from those made unemployed, at least initially.

The overall problems in Europe are: (1) unemployment has grown by nearly 7 million people since 1990 with very little decrease in 1995–6; (2) a long-term unemployment rate of roughly half the unemployed and increasing; (3) high youth unemployment; and (4) in most countries a much higher female than male unemployment rate. What, then, are the causes and hence the cures for the problem? The next section will examine, briefly, the various theories put forward to explain Europe's greatest problem.

EUROPEAN UNEMPLOYMENT: CAUSE AND CURE

The basic conflict of ideas is between the current conventional wisdom, based on new neoclassical economic thought, and post-Keynesian analysis. The former stresses the importance of supply-side factors in the labour market, such as wage flexibility (or, as Thurow (1994) puts it, 'when people talk about flexibility in the Common Market ... they are

talking about wages going down'); and a reduction in all
forms of labour regulation, including indirect costs levied
on employment. These microeconomic variables within the
labour market affect competitiveness, which, in a global context, is important in the loss or creation of jobs. Within this
model, growth, or non-inflationary growth, is generated
through increased competitiveness bringing an increase in
demand for traded commodities through an increase in exports and in import-substitution.[5] At the macroeconomic level
the important variable is seen as inflation, with a belief in
the NAIRU (Non-Accelerating Inflation Rate of Unemployment), where an expansion of monetary demand through
lowering interest rates must be restrained once a certain
level of unemployment has been reached, otherwise there
will be an increase in the price level.[6] Monetary policy should,
therefore, be concerned solely with price stability and operated, preferably, via an independent central bank. Fiscal policy
should therefore, be concentrated on the aim of providing
a low-inflation economy and should avoid public deficits;
even in times of recession a lowering of public expenditure
would be necessary. Hence the current orthodoxy, as we
shall see when we examine the policies of the European
Commission, is to rely on supply-side solution for reducing
the rate of unemployment while macroeconomic policy is
geared to price stability, which is considered to be essential
for monetary union.

Tight monetary and fiscal conditions in most European
countries in the 1980s, followed by the fiscal requirements
for EMU in the 1990s, have resulted in a depressing aggregate demand in Europe, whilst the expansion in the European economy in the second half of the 1980s was based
largely on the sudden growth in world trade resulting from
expansionary policies in the United States.[7] It is based on
these observations of the effects of macroeconomic policy
that there has been an increase in discussion on the positive role that expansionary macroeconomic policy should
play in reducing the rate of unemployment in Europe. James
Meade (1994) points out that Keynesian ideas have turned
full circle, starting with financial policies to encourage expansion for full employment, and now with financial policies aimed at a low rate of inflation with high unemployment,

with the depression in the economy being viewed, as in pre-Keynesian days, as a cyclical 'Act of God'.[8] His solution is to use financial policy to set growth targets for money GDP, which would be high enough to cover any growth in the labour force and also reduce unemployment. His preference is for a low rate of interest as the major policy tool as this would ensure a higher investment to consumption ratio, thus increasing competitiveness and the real demand for labour, and also being more effective in dealing rapidly with unexpected booms and slumps. The problem of external deficits experienced by most Member States with expanding domestic demand could be dealt with if all Member States adopted similar reforms, not just in financial policy but also in the setting of wages to avoid not only inflation but also the inevitable widening of the distribution of income.[9] A more conventional approach (e.g. Davidson 1996) is to develop demand policies to encourage higher consumption of manufactured goods through fiscal or monetary policies, even if they create budget deficits, and dealing with inflationary pressures with incomes policy 'without using the unemployed as cannon fodder'. Global economic prosperity would require one or more major economic blocs to act as the engine of growth. Export-led growth could also be helped by export surplus countries not hoarding but spending their surpluses, for the benefit of all countries and the greater stability of exchange rates.

There is little argument among economists about the need for upgrading the skill levels of the unemployed in Europe through investment in education and training. The loss of low-skill jobs in manufacturing in particular, as a result of structural and technological change, means there is likely to be little demand for unskilled workers, whatever the general macroeconomic situation. One of the most buoyant local labour markets in Europe, the city of Frankfurt, where the number of jobs in 1992 far exceeded the numbers seeking work, nevertheless had 3 per cent of its labour force who were long-term unemployed and largely unskilled (Symes 1995). This form of structural unemployment is unlikely to be alleviated in the short run, for whilst jobs in general are scarce, even low-skill work will be undertaken by higher-skill workers. A general question in training, though, is what kind of training, and who should provide it? The OECD (1994) maintains that there is remarkably meagre evidence for the hypothesis that broad-based training programmes are effective in reducing the level of unemployment by getting participants into work.

As mentioned, the policies of the European Commission tend to follow mainstream economic thought. In the next section the major areas of policy at the micro- and macro-levels are examined.

EU POLICY

The European Council at the Essen meeting in December 1994 requested the Commission, in co-operation with Member States, to review labour market developments in the EU and national policies being followed to address unemployment problems. The areas of policy considered to be of major importance at the Essen meeting were fivefold. They are as follows (CEC 1995a):

1. To improve the employment opportunities for the labour force by promoting investment in vocational training, in particular the acquisition of vocational qualifications by young people. As many people as possible must receive initial and further training which enables them, through life-long learning, to adapt to technological progress in order to reduce the risk of future loss of employment.
2. To increase the employment intensity of growth by:
   (i) more flexible organisation of work, in a way that fulfils both the wishes of employees and the requirements of competition;
   (ii) a wage policy, in the present situation, of wage agreements below increases in productivity to encourage job-creating investment;
   (iii) to promote initiatives, particularly at regional and local level, that create jobs which take account of new requirements, e.g. in the environmental and social service spheres.
3. To reduce non-wage labour costs extensively enough to ensure that there is a noticeable effect on decision con-

cerning the taking on of new employees, and in particular unqualified employees.
4. To avoid policies that are detrimental to the readiness
to work, and moving policy from a passive to an active
labour market policy. The individual incentive to continue seeking employment on the general labour market
must remain. Particular account must be taken of this
when working out income-support measures. The need
for and efficiency of the instruments of labour market
policy must be assessed at regular intervals.
5. Implementing particular measures necessary to help young
people, especially school-leavers who have virtually no
qualifications, by offering them either employment or
training. The fight against long-term unemployment must
be a major aspect of labour market policy. Varying labour market policy measures are necessary according to
the very varied groups and requirements of the long-term
unemployed. Special attention should be paid to the difficult situation of unemployed women and older employees.

The first priority, to try to ensure that all young people
have some form of vocational qualification, is aimed both
at reducing the very high rate of youth unemployment, especially amongst those with only basic educational levels who
are most at risk, and also to avoid a large pool of the unskilled in later years.[10] In addition, there is a recognition
that workers will have to adapt to changing technology, and
the consequent effect on employment, throughout their
working lives. The second priority has a mixture of rationales
within it. The first is interpreted as a means of sharing existing work by reducing the hours of full-time workers; work-
sharing or job-splitting; more part-time work; limiting
overtime; and working short-time during 'periods of depressed
demand' (CEC 1995a). Some of these strategies have already
been implemented in Member States. Examples can be seen
in the four-day week experiment at Volkswagen, and in incentives to firms to implement work-sharing agreements in
France and Belgium. Several countries have taken measures
to promote part-time working to increase the numbers in
employment. There are incentives for older workers to carry
on working part-time (with income maintained to some extent

if an unemployed person is taken on to perform the other part of the job). In Portugal, Spain, Sweden, Finland and Austria, the increase in part-time employment has helped unemployed women in particular, and in France, the Netherlands and Portugal the increase in part-time work was large enough to compensate for the loss of full-time jobs.

Point 2(ii) of the recommendations is aimed at reducing overall labour costs and increasing productivity; and point 2(iii) at increasing employment in labour-intensive areas and also promoting the new ideal that job creation should, as far as possible, be environmentally friendly by increasing employment in clean-up or at least non-polluting activities.[11]

The third priority is, again, aimed at reducing labour costs – this time, the indirect costs of employing workers – on the assumption that lower costs will result in more jobs, particularly for the unskilled. Statutory levies on employers range from 14 per cent to 34 per cent across Member States. Taxes on employment, which include employers' and employees' social contributions and payroll taxes, varied from 28 per cent of GDP in Portugal to 48 per cent of GDP in Denmark in 1992. Between 1980 and 1992 total taxes on labour rose from around 35 per cent to 40 per cent, the United Kingdom being the only country where it declined. In Belgium, Ireland and the United Kingdom, employers' social contributions for those on low pay were reduced in 1994. In France the five-year law on employment, introduced in 1993, provided an exemption of some employment tax on employees earning up to 1.3 times the statutory minimum wage. It should be noted, however, that indirect labour costs in the United States and Japan were around 22 per cent of total labour costs, much higher than in Denmark, Greece, Ireland, Luxembourg and the United Kingdom. There is no clear relationship between unemployment or LTU levels and the ratio of indirect labour costs; Portugal, Sweden, Austria and the Netherlands had relatively high indirect costs but lower than average unemployment and LTU rates.[12]

The fourth priority, that tax and social security policy in Member States should not inhibit the unemployed from seeking work, is again aimed largely at the low-paid/low-skill sectors, including the young. In all Member States families with children are entitled to allowances and benefits, and in many countries to some tax relief. At the bottom end of the earnings scale, in 1993 the average deduction in tax and social insurance for single people on 50 per cent of average earnings varied from 22 per cent in the United Kingdom to 44 per cent in Belgium, and around 40 per cent in France and Denmark (although housing benefit in France would raise disposable income by 10 per cent on average). At even lower levels of earnings, in ten Member States overall deductions were around 30–40 per cent of earnings for single people. The relatively high rates of deductions may act as a disincentive to the young and single on low pay. For couples and families in the United Kingdom, Italy and Luxembourg family benefits and supplements to income are available to bring disposable income up to an acceptable standard for the low paid. In Denmark, Germany, France, the Netherlands and the United Kingdom, housing benefit for those on low income is available, but although it raises disposable income, it may act as a barrier to workers seeking employment, in so far as they may seek part-time, low-paid work in order to avoid loss of benefit. The general effect of Member States' raising income levels to those on low pay is to relieve employers of the need to ensure acceptable wage rates, i.e. their 'competitiveness' is subsidised by the state. In cases where there is a single cut-off rate for social subsidies, low-paid workers will suffer a disincentive to seek work. The Essen recommendation aimed to ensure that the effects on disposable income of Member States' tax and social protection policies should minimise the unemployment trap that may be otherwise created.

The fifth priority is already enshrined in the disbursement of funds under the Community Structural Fund (CSF) system – helping those most disadvantaged in the labour market: the young, the long-term unemployed, women and older workers. Objective 3, covering the period 1994–9 (previously Objectives 3 and 4), is aimed directly at the young and long-term unemployed. Funds are available from the Commission for training programmes for these two groups, with an 85 per cent subsidy in Objective 1 regions, and a 50 per cent subsidy elsewhere with some flexibility allowing higher percentages to be granted in special circumstances. In 1990–2

CSF funds for the young and LTU went largely to basic training and updating of skills, not to higher-level training. The
funds are available to governments in the Member States
and not to employers as a subsidy for training in the
workplace. Whilst the Commission encourages training to
be linked to local labour market needs, the success rate from
this type of training is low, especially in times of recession
and when job losses are occurring in local labour markets.[13]
The long-term unemployed, in particular, as we have seen,
are last in the queue for any new employment even if they
have basic training. More is needed in the form of higher
skills training over a longer period, together with help in
confidence building and work experience if the LTU are
not to remain at a permanent disadvantage. But the question that must be answered is, what is the purpose of training millions of workers of there are not millions of new
jobs forthcoming, nor are likely to be in the near future?
The macroeconomic conditions for job creation are simply
not there, and it is a more than futile hope that they will
be without any serious action on macroeconomic policy.

So what is the policy of the Directorate General for Economic and Financial Affairs? Recommendations put forward
in 1995 (CEC 1995b) saw the appropriate macroeconomic
framework for Europe as being one of stable monetary policy
not undermined by budgetary and wage developments;
consolidation of public finances in Member States, i.e. a
reduction in public deficits to meet convergence criteria;
and wage trends consistent with price stability, i.e. below
increases in productivity in order to increase profitability in
the private sector and therefore induce employment-creat-
ing investment. The main task is very clear; that control of
inflation is of paramount importance and that this is best
achieved by tight fiscal and monetary policy and a further
reductions in wage costs. 'The economic recovery, if it
progresses as predicted, will absorb the cyclical component
of unemployment by 1997.' This is assumed to be a reduction of less than 2 per cent of unemployment rate, in other
words, the concept of NAIRU is well entrenched within the
Directorate. Fears are also expressed concerning the potential impact of growth on 'weakening the commitment [of
Member States] to improvement of the budget deficit...

and a reluctance to implement measures which are necessary to remove labour market imperfections'. Growth, which is thought necessary for job creation, is to be obtained from greater competitiveness and 'more active and efficient labour market policies'; a pure new neoclassical prescription. Growth, however, did not develop as expected in 1995 and a later statement (CEC 1996) stressed the need to 'relaunch the recovery process', achieve a high degree of sustainable convergence and significantly reduce the 'alarming unemployment total'. It was hoped that this could be done by easing monetary conditions, with the proviso that this could only be achieved in the context of further reductions in budget deficits and continuing adequate wage developments. Although there is some recognition here that demand may need to be stimulated by a reduction in interest rates, there is extreme caution and a failure to recognise that unless the easing of monetary conditions was quite substantial, it would be cancelled out by the 'pressing need for fiscal consolidation'.

Since competitiveness in world markets is clearly seen as the key to growth, let us look at the problems faced in Europe by the development of the global economy.

EUROPE AND THE GLOBAL ECONOMY

The freeing of financial markets in the 1970s and early 1980s and the reduction in trade barriers resulted in large flows of investment funds, particularly institutional investment funds, to newly industrialised countries, with consequent losses in manufacturing employment in Europe. Multinational enterprises sought lowest cost locations for production, leaving Europe with head office status in many cases. The economic miracle of the East Asian countries, in particular Singapore, Taiwan, Malaysia and Hong Kong, occurred through export-led growth, as it had done in Japan two decades earlier.

The argument is made that the countries of the Pacific rim are successful because of low wages and a deregulated labour market. This may once have been the case in some of these countries, but Japan grew under a highly trade protectionist framework and has a highly developed welfare state; Singapore has a highly regulated labour market, high social contributions and a payments system similar in concept to Meade's Labour Capital Partnership; Korea has wage levels far in excess of those in Britain for example.[14] Taiwan and Hong Kong also have wage levels at similar rates to the wealthier countries in Europe. China is thought to be the current threat, but as yet has made little or no impact on the European market. A reduction in wage costs of the unskilled in Europe is going to make little impact on competitiveness in manufacturing; increasing investment in new technology may, but this will lower employment intensity. One of the problems that does exist in this global setting is the lack of flowback of the export surpluses of these growth economies to Europe on any great scale, and the tendency to hoard surpluses (Davidson 1996).

On the other hand, Europe has one great advantage in the context of the global economy. It is the world's largest market in terms of purchasing power. Although it is not as large as China in terms of population, it has a better educated population and better infrastructure. The fact that it is the largest world market (and is likely to grow with an expansion of membership) will, in Thurow's analysis (1994), mean that Europe will write the rules for world trade in the century ahead, as Britain did in the nineteenth century and the United States in the twentieth. As he points out, Most Favoured Nation (MFN) status, where any one country must extend the same trading regulations to all countries as it applies to its most favoured trading partner(s), and which was at the heart of past GATT agreements to free world trade, is not in fact practised. In any case, there is an exceptional clause for common markets where the ultimate goal is political unification. So the EU may well set various increasing quality standards that involve free trade within, but management of trade without. At the G7 Employment Summit at Lille in April 1996, there was much discussion over whether social clauses protecting workers should be included in future trade agreements. President Chirac stated France's position that the liberalisation of world trade and the development of employment could not be disassociated from respect for universal labour standards, such as the freedom of trade unions and collective bargaining and the exploitation of young workers. Differences in wage levels, social security and labour laws would be 'less and less tolerated as international competition grows in intensity'. The respect accorded to free market capitalist philosophy, free trade and competitiveness are paper-thin and crumbling in many Member States. One could argue that a truly global economy will bring the greatest benefit in terms of total world income through comparative advantage, but it is difficult to persuade a low-growth, high-unemployment Europe that this will remain in their interest, or that it fails to protect the welfare of its weaker citizens and thus abandons the European ideal of increased social cohesion.

The reality is, one way or another, that Europe as a whole will not end up as victims of the global economy. This is not, however, to say that it will only survive in the context of high protectionism. Europe should and can pay its way in a global economy through developing a high knowledge-based society, and through technological innovation and investment that will enhance productivity and competitiveness in manufacturing industry, albeit initially with a lower level of manufacturing employment.

CONCLUSION: THE FUTURE

Europe is suffering from a conflict of aims. On the one hand, it wishes to see the totally unacceptable level of unemployment reduced; it also wishes to implement a single currency, the prerequisites for which were determined, under the Maastricht Treaty, as nominal convergence of inflation and interest rates through tight fiscal policy and control of monetary policy both designed for price stability. This is the crux of the problem. The Directorate in charge of employment policy is geared to carrying out microeconomic measures to upgrade skills and provide the unemployed workforce with the means of coping with technological change, and devising the best strategies to get the long-term unemployed into employment. While this is very worthwhile and essential for the future competitiveness of Europe and the sustainability of employment in the long run, in the short to medium term raising the quality and increasing the occupational flexibility of the workforce will do little in the context of slow employment growth. Macroeconomic policy, as seen in the statement above, of the Directorate General for Economic and Financial Affairs, is effectively constraining the growth of employment through higher than necessary real interest rates and fiscal contraction. The hope of an export-led recovery occurring in the short run is a mirage. However much competitiveness is increased, the stagnation in Europe's economy is acting as a brake on world trade generally, since Europe is the largest single world market. Without an increase in demand within the EU all the training will result in nothing more than a more highly skilled, unemployed workforce. It seems unlikely that the general drift of macroeconomic policy will change. Germany and France in particular are keen to push a single currency through as soon as possible, on the basis of the given convergence criteria. Finance ministers of the more prosperous countries are keen that fiscal consolidation should be adhered to by the rest, in order to avoid the problems suffered through competitive devaluations of their currency.[15] As it stands, despite the current statements on a potential easing of monetary policy, there is unlikely to be any significant change in the level of European unemployment in the short term. The long term will depend on whether or not the 1996 IGC in Turin decides on a change in policy direction that will accommodate the fact that most Europeans wish to maintain a welfare state, and will not tolerate a large proportion of their citizens locked into long-term unemployment or low-paid work. A decision to defer the date for monetary union (it is unlikely that the nominal convergence criteria will be altered to take account of real economy factors) may ease the situation on employment, or at least allow for an effective reduction in real interest rates. The real problem lies in the views of Member States on what constitutes a good society, and whether the economy is there to serve the needs of people or the people there to serve the needs of free markets. It is to be hoped that some accommodation of views will emerge from the IGC which will have a positive effect on Europe's unemployed millions.

NOTES

1. This loss of six million jobs refers to the EU as a whole, which includes the new members, Austria, Sweden and Finland, and also Eastern Germany.
2. 'Employment in Europe 1995'. Office for Official Publications of the European Committee, Luxembourg.
3. The statistical measure of the disparity in unemployment rates (standard deviation weighted by the labour force) showed that disparities between member states rose from 4.1 to 4.6 (1985–94).
4. Figures from the *Economist*, 6 April 1996, for the first quarter of 1996.
5. Davidson (1996) gives examples from the United States as being calculated at around 6 per cent unemployment by both the New Keynesian economist Alan Blinder and Alan Greenspan of the Federal Reserve Bank. It is generally thought to be higher in Europe, which is more prone to wage inflation than the United States.
6. This so-called neo-Keynesian preference for expansion via export-led growth is the rationale for increased competitiveness in EC policy statements.
7. For a further discussion of research on the role of supply side factors and monetary policy, see Symes (1995).
8. 'There is often a strange general tendency to assume that (much higher output with a large number employed) will automatically materialise without any very profound analysis of the reason why, together with a rather superficial reminder that one will need to prevent an excessive inflation of money prices' (Meade 1994).
9. Meade's solution to these problems lies in a form of pay based on profit-sharing (Labour–Capital Partnership) and in a Citizen's Income for all members of society with provisions that would remove disincentives to work.
10. It was found that in Germany those under 20 years of age suffered virtually no unemployment because of the system of dual training in vocational schools and firms, for a range of professional skills. Hence those in their twenties also had low rates of unemployment (Symes 1995).
11. The percentage of employment in polluting as opposed to eco-friendly activities is greater in all Member States, but varies between them. Ireland, Spain and Portugal have a lower relative number in polluting activities, while the more developed countries – Luxembourg, the Netherlands and Germany – have over 15 per cent of their workforce in polluting industries (see CEC 1995a).
12. This idea has, however, widespread, acceptance. Meade (1994) goes so far as to say that all indirect labour costs should be abolished and replaced by taxes on income.
13. For a further discussion on the effects of basic training programmes in the EU, see Symes (1995) and the *Economist*, 6 April 1996.
14. Recently, a Korean car firm had to increase wages that were acceptable to British workers in order to be in line with its own domestic

workers who feared 'social dumping' through low labour costs in the United Kingdom.
15. Meeting of Finance Ministers of Member States, April 1996 in Verona.

REFERENCES

Budd A., Levine P. and Smith P. (1986), 'The Problem of Long-term Unemployment', *Economic Outlook 1985–89*, 10 (5), London Business School Centre for Economic Forecasting.

CEC (1993), *Growth, Competitiveness, Employment: The Challenges and Ways, Forward into the 21st Century*, White Paper, Luxembourg.

CEC (1995a), *Employment in Europe*, Directorate General for Employment, Industrial Relations and Social Affairs, Luxembourg.

CEC (1995b), *European Economy*, No. 60, Directorate General for Economic and Financial Affairs, Brussels.

CEC (1996), *Annual Economic Report*, Brussels.

Davidson, P. (1996), 'The Viability of Keynesian Demand Management in an Open Economy Context', *Oxford International Review of Applied Economics*, Vol. 10, No. 1, pp. 91–105.

Jackman, R. (1992), 'An Economy of Unemployment', in E. McLaughlin (ed.), *Understanding Unemployment*, Routledge, London.

Meade, J.E. (1994) *Full Employment Regained?*, Cambridge University Press, Cambridge.

OECD (1994), *Jobs Study: Unemployment in the OECD Area 1950–1995*, OECD, Paris.

Symes, V. (1995), *Unemployment in Europe: Problems and Policies*, Routledge, London.

Thurow, L. (1994), 'New Game, New Rules, New Strategies', *RSA Journal*, November 1994.

12 Ageing Populations in Europe: Demographic Trends and Policy Issues
Jane Littlewood

INTRODUCTION

This chapter is primarily concerned with the social policy implications of the 'greying' of the population of the European Union (EU). Consequently, the major demographic changes which have taken place in the EU will be considered in the first part of the chapter. However, it must be said at the outset that the 'science' of demography is somewhat imprecise. Specifically, although it is possible to detect general trends over long periods of time, there may be some short-term fluctuations which go against these general trends. Furthermore, casting forward population projections is almost always fraught with difficulty.

Also, thorough investigation is not always possible due to difficulties in locating reliable statistical evidence. However, the UN demographic yearbooks are available from 1948 onwards, and Eurostats are available from the 1960's onwards. Whilst there are some residual problems associated with different age groupings and census years, the statistics available are certainly accurate enough to detect general trends. As Taylor-Gooby (1992) indicates:

> estimates of the young population for the last years of this century and the early years of the next must be uncertain, as must calculations of the working population from the second quarter of the next century onwards. However, estimates of the elderly population over the next sixty or seventy years and of the working age population for the next thirty or so can be treated with some confidence (assuming the absence of cataclysms, health care

miracles or mass emigration to Mars) because they are based on knowledge of changes which have already taken place

(Taylor-Gooby 1992: 68)

The second part of the chapter is concerned with trends in expenditure on social protection. It will be shown that whilst a general trend towards an increased percentage of GDP being spent on social protection can be identified, the share of social protection being spent upon elderly EU citizens has, in general terms, remained fairly constant. Furthermore, a trend towards increasing the rate of social contributions will be identified.

The final part of the chapter looks at policy issues and alternatives for the future. It argues that, at least in terms of the implications for social protection that a greying population implies, the situation is not as intractable as some commentators (particularly from within the context of the United Kingdom) have implied. However, whether the full range of policy alternatives will be developed within the European context remains to be seen.

DEMOGRAPHY AND DEMOGRAPHIC TRENDS IN THE EU

As Taylor-Gooby has indicated, most discussions about demographic change are located within the context of the 'limits' of social policy and the necessity for a change in policy initiatives. It is within this context that the interpretation of the OECD's authoritative report *Ageing Populations* (1988) must be interpreted. Trends in the age structure of populations, particularly the greying of populations, tend to attract great interest in the cross-national policy community, and this interest tends to be associated with the need to limit the state provision of social protection.

Ageing Populations (1988) identifies two phenomena whose general impact will vary in both force and timing in different countries. The first phenomenon is the 'demographic transition' associated with the development of mature industrial societies. At its most general level this transition involves the following trends: a substantial decline in mortality rates and a substantial decline in fertility rates to below the level at which any given population can be maintained, i.e. a total fertility rate (TFR) of less than 2:1. This transition results in the ageing of any given population.

The second phenomenon is the post-war 'baby-boom'. This boom is superimposed on already ageing populations. TFRs rose in most countries in the 1940s and this rise will inevitably lead to an 'additional' cohort of elderly people, largely falling (depending upon the country) in the first 25 years of the next century.

In an article entitled 'Age-Structure Changes in 1950–1990' (UN 1993) the population division of the UN Secretariat presented a model of demographic transitions which explains this demographic shift in four broad stages.

Stage 1: This is a stationary stage before demographic transition. Life expectancy at birth is between 20 and 30 years. The average number of live births per woman is between 6 and 8. High mortality and fertility levels lead to a young population, whose structure is relatively stable.

Stage 2: Generally speaking, a decline in mortality precedes a decline in fertility. When mortality rates are very high, any decline in mortality is typically greater among the younger age groups. Consequently, when mortality begins to decline, although the population increases at all levels, it increases especially amongst the very young. Therefore, the population becomes even younger. In addition, improvements in health care lead to even higher fertility rates and an even younger population. This effect tends to be strongest in the early years of change, so cohorts of those who were very young children when the decline in mortality began and those born immediately after tend to be larger. These cohorts then work through the system providing a bulge in the population at the stage they have reached at any given time.

Stage 3: This usually occurs several decades after the start of the decline in mortality rates. This stage sees the beginning of a significant fall in fertility resulting in a slowing in the growth of numbers of children in any given population and consequently the proportion of elderly people starts to rise. This stage may be characterised as 'fertility-dominated' ageing. At stage 3 the impact of a decline in fertility tends to exceed that of a decline in mortality. Specifically, fertility decline is the turning point from an increasingly younger to an increasingly older population. Fertility decline is also a turning point from a rising to a falling growth rate of total population.

Stage 4: After fertility reaches the region of population replacement level (i.e. TFR is 2:1) mortality decline replaces fertility decline as the major driving force behind the further ageing of the population. This shift from 'fertility-dominated' to 'mortality-dominated' ageing occurs for three reasons: Specifically:

1. Any given decline in fertility generally slows after reaching the region of replacement level.
2. Significant mortality reduction becomes increasingly limited to the older age ranges, i.e. elderly people simply live longer.
3. The ageing of the population itself begins to amplify the effect of mortality decline on population ageing, i.e. as the number of elderly people increases the numerical impact changes in its proportion on the entire age distribution and therefore becomes more significant.

However, it must also be noted that the age structure of any population reflects not only fertility and mortality but also migration patterns over the previous 8–10 decades.

On a world-wide scale 'greying populations' do not appear to present any particular problems. For example, in the mid-1990s the world's population fell into the following age groups (UN 1991).

Under 15 years	32%
15–24 years	19%
65 years+	6%
Median age	24 years

However, the situation in Europe is somewhat different. Specifically:

Under 15 years	19.6%
15–24 years	15.0%
65 years+	13.4%
Median age	35 years

Furthermore, a more detailed consideration of the position of the EU countries would appear to indicate that these countries, to a greater or lesser extent, have (a) reached stage 4 in their demographic development and (b) will all be affected, albeit to different extents, by a 'baby boom bulge' of elderly citizens in the first 25 years of the 21st century. Table 12.1 shows changes in the population structure over time.

Table 12.1 clearly shows a general trend towards a smaller percentage of the population under 15, which can be detected in all countries for which data are available. However, this trend does not necessarily represent a smooth and inevitable transition. Specifically, the decline seems sharpest in the years between 1975 and 1985 and seems to have been particularly marked in (West) Germany, where it declined by 7.7 per cent. In contrast, the decline in France was much slower (2.7 per cent). However, after 1985 some countries saw an increase in the percentage of under 15s in the population. Whilst Germany saw the sharpest rise (influenced possibly by the effects of reunification), both Luxembourg and the United Kingdom also saw small rises, whilst the rate of decline slowed in other countries. The exception to this general trend is Ireland, which appears to be somewhat behind the rest of the EU in both starting and slowing its rate of decline in the under 15 population. Thus, the years 1971–5 saw no change in the percentage of the population under 15, while the decline between 1985 and 1993 was sharper than in other EU countries. Nevertheless, Ireland still has a proportionately younger population, having started at a higher level in 1971.

Life expectancy at birth has also risen over the same period of time (Table 12.2).

However, it must be said that whilst life expectancy at birth has risen in all Member States, the actual rate of increase has been much less in some societies than others, resulting in a convergence which may be interpreted as a possible

Table 12.1 Population by Age Groups (%)

	Years	1970	1975	1980	1985	1993
Belgium	0–14	23.6	22.2	20.0	18.8	18.2
	15–44	40.3	41.4	42.8	43.6	43.7
	45–64	22.6	22.5	22.8	23.4	22.7
	65+	13.4	13.9	14.4	13.8	15.4
Denmark	0–14	23.2	22.6	20.8	18.4	17.0
	15–44	41.2	41.8	43.4	45.2	43.9
	45–64	23.2	22.2	21.3	21.3	23.6
	65+	12.4	13.4	14.4	15.1	15.5
France	0–14	25.1	23.9	22.3	22.1	19.9
	15–44	41.5	42.0	42.8	44.0	44.4
	45–64	21.0	20.6	20.9	21.9	21.1
	65+	12.6	13.5	14.0	13.0	14.5
Germany*	0–14	23.2*	21.5*	18.2*	15.1*	16.3
	15–44	42.4	–	40.9	41.2	42.8
	45–64	22.8	21.9	21.9	25.4	25.2
	65+	13.2	14.4	15.5	14.8	15.0
Greece	0–14	25.3	–	22.8	20.9	18.1
	15–44	42.4	–	40.9	41.2	42.8
	45–64	21.2	–	23.1	24.5	24.7
	65+	10.9	–	13.1	13.4	14.3
Ireland	0–14	31.3	31.3	30.4	29.2	26.3
	15–44	37.2	38.4	41.4	43.2	44.4
	45–64	20.4	19.9	17.4	16.8	17.6
	65+	11.1	10.9	10.7	10.8	11.4
Italy	0–14	24.4	24.1	22.0	19.3	16.3
	15–44	41.9	41.4	42.1	43.4	45.0
	45–64	22.4	22.3	22.2	23.9	23.3
	65+	11.3	12.2	13.5	13.2	13.6
Luxembourg	0–14	22.1	20.2	19.0	17.3	17.9
	15–44	41.8	43.9	44.7	45.5	45.2
	45–64	23.4	22.9	22.2	23.9	23.3
	65+	12.6	13.0	13.5	13.2	13.6
Netherlands	0–14	27.2	25.3	22.3	18.6	18.3
	15–44	42.6	44.1	46.3	48.4	46.8
	45–64	19.8	19.8	19.9	20.5	21.9
	65+	10.3	10.8	11.5	12.5	13.0
Portugal	0–14	26.4	24.0	–	–	24.1
	15–44	40.8	–	42.8	42.7	44.5
	45–64	20.9	–	20.6	21.8	22.5
	65+	9.6	–	10.3	12.0	14.1

Table 12.1   Continued

	Years	1970	1975	1980	1985	1993
Spain	0–14	27.7	–	25.9	23.1	18.9
	15–44	41.9	–	41.5	43.0	45.8
	45–64	20.5	–	21.8	21.9	21.9
	65+	9.6	–	10.3	12.0	14.1
United Kingdom	0–14	24.1	23.3	20.7	19.2	19.4
	15–44	38.6	39.4	41.8	43.7	42.7
	45–64	24.2	23.3	22.4	22.0	22.1
	65+	13.2	14.2	15.1	15.1	15.8

Note: * Most recent year for which data are available.
Sources: Eurostat Census of Population 1968–77 (1977), Eurostats 1960–76 (1977), Eurostats (1984), Eurostats (1989), Council of Europe Stats (1993), UN Demographic Yearbook (1971), UN Demographic Yearbook (Special Issue) (1991).

Table 12.2   Life Expectancy at Birth, 1970–91

Country	1970 or 1971	1991*	Increase
Belgium	71.0	75.7	4.7
Denmark	73.5	75.4	1.9
France	72.9	77.7	4.8
Germany	70.5	75.7	5.2
Greece	73.8	77.4	3.6
Ireland	70.7	75.0	4.3
Italy	71.6	77.2	5.6
Luxembourg	69.7	76.1	6.4
Netherlands	73.7	77.3	3.6
Portugal	67.0	74.4	7.4
Spain	72.8	77.0	4.2
United Kingdom	71.8	76.4	4.6

Note: * Or most recent year for which data is available.
Source: European Commission Report on the State of Health in the EC (1995).

sign of a ceiling effect to what is achievable in terms of further extending life expectancy amongst EU citizens. Nevertheless, as Simons (1992) points out, the possibility of an increase amongst the very old (80+ years) projected for the first half of the 21st century will almost certainly be associated with increased costs in the areas of health and welfare provision.

Fertility rates in the EU have, and have continued, to decline. The population replacement level of 2:1 has not been reached in Europe as a whole since the mid-1970s. Table 12.3 gives EU TFRs for 1960–88.

Despite small upturns in the TFR in Belgium, Denmark, Luxembourg and the Netherlands, the general decline in fertility in the EU appears to be continuing into the 1990s. A comparison of EU total fertility rates is given in Table 12.4.

Also, marriage trends do not give rise to optimism. The Council of Europe (1993) has identified two major trends: (1) marriage appears to be less popular and that 'consensual unions' are increasing; (2) marriage (and childbearing) tends to occur later. Both these trends are most marked in Northern Europe, especially Sweden and Denmark, followed by Western Europe. However, they are also found to a lesser degree in Southern and Central Europe. An increase in the number of children born outside marriage has also been noted. 'Recent Demographic Developments in Europe' (1993) makes an interesting link between the number of births occurring outside marriage and the given countries fertility rate. Specifically:

> The countries with the highest proportion of births outside marriage are also those showing the highest rise in birth rates (Iceland, Sweden, Norway) while those with low proportions of extra-marital births have the lowest fertility (Italy, Spain Greece).
>
> (Council of Europe 1993: 15)

However, one extremely uncertain factor which may affect the demographic profile of any given country is migration. International migration is notoriously difficult to predict due to its relationship to economic and political circumstances. Migration is often characterised by short-term fluctuations.

During the first half of the 1980s net migration declined throughout Western, Northern and Southern Europe because of depressed economic conditions. However, economic recovery coupled with the political events associated with the breakdown of the former Soviet Union and the Communist bloc in Eastern and Central Europe reversed this trend in the late 1980s.

Table 12.3 Fertility for the EU-12, 1960–88

Year	Total Fertility Rate
1960	2.63
1965	2.77
1970	2.45
1975	2.08
1980	1.87
1985	1.62
1988	1.60

Source: Eurostats (1989).

Table 12.4 A Comparison of EU Total Fertility Rates, 1988–94

Country	1988	1994
Austria	–	1.45
Belgium (1986)	1.54	1.55
Denmark	1.56	1.81
Finland	–	1.85
France	1.82	1.66
Germany	1.42	1.26
Greece	1.52	1.38
Ireland	2.17	1.86
Italy	1.34	1.19
Luxembourg	1.51	1.72
Netherlands	1.55	1.56 (est.)
Portugal	1.53	1.44
Spain	1.38	1.22
Sweden	–	1.89
United Kingdom	1.84	1.74

EU-15 average TFR = 1.45.
EU-12 average TFR = 1.60.
Source: Adapted from Eurostats 1990 and UNESCO, *Statistical Yearbook* (1994).

The main direction of migration in Europe is east to west, with many migrants being asylum-seekers mainly from Central and Eastern Europe. The main destination for migrants has been Germany, which in 1991 owed its increase in population entirely to net inward migration. Indeed, inward migration even compensated for a small natural decrease (i.e. deaths exceeding births) in the population. In 1992, Germany again attracted migrants, receiving 61 per cent more than in 1991.

According to the Council of Europe (1993), in 1992 Austria owed 74 per cent of its population growth to migration, Denmark owed 61 per cent, Finland 33 per cent, Greece 96 per cent and Italy 85 per cent. Since 1989 net migration in Europe has been higher than natural growth and is therefore the main component of population growth. Thus, it would appear that migration cannot easily be dismissed. Indeed, if fertility and mortality continue to decline, migrants may make up an even larger proportion of the working population in many European countries. However, any increase in the migrant population on such a scale has enormous social policy implications, which extend far beyond issues associated with income maintenance, health and welfare spending.

To summarise, other relevant trends in the EU include the declining popularity of marriage, rising divorce rates and the increasing importance of inward migration for many EU countries in order to prevent overall population decline.

The 'greying' of the EU population raises potentially problematic policy issues associated with a larger elderly population being supported financially by a smaller working-age population. Consequently, spending patterns on the social care of the elderly are the concern of the second part of this chapter.

SOCIAL PROTECTION BENEFITS AND AGEING POPULATIONS

Increased spending on social care may be expected as more and more people live into very old age. Indeed, there is some evidence that this trend may already be occurring. Table 12.5 shows social protection expenditure as a proportion of GDP.

Overall, then, the trend in the EU between 1970 and 1983 was to increase the percentage of the GDP spent on social protection.

However, since 1983 the total expenditure on social protection as a percentage of GDP has shown considerable variation between countries, with the countries of Southern Europe (particularly Portugal and Greece) spending a much lower percentage of their GDP on social protection than

Table 12.5 Social Protection Expenditure as percentage of GDP, 1970–83

Country	1970	1975	1980	1983
Belgium	18.7	24.2	28.1	31.9
Denmark	19.6	25.8	28.7	30.2
France	19.2	22.9	25.9	28.8
Ireland	13.2	19.7	21.0	24.6
Italy	17.4	22.6	22.8	27.3
Luxembourg	15.9	22.3	25.9	29.3
Netherlands	20.8	28.1	30.4	34.0
United Kingdom	15.9	19.4	21.4	23.7
West Germany	21.5	29.8	28.5	28.9
EU-9	19.0 (est.)	24.7	25.8	28.0

Source: Eurostat, *Social Protection Statistical Bulletin*, 1 (1985) and Eurostat, *Social Protection Bulletin* 1 (1984), Table 1.

the countries of Northern Europe, particularly Sweden, which has the highest percentage of GDP spent on social protection.

Although the general trend seems to have been for the percentage of GDP spent on social protection to rise, this rise has been inconsistent, indeed in some years it has even fallen, (e.g. Belgium between 1985 and 1990, when the proportion fell by just over 2 per cent). Table 12.6 illustrates this point. However, it is interesting to note that there has been relatively little change in the proportion of social protection benefits spent on the elderly citizens (see Table 12.7). Furthermore, whilst the figures for 1985–92 are not directly comparable (i.e. the figures for 1985–92 include survivors' benefits alongside old age benefits), the trends noted between 1975 and 1983 seem to be continuing. In short, there is very little change in the actual proportion of social protection benefits being spent on old age. Table 12.8 shows social protection spending between 1985–92.

Other spending went on work-related accidents and illness, invalidity and disability benefits, as well as some miscellaneous benefits.

Obviously, whilst falling fertility rates and the decline in the popularity of marriage may lead to the possibility of making financial savings on education, and family and children's policies, the situation is still potentially problematic. Spending on maternity and family policies in the EU is, on

Table 12.6 Total Expenditure on Social Protection in Current Prices, percentage of GDP

	1985	1990	1992
EU-12	26.1	25.3	27.1
Belgium	29.3	27.0	27.8
Denmark	27.8	29.6	31.4
France	28.8	27.6	29.2
Germany	28.4	27.0	27.3
Greece	19.4	20.5	19.3
Ireland	23.8	19.7	21.6
Italy	22.6	23.3	25.6
Luxembourg	25.5	25.9	28.0
Netherlands	31.3	32.2	33.0
Portugal	14.2	14.9	17.6
Spain	20.2	20.6	22.5
United Kingdom	24.3	22.7	27.2
Austria	–	26.7	28.2
Finland	–	26.1	35.4
Sweden	–	35.8	40.0

Source: Eurostat Year Book (1995).

Table 12.7 Social Protection Benefits by Selected Function, percentage of Total Benefits, 1975–83

Year	Sickness	Old Age	Family	Unemployment
1975				
Belgium	22.6	26.5	15.0	7.8
Denmark	29.4	31.9	11.2	9.4
France	27.6	35.5	12.6	3.7
Germany	28.0	30.3	8.9	4.5
Ireland	36.2	25.0	10.9	10.2
Luxembourg	23.1	32.6	8.8	0.2
Italy	23.8	31.8	11.7	2.2
Netherlands	30.1	29.4	10.4	6.3
United Kingdom	25.2	43.0	9.1	5.6
EU-9	26.7	33.7	10.6	4.6
1980				
Belgium	22.1	26.2	11.8	11.3
Denmark	26.8	35.0	10.0	10.8
France	25.7	34.8	10.7	6.7
Germany	29.2	29.3	7.5	3.3
Ireland	36.0	26.4	8.7	8.2
Luxembourg	23.6	30.4	8.0	1.8

Table 12.7 Continued

Year	Sickness	Old Age	Family	Unemployment
Italy	23.2	33.9	7.3	2.4
Netherlands	29.1	28.2	9.3	6.1
United Kingdom	23.0	40.6	11.5	8.5
EU-9	26.0	33.1	9.2	5.5
1983				
Belgium	21.9	27.0	9.9	14.2
Denmark	23.5	34.3	9.4	13.7
France	24.9	34.0	9.6	9.8
Germany	27.0	29.8	6.5	7.1
Ireland	29.0	24.9	9.4	13.1
Luxembourg	22.8	26.7	7.6	3.1
Italy	22.5	34.7	6.9	3.2
Netherlands	25.6	27.0	8.1	12.7
United Kingdom	20.3	40.6	10.6	10.1
EU-9	24.1	33.3	8.3	8.4

Source: Eurostats 1995.

Table 12.8 Social Protection Benefits by Function, Current Prices, percentage of Total Benefits

Year	Unemployment and the Promotion of Employment	Health	Old Age and Survivors	Maternity and Family
1985				
EU-12	8.1	23.7	44.8	8.7
Belgium	13.3	20.3	42.7	9.7
Denmark	15.3	22.1	37.2	10.5
France	6.0	24.3	45.6	11.1
Germany	6.6	27.5	42.5	7.6
Greece	2.3	10.5	65.5	3.2
Ireland	14.0	29.1	27.7	16.6
Italy	3.4	22.4	58.7	5.8
Luxembourg	1.3	23.8	47.3	9.5
Netherlands	11.8	20.6	33.1	7.6
Portugal	2.6	33.9	37.3	7.4
Spain	19.0	23.6	43.3	2.6
United Kingdom	10.8	19.0	41.9	11.6
Finland	–	–	–	–
Sweden	–	–	–	–

continued on page 262

Table 12.8 Continued

Year	Unemployment and the Promotion of Employment	Health	Old Age and Survivors	Maternity and Family
1990				
EU-12	6.7	24.6	45.8	8.0
Belgium	11.1	23.2	43.9	9.0
Denmark	15.3	19.7	36.6	12.1
France	6.6	26.5	44.4	10.0
Germany	6.1	28.1	42.1	8.1
Greece	2.9	10.5	68.2	1.7
Ireland	12.6	28.6	28.8	17.5
Italy	1.8	21.7	61.7	5.1
Luxembourg	0.8	24.5	46.8	11.2
Netherlands	8.3	21.5	37.1	5.9
Portugal	2.7	28.7	42.6	6.7
Spain	17.0	26.0	42.7	1.7
United Kingdom	5.8	20.6	43.0	10.8
Finland	5.5	26.6	35.7	13.5
Sweden	4.7	36.1	40.8	15.5
1992				
EU-12	7.2	25.3	44.8	7.8
Belgium	11.4	23.5	44.7	8.1
Denmark	17.2	19.2	35.1	12.0
France	7.7	26.6	44.1	9.5
Germany	6.2	29.2	40.6	8.9
Greece	5.3	9.3	69.0	1.7
Ireland	14.6	29.1	27.2	17.4
Italy	1.7	22.9	62.8	3.9
Luxembourg	0.8	24.4	48.4	11.1
Netherlands	8.4	21.9	36.9	5.4
Portugal	5.0	31.2	38.8	5.6
Spain	18.5	25.7	41.3	1.8
United Kingdom	6.0	21.1	39.4	10.9
Finland	14.0	21.5	33.1	12.7
Sweden	8.5	24.8	47.8	16.0

Source: Eurostat Yearbook (1995).

average, only 10 per cent of the total spending on social protection. Paradoxically, by far the largest proportion of social spending goes on old age and survivors' benefits and health care – the very areas where spending will need to increase further.

This trend towards more spending on social protection obviously needs to be financed. Indeed, the rate of social contributions in the EU-15 has been rising since 1989, when it was 13.7 per cent of GDP, to 14.2 per cent in 1991 and

Table 12.9 Social Contributions in the Member States of the EU, percentage of GDP

	1991	1994
Austria	13.8	15.2
Belgium	15.9	15.9
Denmark	1.5	1.7
Finland	13.0	14.7
France	19.3	19.3
Germany	17.0	18.2
Ireland	5.7	5.7
Italy	13.1	13.2
Luxembourg	11.7	12.8
Netherlands	18.0	19.8
Portugal	10.2	10.4 (1993)
Spain	12.4	13.0
Sweden	15.1	13.8
United Kingdom	6.7	6.6

Note: The German figures include the new Länder.
Source: Adapted from Eurostat key figures, 06/95.

15 per cent in 1994 (Eurostat 1995). However, individual countries show variations, as Table 12.9 illustrates.

This general growth in the EU is accounted for by increases in employee contributions, i.e. 4.3 per cent of GDP in 1989, 4.5 per cent in 1991 and 5.3 per cent in 1994 (Eurostat 1995). In addition, the rate of social contributions paid by the self-employed and non-employed has increased from 1.4 per cent in 1989 to 1.5 per cent in 1991 to 1.8 per cent in 1994. Thus, it would seem that in Europe as a whole, there is a growing and already established trend towards individuals and employers shouldering more responsibility for meeting the rising costs of social protection.

POLICY ISSUES RAISED BY DEMOGRAPHIC TRENDS

The main issue which has already been noted is the question of financing an ageing population. However, it must be noted at the outset that dependency in old age is, in some ways, a social construct rather than a social fact (Phillipson and Walker 1986). Specifically, Townsend (1986) has argued that:

the dependency of the elderly has been structured by long term economic and social policies. Elderly people are perceived and treated as more dependent than they are or need to be by the state, and this outcome has been fostered by the rapidly developing institutions of retirement, income maintenance, residential and domiciliary care which comprise a subordinate but necessary part of the overall management of state policy. In short, ageism has been and is being institutionalised in modern society. There are forms of discrimination against the elderly which are as deep as forms of discrimination against women and ethnic minorities.

(Townsend 1986: 15)

It must be said that many elderly citizens have enjoyed better health and social care than their predecessors and can look forward to active and independent living on retirement. Nevertheless, there will still be significant numbers of very elderly EU citizens who will eventually become dependent. If it is accepted that Europe cannot support its dependent ageing population, then a number of policy measures must be considered. However, some authors, notably Taylor-Gooby (1992), cast doubt on the intractability of the problems posed by ageing populations. Specifically, Taylor-Gooby raises the following pertinent issues:

The changes in population structure raise serious questions for social policy. However, it is premature to draw the conclusions reached by some policy makers in the UK and the USA, that demographic change incapacitates the welfare state. There are three reasons for this. First, the calculations typified by the OECD report pay little attention to previous experience in coping with the impact of change. Second, they may be an incomplete guide to the future because they say little about relevant social changes. Third, the whole question of how ageing is related to dependency requires more detailed consideration.

(Taylor-Gooby 1992: 72)

One of the important social changes Taylor-Gooby identifies is changes in patterns of employment. Whilst, to a certain extent, long-term changes are unknown and unknowable,

Symes has indicated in Chapter 11 of this volume that increased rates of labour market participation have, and may still, offset the influence of demographic transition. Overall, Taylor-Gooby finds it reasonable to conclude that 'demographic pressures will not prove insuperable in most countries, unless there is a complete and unprecedented economic collapse' (Taylor-Gooby 1992: 73).

This relative optimism was also reflected in an international symposium on population convened by the United Nations in 1987. The report (United Nations 1988) made the following points:

1. Whilst the share of total income spent upon the elderly would increase, this would be offset by a rise in the absolute levels of after-tax income per worker (due to increased productivity and a reduced burden of youth dependency).
2. The funding of pensions is problematic but not insoluble.
3. A reduced burden of child care in an ageing population could help people to pay higher contribution rates.
4. Raising the age of pension eligibility would substantially reduce the expenditures of pension schemes (by 50 per cent in some cases).

A more recent report (OECD 1995) identifies two dimensions of policy responses in connection with ageing populations, i.e.:

1. To restore sound public finance in the medium term so that it is possible to cope with demographic pressures when they begin to be felt.
2. To review pension and healthcare policies.

In connection with the latter dimension, the following policy options are identified:

For pension schemes options include raising contributions, reducing pension payments and, perhaps most effective, increasing the age of retirement. For health it will be necessary to explore ways of delivering care for the frail elderly in a more cost-effective manner.

(OECD 1995: 33)

In terms of pension schemes Chassard and Quintin (1992) have explored the foundations and implications of the policy of convergence, i.e. the convergence of policy for social protection based on common objectives but respecting the diversity of EU schemes. The main lines of possible reform they outline are: (1) later eligibility for pensions; (2) more stringent conditions of eligibility; and (3) less favourable computation of the benefit payable.

Chassard and Quintin argue that reform of such a nature would make it possible to limit any increase in contributions or state support. Indeed, there is also evidence to suggest that relevant reforms are already taking place in France, Portugal, Italy, the Netherlands, Ireland, Germany and the United Kingdom (Missoc 1994).

In terms of policy provisions for the dependent elderly, Henrad (1991) compares the solutions adopted by several EU countries in the sectors of housing, home care services, residential and nursing homes. Henrad argues that a real medico-social policy has been worked out only in Denmark and the Netherlands. France and the United Kingdom have developed policies, but have not provided corresponding resources. Alternatively, in Germany and Italy there is no clearly defined policy at all.

Clearly, whilst relevant policy options are being pursued, longer-term demographic issues may prove to be more difficult to address. For example, Doring *et al.* (1994) looked at old age security for women in 12 EC countries in order to ascertain the extent to which elderly women received minimum pensions of their own. Doring *et al.* found that only in the Netherlands and the United Kingdom do the majority of women receive pensions of their own, and it is only in the Netherlands that these pensions are enough to guarantee a minimum of subsistence. In other countries 'a relatively high fraction' of elderly women depend on intra-family transfers from spouses or survivors' pensions. Doring *et al.* (1994) conclude that none of the countries in their study has introduced a social security system based on universality and a guaranteed minimum. The previously mentioned demographic trend towards rising divorce rates may serve to complicate even more the issues associated with the pension rights of women.

Furthermore, whilst an increase in the participation of women in the labour market is offsetting the demographic transition, women's work is traditionally low-paid and low-status. It is also more likely to be part-time and is often below the tax threshold. If these patterns of employment continue, then it seems unlikely that the revenue raised will be sufficient to meet pension needs.

Women are also responsible for the bulk of childcare and informal social care of the elderly. Indeed, it is also women who form the majority of the 'old' elderly (i.e. 80+ years) EU citizens. Taylor-Gooby (1992: 84), in highlighting the relevance of political choice and planning, suggests that one option would be that 'for example, informal social care can be brought within the sphere of paid employment'. Alternatively, Parry (1995) is relatively pessimistic and argues that:

> The length of perspective necessary to see the value of social protection is usually denied to governments which have to manage budgets year to year and win elections at frequent intervals. The result tends to be a periodical concern with worst-case scenarios in which the working age population seems to be overwhelmed by children or the elderly.
>
> (Parry 1995: 394)

Another policy of long-term importance would seem to be that of encouraging people to have more children. Simons (1992) argues that according to responses to a 1986 UN survey, nine European countries (Bulgaria, East Germany, Hungary, Romania, Greece, France, West Germany, Liechtenstein and Monaco) all felt that their fertility rates were too low, and all except West Germany had instituted pro-natalist policies. However, the effects of such policies are more likely to have a temporary effect on the timing of births rather than an effect on completed family size.

Sweden is perhaps the classic case of a country exhibiting pro-natalist policies. Policies have been introduced which aim to make it easy for women to have children and yet still take up paid employment. Sweden's relatively high fertility rate does imply that the pro-natalist policies have been successful, but whether the effects can be sustained is uncertain.

Indeed, the most recent evidence (Eurostat No. 8, 1995) suggests that the TFR in Sweden, which had reached the population replacement threshold in 1990, is now falling towards the levels of other Northern European countries. Alternatively, France also has a number of pro-natalist policies and yet has broadly similar trends in fertility rates to the United Kingdom which gives little practical help to families.

One solution to the problems posed by ageing populations which has been the subject of much discussion in the press involves substituting informal, voluntary or private measures for pensions and social care. Indeed, there are indications that this process has already begun and will continue. Recent interest in Asia's 'growth miracle' are of interest. Specifically, 'Adopting an Asian approach to ensuring that baby-boomers save for their old age would not, in itself, free Europe from the trap of low savings and growth rates. But it might stop us from moving ever further in the wrong direction' (Flanders 1995: 25).

Obviously, the route to a private welfare system is fraught with problems and may, paradoxically, rely on more welfare state involvement rather than less. What happens to the low paid and the unemployed who cannot afford private provision?

To conclude, current responses to demographic challenges vary. For example, in funded schemes where deficits are visible (e.g. France) corrective action involving increased contributions are likely. Alternatively, in Germany there remains some potential through increasing the typically low rate of female participation in the workforce, increasing the retirement age and making pensions less generous (e.g. Pensions Reform Act 1992). However, Parry (1995) is of the opinion that the major problems may occur in Southern Europe where the political consensus needed to deal with deficits may be lacking and 'the demands for social benefits are an important reason why the discipline required for a common European currency may not be met' (Parry 1995: 395). Parry is also of the opinion that the ideological force of social provision for the elderly will be lost in larger political and economic contexts because, in terms of social policy, the EU may prove to be a poor integrative mechanism. Parry, like Taylor-Gooby (1992), sees the problem as a one of political will as much as structural inequalities and administrative weaknesses. Specifically:

> For its part, the welfare state may never be able to offer the technical instruments or the philosophical impetus it provided in that happier post-war age when reconstruction rather than deconstruction was the watchword, and everything seemed possible in the delicate area where state action and individual behaviour interact in search of end-states of happiness and growth,

(Parry 1995: 398)

REFERENCES

Baker, J. (1986), 'Comparing National Priorities: Family and Population Policy in Britain and France', *Journal of Social Policy*, Vol. 15, No. 5, pp. 421–42.

Barr, N. (1991), 'The Objectives and Attainments of Pension Schemes', in Thomas and Dorothy Wilson (eds.), *In the State and Social Welfare*, Longman, London.

Brauns, H-J. and Kramer, D. (1989), 'West Germany: The Break-up of Consensus and the Demographic Threat', in B. Munday (ed.), *The Crisis in Welfare*, Harvester-Wheatsheaf, Hemel Hempstead.

Brooke-Ross, R. (1987), 'Elderly People's Care in Germany', *Social Policy and Administration*, Vol. 21, No. 3 (Autumn), pp. 244–51.

Butler, A. (1986), 'Housing and the Elderly in Europe', *Social Policy and Administration*, Vol. 20, No. 2 (Summer), pp. 136–52.

Chassard, Y. and Quintin, O. (1992), 'Social Protection in the European Community: Towards a Convergence of Policies', in *International Social Security Review*, Vol. 45, pp. 91–108.

Ginn, J. (1993), 'Grey Power: Age-based Organisations' Response to Structure Inequalities', *Critical Social Policy*, Issue 38 (Autumn), pp. 23–47.

Gray, B. (1986), 'Status and Stereotypes – Past and Present Attitudes to Old People in Western Society', *Social Policy and Administration*, Vol. 20, No. 2 (Summer), pp. 153–68.

Guillemard, A-M. (1986), 'Social Policy and Ageing in France' in C. Phillipson and W. Walker (eds.), *Ageing and Social Policy: A Critical Assessment*, Gower, Aldershot.

van Gunsteren, Herman and Rein, Martin (1985), 'The Dialectic of Public and Private Pensions', *Journal of Social Policy*, Vol. 14, No. 1, pp. 129–49.

Doring, D., Hauser, R., Rolf, G. and Tibitanzl, F. (1994), 'Old-age Security for Women in the 12 EC Countries', *Journal of European Social Policy*, Vol. 4, No. 1, pp. 1–18.

Flanders, S. (1995), 'Why States Must Grow: Growing Older and Growing Slower', *Financial Times*, 6 November, p. 25.

Henrad, J. C. (1991), 'Care for Elderly People in the European Community', *Social Policy and Administration*, Vol. 25, No. 3, September, pp. 184–92.

Parry, R. (1995), Redefining the Welfare State', in J. Haywood and E.C. Page, *Governing the New Europe*, Polity Press, Cambridge, pp. 374–400.

Petersen, J. H. (1991), 'Problems of Pension Policy: American, British, Danish and German Ideas', *Social Policy and Administration*, Vol. 25, No. 3, September, pp. 249–60.

Phillipson, C. and A. Walker (1986), *Agency and Social Policy*, Gower, Aldershot.

Simons, J. (1992), 'Europe's Ageing Population – Demographic Trends', in J. Bailley (ed.), Social Europe, Longman, London, pp. 50–69.

Stahlberg, A-C. (1991), 'Lessons from the Swedish Pension System', in Thomas and Dorothy Wilson (eds.), *The State and Social Welfare*, Longman, London.

Stahlberg, A-C. (1993), 'Pension Reforms in Sweden', *Benefits*, Issue 6, Jan/Feb, pp. 11–15.

Taylor-Gooby, P. (1992), *Social Change and Social Welfare*, Harvester-Wheatsheaf, Hemel Hempstead.

Tester, S. (1994), 'Implications of Subsidiary for the Care of Older People in Germany', *Social Policy and Administration*, Vol. 28, No. 3, September, pp. 251–62.

Townsend, P. (1986), 'Ageism and Social Policy', C. Philipson and A. Walker (eds.) *Ageing and Social Policy: A Critical Assessment*, Gower, Aldershot.

Walker, A. (1993), 'Achieving (or not Achieving) Economic Security in Old Age: the EC's Pension Systems Compared', *Benefits*, Issue 8, Sept./Oct., pp. 4–8.

Other Reports and Statistical Sources

OECD Reports
'Effects of Ageing Populations on Government Budgets' (1995), in *Economic Outlook*, 57, June (OECD, Paris).

OECD (1988), *Ageing Populations*, Organisation for Economic Co-operation and development (Paris).

EU Publications
Social Protection in the Member States of the European Union. Situation in July 1994 and evolution. From MISSOC, the Directorate General of Employment, Industrial Relations and Social Affairs, published by the Office for Official Publications of the European Communities (Luxembourg, 1995).

Eurostat Demographic Statistics, Eurostats 1960–76, published for the Office for Official Publications of the European Communities (Luxembourg, 1977).

Eurostat Demographic Statistics, Eurostats, 1984, 1989, 1990 all published by the Office for Official Publications of the European Communities (Luxembourg).

Eurostat Census of Populations 1968–77, published by the Office for Official Publications of the European Communities (Luxembourg, 1977).

Eurostat Year Book 1995, published by the Office for Official Publications of the European Communities (Luxembourg, 1995).

Eurostat Social Protection Statistical Bulletin, European System on Integrated Social Protection Statistics (ESSPROS), Eurostat 1 (Luxembourg, 1985).

Eurostat Social Protection Statistical Bulletin 1, (Luxembourg, 1984).

Eurostat Key Figures 06/95, published by the Office for Official Publications of the European Communities (Luxembourg, 1995).

Eurostat Statistics in Focus, Population and Social Conditions, Eurostat No. 8, published by the Office for Official Publication of the European Communities (Luxembourg, 1995).

MISSOC (1994), Social Protection in the Member States of the European Union, Situation at 1st July, the Directorate General in Employment, Industrial Relations and Social Affairs, Office of Official Publications for the European Communities, Luxembourg..

Council of Europe Publications
Recent Demographic Developments in Europe, published by the Council of Europe Publishing and Documentation Service (Strasbourg, 1993).

United Nations Publications
'Age-Structure Changes in 1950–1990', In the *United Nations Demographic Year Book 1991*, Special Issue on Age and Ageing, published by the Department for Economic and Social Information and Policy Analysis of the United Nations (New York, 1993).

United Nations Demographic Yearbook, published by the Department for Economic and Social Information and Policy Analysis of the United Nations (New York, 1971).

UNESCO Statistical Year Book, published in 1994 by the United Nations Education, Scientific and Cultural Organisation (Paris, 1994).

13 Health Policy and the European Union

Ed Randall

INTRODUCTION

Observers of the European health scene often begin a review of European Community (EC) (now European Union
(EU)) health policies by acknowledging the vast range of
health issues and the diversity of policies that are relevant
to them (ter Kuile 1992). There are very few human activities which fail to provide an opportunity for aspiring health
policy-makers to proffer an opinion or come up with policy
recommendations that cross national boundaries. Diseases
like AIDS do not recognise international borders and
industrial processes that give rise to health endangering pol-
lutants do not respect frontiers. Many industrial and commercial concerns depend for their economic survival upon
purchases made by health care systems and operate in more
than one country. Health care organisations are themselves
major purchasers of services supplied by entrepreneurs keen
to operate beyond their own domestic markets.

Even though the emphasis in EC public policy-making was
on economic development and integration, officials based
in Brussels and Luxembourg – and the political leaders of
Member States – frequently discovered good reasons for the
EC to formulate policies which would have major implications for Europe's health services. The scale of European
spending on medical services (both public and private), and
the enormous numbers of people employed both directly
and indirectly by health care systems, meant that European
legislation and regulation affected the delivery and organisation of medical services – even when the EC had no direct
responsibility for making and implementing health policy.

Despite some reluctance on the part of EC Member States,
particularly the United Kingdom, to support the develop-

ment and strengthening of Europe's political and social dimensions, health issues have attracted the interest of EC institutions over a long period. There are common problems and concerns which have inspired and sustained the belief that the EC/EU can successfully encourage co-operation and collaboration, and even venture out to play a leading role in some areas of health policy. Perhaps this reflects the view that if it is reasonable to expect any organisation to facilitate co-operation and collaboration between European societies in the field of health policy, then it is the European Commission to which we should turn. The Commission is well placed to establish and influence co-operation within the EU.

The Commission drafts European legislation for consideration by the European Parliament and the Council of Ministers, and it is responsible for European Directives which are binding on Member States. Even if it were to confine itself narrowly to labour market and trade issues, it could hardly fail to have an impact on the health services available to EU citizens, a point made by the European Healthcare Management Association (EHMA), which has observed that the move towards a single market in Europe has had a substantial impact on the health care sector (EHMA 1994a). The EHMA makes the case that economic concerns can determine policy developments that are relevant to health and health services. Domestic health services markets have been opened up to EU-wide competition for construction contracts and the supply of medical goods and equipment. European Community 'rules in this area require public contracts above a certain monetary value to be open to competition between companies in all Members States' (EHMA 1994a: 8). And those who have the responsibility for opening up Europe's markets quickly find themselves assailed from all sides with arguments about how trade needs to be fair, not just open. The European Commission's role in driving forward the single European market (SEM) has meant that it has had an expanding role in setting standards so that competition is seen to be both fair and safe and in the interests of consumers. The Commission is now a major influence in the health field even when it is addressing some other policy area.

Social Policy and Health Policy in Europe – Going Beyond The Marketplace

Whilst economic considerations have been predominant in European public policy-making the representatives of most of the Member States of the EC have wanted to do more than bring about economic integration. There is persuasive evidence of a longstanding aspiration to advance the cause of social and political union. This aspiration has extended to a desire to improve and protect the health of EU citizens.

The European Social Charter on the Fundamental Rights of Workers, first agreed in Turin in 1961, has been developed within the EC since 1965, when it first operated officially as a guide for the actions and policies of Member States in the social field. The Charter included, amongst the entitlements of workers, an entitlement to medical assistance. The European Social Charter was itself the basis for the European Community's Social Charter, adopted by all EC Member States in December 1989, with the sole exception of the United Kingdom. It is reflected in the Social Chapter of the Maastricht Treaty from which the United Kingdom was once again an absentee (Bainbridge 1995). The United Kingdom's absence indicates more than a reluctance to be part of an ever-deeper Union. There are tremendous difficulties in formulating social policies for the whole of the EU, and in going beyond policies in the health field which have been developed as an adjunct to economic co-operation and integration. However, there should be no disguising the fact that the United Kingdom's reluctance to join also reflects the hostility of some powerful British politicians to membership of a club that aims at the social and political – not just the economic – integration of European nation states.

Getting Europe's Institution Involved In Health

The reasoning which would appear to lie behind the willingness of the majority of Member States to give the EC/EU a clearer and stronger social dimension, including the development of a European public health policy, is reflected in the *Commission Communication on the Framework for Action in the Field of Public Health* (Commission of the European Communities [CECs] 1993a). There is a belief that the EU Member States face common health problems which multinational teamwork will help them to tackle more effectively; and that there is considerable scope for working together and significant benefits to be obtained from doing so. To adapt, just a little, the Commission's statement setting out the common health problems identified in its 1993 Communication, we can point to:

- the common challenge of providing for the health needs of ageing populations in Member States;
- the existence of a shared interest in providing for increasing population mobility in the Community and between Member States;
- the changes in the environment and work setting which have to be faced in all the Member States;
- the challenge of meeting rising expectations about what health services can and should deliver; and
- the need to tackle Community wide socioeconomic problems, most notably the problems of social exclusion (which have a major health component).
  (CECs 1993a: 1c)

And, we might add, a universal anxiety about the cost of medical services and a shared determination to find ways and means of keeping the costs of health programmes under control.

The response of the Commission to such shared concerns is to argue that a 'Community approach' focused on common concerns and problems is essential. The role of the EU is to facilitate the establishment of common objectives and networks; to assist in the exchange of information and personnel; to help improve data systems and offer, albeit limited, financial support for innovative and shared health programmes and projects; to produce an annual Community health report and to encourage and promote efforts to reduce and contain health care costs. The Commission has identified the mechanisms it will employ to support the 'Community approach' as: 'Consultation and participation; promotion of programme and policy coordination; cooperation with international organisations; health education and promotion; support for research and the training of health professionals' (CECs 1993a: 1d).

The Commission as Information Provider

The belief that the Commission, on behalf of the EU, can play an important part in co-ordinating efforts to improve health throughout Europe has been given a tangible expression in the work that the Commission has been doing, in recent years, in producing a European health report (CECs 1995). This document is meant to embody the 'Community approach'. The Commission's work on the state of health in the EU is clearly designed to underpin the specific public health programmes and campaigns in which it has been involved and to build an EU-wide appreciation of European health issues, as well as defining certain health issues as issues for the EU as a whole. As Smith (1992) argues, what has been of concern to epidemiologists is of increasing interest to a growing number of ordinary Europeans: 'Pressure will come increasingly on European countries to bring their health services and the health of their citizens up to at least European average levels' (Smith 1992: 14).

The Commission's *Report on the State of Health in the European Community* should help to stimulate interest in what is happening in different European countries. The report identifies similarities and differences in the health of Europe's national populations. It also identifies major gaps in our knowledge, which co-operation between Member States might begin to address (CECs 1995): 'Differences in death rates between social groups are present in all countries. . . . However, data on the pattern of use or uptake [of services] by social groups are generally not available' (CECs 1995: 8).

Some of the principal observations of the report provide a useful backcloth to this chapter on European health policy. Infant mortality rates have fallen throughout the EU, but substantial variations between and within Member States remain (see Figure 13.1). Similarly, life expectancy at birth has risen in all Member States, but the rate of increase has been much less in some societies than others, resulting in a convergence, suggesting that we may be approaching a ceil-

Figure 13.1 Infant Mortality Rates per 1000 Live Births by Member State

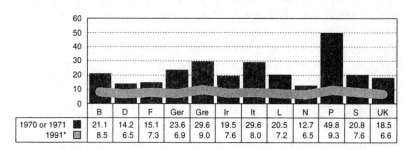

	B	D	F	Ger	Gre	Ir	It	L	N	P	S	UK
1970 or 1971	21.1	14.2	15.1	23.6	29.6	19.5	29.6	20.5	12.7	49.8	20.8	18.5
1991*	8.5	6.5	7.3	6.9	9.0	7.6	8.0	7.2	6.5	9.3	7.6	6.6

Note. * Or most recent year for which data are available.
Source. European Commission Report on the State of Health in the EC (1995).

Figure 13.2 Life Expectancy at Birth, in Years by Member State

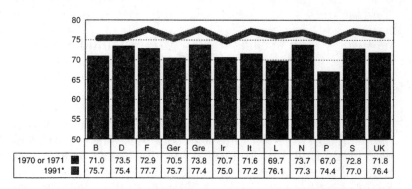

	B	D	F	Ger	Gre	Ir	It	L	N	P	S	UK
1970 or 1971	71.0	73.5	72.9	70.5	73.8	70.7	71.6	69.7	73.7	67.0	72.8	71.8
1991*	75.7	75.4	77.7	75.7	77.4	75.0	77.2	76.1	77.3	74.4	77.0	76.4

Note: *Or most recent year for which data are available.
Source: European Commission Report on the State of Health in the EC (1995).

ing on what is achievable (see Figure 13.2). There are striking differences between Member States in the patterns of mortality from diseases of the circulatory system and malignant neoplasms and in the changes in mortality rates for these diseases – differences which echo differences in diet and personal behaviour and the environment, and which may reflect the way in which these factors interact in different

European societies (see Figures 13.3 and 13.4). The belief of Commission staff engaged in disseminating information about patterns of disease in different Members States appears to be that there are great opportunities for health policy-makers to learn more and make greater use of information about variations in mortality rates between Member States if health service and epidemiological data can be shared and compared more easily.

Much of the optimism that there seems to be in the Commission about the potential future role of European health policy rests on the belief that shared information can play a critical part in enhancing the prospects of concerted and effective action in the health field. If a European public opinion concerned with health issues can be fostered and encouraged, then Member States may find the arguments for generalising the best and most successful health programmes throughout the EU more convincing.

THE EVOLUTION OF EUROPE'S HEALTH-RELATED POLICIES

Health Policy Piecemeal

The Maastricht Treaty, which established the EU and which came into force in November 1993, committed the EU and its Commission to developing EU-wide policies aimed at improving the health of all its citizens. Prior to the Treaty on European Union the EC and its institutions had no specific authority to make or implement policies which had the improvement or protection of public health as their principal aim. This did not prevent the development of policies which were relevant to the delivery of health services and to public health throughout the EU, but the lack of any explicit authority to do so for its own sake meant that the Commission's involvement in the field of health had to be carefully justified in terms of its relevance to economic, employment and commercial considerations.

The absence of a clear legal basis for developing European health policy in the Treaty of Rome resulted in a piecemeal approach to health issues. The EC was able to pursue the

Figure 13.3 Standardised Death Rates, Diseases of Circulatory System*

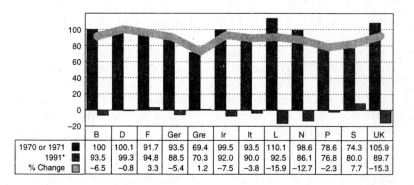

	B	D	F	Ger	Gre	Ir	It	L	N	P	S	UK
1970 or 1971	116.4	96.5	74.8	101.7	68.3	149.3	96.7	149.5	99.3	109	93.3	140.5
1991*	58.6	66.3	40.6	74.1	65.6	87.3	51.5	63.6	60.4	64.9	51.3	79.3
% Change	−39.1	−31.3	−45.8	−27.2	−3.9	−41.6	−46.7	−57.4	−39.1	−40.4	−45.1	−43.5

Notes: * 0–64 years, per 100 000.
** Or most recent year for which data are available.
Source: European Commission Report on the State of Health in the EC (1995).

Figure 13.4 Standardised Death Rates, Malignant Neoplasms*

	B	D	F	Ger	Gre	Ir	It	L	N	P	S	UK
1970 or 1971	100	100.1	91.7	93.5	69.4	99.5	93.5	110.1	98.6	78.6	74.3	105.9
1991*	93.5	99.3	94.8	88.5	70.3	92.0	90.0	92.5	86.1	76.8	80.0	89.7
% Change	−6.5	−0.8	3.3	−5.4	1.2	−7.5	−3.8	−15.9	−12.7	−2.3	7.7	−15.3

Notes: * 0–64 years, per 100 000.
** Or most recent year for which data are available.
Source: European Commission Report on the State of Health in the EC (1995).

social dimension of its common market most vigorously in asserting workers' rights and, in the health field, this meant promoting health and safety at work. In its 1993 framework statement on safety, hygiene and health protection at work the Commission claimed that it had been striving over a period of 30 years to 'reduce to a minimum both work accidents and occupational diseases' (CECs 1993b: 2). Community action was designed to cut the annual death toll from occupational accidents, put at 8000 per annum across the EU and the economic losses associated with accidents and occupational diseases – losses that the Commission conservatively estimated at ECU 26 000 million in 1991 (CECs 1993b).

Safety and Health at Work

The involvement of the EC in promoting safety and protecting health at work can be traced back to the Rome Treaty of 1957. Whilst the 1951 Paris Treaty, which created the European Coal and Steel Community, offered some scope for the development of Community activity in the field of health, it was not until 1957 that any positive action was taken. The treaty establishing the European Atomic Energy Community (EAEC), which included Articles on health and safety, was signed and, in the same year, a research programme was launched into occupational safety and health in the coal and steel industries of member states and the Safety and Health Commission was established alongside an Advisory Committee on Safety, Hygiene and Health Protection at Work. The EC had started to develop a health competence in a practical as well as a legal sense, enabling it to deal with health and safety in the workplace across Europe. The two bodies were deeply involved in the development of the action programmes in 1979 and 1984 which resulted in new European health and safety legislation (CECs 1993b).

The Single European Act (SEA), which came into effect in July 1987 and which provided for the creation of an SEM in goods and services by 1993, gave a boost to the EC's involvement in the health field. Article 118a, an SEA supplement to the EC Treaty, emphasised the role of the EC in improving the health and safety of workers, and it introduced qualified majority voting for decisions on Community legislation directed to making the workplace safer and healthier. The result was, in the Commission's own words, 'the adoption of a significant amount of safety and health legislation and a new level of awareness on these issues' (CECs 1993b: 2). However, even though references to social as well as economic partnership are widespread in contemporary

Commission documents, the Commission takes great care to explain that its activities (in relation to health and safety at work) have a powerful economic rationale. The Commission's 1993 Communication on its safety and health at work activities explained that its programme of work was intended to minimise economic losses and to improve competitiveness as well as facilitate the free movement of workers within the ECC community by establishing a common minimum set of standards in workplaces throughout the EU (CECs 1993b).

The expansion of the EU's role in safety and health at work was confirmed by the European Council in October 1993 when the establishment of a new European Agency, for safety and health at work was agreed. This Agency is charged with collecting and analysing information on occupational safety and health and promoting best practice throughout the EU (CECs 1993b). The importance of occupational health issues can be gauged from Commission data showing that: 'Of the 120 million or so workers in the Community, almost 10 million are victims of work accidents or occupational diseases each year' (CECs 1993b: 2).

What's Mine Is Yours

The SEA did more in the health field than provide a boost to the Commission's work on safety and health at work. It also gave momentum to the process of harmonisation in the training and education of health workers.

Attempts to develop a system for mutual recognition of professional qualifications throughout the EC had been going on for some time before the SEA came into force. Although the Treaty of Rome was intended to ease and encourage the movement of labour between Member States, it did not prove easy to evolve arrangements for the reciprocal recognition of professional qualifications. The medical profession were the first professional group for whom a means of recognising qualifications, obtained in different member countries, was established. As Brearly notes, 'it took some 18 years from the signing of the [Treaty of Rome] to agree the medical directives upon which the mutual recognition of medical qualifications could be based' (Brearly 1992: 30).

Brearly records that the earliest attempts to facilitate the free movement of medical labour were frustrated by attempts to reach a precise agreement on 'the duration and content [of] the training which doctors had to undergo if their qualifications were to be recognised throughout the community' (ibid.). The approach adopted assumed that a professional title, such as medical doctor, in one country could be relied upon in all other Member States. Brearly has argued that this lowest common denominator approach may have inhibited rather than stimulated improvements in medical education throughout the EC. He does acknowledge that a Directive (issued in 1986), making general practice training mandatory, 'represents a genuine advance in training standards' even though 'several countries are experiencing difficulties with its implementation' (Brearly 1992: 30).

The content and standards of medical education in Europe are clearly matters of considerable importance. The Commission has a long history of involvement in facilitating discussions amongst Member States about them. Any EU health policy in the future seems certain to entail a consideration of how public health goals can best be reflected in the education of the most expensive health workers in the EU.

Stallknect (1992), in her account of *Nursing in Europe*, argues that even though the political engine for harmonisation of standards in nurse education and mutual recognition of qualifications has been the labour market policy of the EC, the results for nurses and nursing have been beneficial. The need to agree minimum standards of education for nurses to facilitate free movement within the EC 'forced the professional associations representing nurses and other health professionals to reassess their attitudes' (Stallknect 1992: 59). And, despite apprehension that the adoption of a common set of minimum standards for nurse education in Europe would erode efforts to improve nurse education, she concludes that 'In most of the countries of the EC educational programmes [for nurses] have continued to evolve and improve, (ibid.: 60). Stallknect considers that the EC's efforts to achieve mutual recognition of qualifications and the stimulus given to harmonisation of training led nurses to 'extend their cooperation into other areas' (ibid.). The EC's efforts in promoting free movement of labour are presented by Stallknect as providing some of the political and professional collateral needed to raise the status and pay of nurses throughout Europe and to generalise the best standards of nursing in Europe.

The EC and the European Pharmaceuticals Market

The SEA has also played an important part in another area of health-related European policy-making by shaping and regulating the European market in pharmaceuticals. A market valued at £20 000 million in 1987 (Burstall 1990).

Prescription drugs are very big business in Europe and a major expense for European health care systems, coming second only to staffing costs in health care systems' budgets. EU policies on the trade in pharmaceuticals 'influence the prescribing rights of the Community's 600 000 practising doctors and the access to treatment of many of its 350 million citizens' (Taylor 1992). The EU is now involved in every aspect of the sale, production and use of drugs.

The application of the principles of a single market to the pharmaceutical industry set the European Commission an exceptionally demanding task. There are wide variations in the cost, use and volume of pharmaceuticals prescribed in European countries. The SEA requires the European Commission to harmonise national regulations and create, so far as possible, a level playing field for the trade in medicines. The objective is to develop a market in which purchasers of pharmaceuticals can make their decisions on the basis of good information about the efficacy of drugs and in which manufacturers can be sure that they will be dealt with even-handedly by national authorities. The regulation of the pharmaceutical industry and the creation of an EU-wide market in accordance with the SEA has been such a complex task that a European Medicines Evaluation Agency has been established to deal with it. Based in London, it came into operation in 1995 and offers a 'centralized Union-wide registration procedure for new medicinal products' (Bainbridge 1995: 193). It builds on EC actions affecting the pharmaceutical industry going back to 1965, including the 1989 'transparency' Directive, which was designed to ensure that 'national decisions on medicine pricing and reimbursement are fair and made on a visible basis' (Taylor 1992).

A Kaleidoscope of Community Policy and Activity

Although the three broad areas of Community policy discussed above are most often represented as the principal means by which the EC gained influence and developed its competence in the health field, there are many other ways – apart from specific health programmes (discussed below) – in which the EC has had an impact on health services and the health status of EC residents.

Reflecting the opening paragraph of this chapter, the EC has been deeply involved in setting standards for and regulating actions which have an impact on the environment. In a document entitled *Towards Sustainability*, which was adopted as official policy by the Council at the beginning of 1993, the EU has been provided with a ringing declaration about a great range of environmental objectives and proposals which are intended to: improve the quality of water, air and soil, control dangerous substances and industrial activities; monitor radiation; and control pollution and the disposal of waste throughout the EU (CECs 1993a).

The EC's interest in the relationship between foodstuffs and well-being has a 30-year history. Community regulations include policies on food labelling and consumer education and information aimed at improving public health by making it possible for people to make informed decisions about what they purchase and eat. Consumer protection measures are based on a number of European Directives which apply to numerous goods, including machines and toys as well as medical products. The EC has also been particularly active in promoting research and the development of information technology, particularly where it is relevant to health.

In fact, the EU, through its administrative and policy-making machinery, is now involved in a staggering range of health issues. The list includes the regulation of tobacco advertising, the promotion of measures to achieve European self-sufficiency in human blood products, action to improve the treatment provided to victims of poisonings, the issuing of Directives on the confidentiality of personal information and the fostering of co-operation to ensure that the numbers of qualified doctors in the EU match the numbers required by the health care system in individual Member States (see CECs 1993a; and HoC Health Committee 1992). Such a diversity of activities and responsibilities suggests that there is considerable scope for conflict and rivalry – as well as co-operation – between the EU's institutions and the governments and institutions of Member States.

PUBLIC HEALTH MAKES IT WAY ONTO THE EUROPEAN AGENDA

Europe Against Cancer

Despite the fact that prior to 1993 the European Commission had no specific authority to tackle what Commission papers now refer to as 'major health scourges', EU public health campaigns were launched against cancers, AIDS and drug dependency. The framing of a public health role for the Commission depended on a liberal interpretation of general powers available under the Treaty of Rome (HoC 1992) and the support of European Heads of State and the very strong support of at least one major European political leader for launching an EC-wide public health initiative. Chris Ham (1992: 138), in his account of EC involvement in health issues, reports that 'Europe against Cancer... is believed to have originated through the interest of President Mitterrand.'

Europe against Cancer is the best known and longest running special EC public health programme. The first cancer programme (an Action Plan covering the period 1987–9) was targeted at known carcinogens and behaviours associated with risk (CECs 1993a). It was intended to provide support for screening programmes, public education about risky behaviours and it sought to popularise a 'ten-point Code against Cancer' (see Figure 13.5).

The Commission's 1994 proposal for a third Action Plan (1995–9) to combat cancer trumpets the success and wide support for the first two Action Plans, whilst carefully noting that the Commission's role is intended to be that of a 'catalyst and a stimulant to Member States' own national actions against cancer' (CECs 1994a: 30).

Figure 13.5

EUROPEAN CODE AGAINST CANCER

Committee of Cancer Experts:

'If the European Code were respected, there would be a significant reduction in the number of deaths from cancer in the Community; the decrease could be about 15% by the year 2000'

CERTAIN CANCERS MAY BE AVOIDED:

1. Do not smoke
   Smokers, stop as quickly as possible and do not smoke in the presence of others
2. Moderate your consumption of alcoholic drinks, beers, wines or spirits
3. Avoid excessive exposure to the sun
4. Follow health and safety instructions at work concerning production, handling, or use of any substance which may cause cancer.

> Your general health will benefit from following two commandments which may also reduce the risk of some cancers:

5. Frequently eat fresh fruit and vegetables and cereals with a high fibre content
6. Avoid becoming overweight and limit your intake of fatty foods

MORE CANCERS WILL BE CURED IF DETECTED EARLY

7. See a doctor if you notice an unexplained change: appearance of a lump, a change in a mole or abnormal bleeding
8. See a doctor if you have persistent problems, such as persistent cough, a persistent hoarseness, a change in bowel habits or an unexplained weight loss

> For women:

9. Have a cervical smear regularly
10. Check your breasts regularly and, if possible, undergo mammography at regular intervals above the age of 50

Based on *European File*, September 1990, 11–12/90, page 7.

The formulation of policy in relation to tobacco advertising has been particularly problematic for the Commission. The case for the Commission, the Council and the Parliament to act more decisively – even if that means confrontation and trouble with the governments of some Member States – has been made forcefully by the Economic and Social Committee (which has the role of advising the Council of Ministers on draft European legislation). In an Opinion issued in September 1994, on the Commission's Action Plan (1995–9) to combat cancer, the Economic and Social Committee observed that 'this is not the first time that the Committee has had to lament the blatant contradiction between the anti-smoking campaign and the Community funding of tobacco producers' (ESC 1994: para. 3.4.3).

European health-related research, supported by the Commission, has also cast the health services of some Member States in an unfavourable light. The *Independent*'s medical editor reported that:

> Delays in getting treatment, rather than the treatment itself, may account for poor results for breast, lung, ovary and cervical cancer in women and stomach and colon cancer in both sexes. The proportion of British patients with stomach cancer surviving for five years after diagnosis is about half the European average.
>
> (Hall 1995: 6)

Hall goes on to quote Michael Coleman of the London School of Hygiene and Tropical Medicine, who drew attention to 'evidence in the medical press that shows there is at least concern about the efficiency and speed at which GPs arrange for patients to be seen in hospital'.

It may prove very difficult for European Commission staff to avoid conflicts with the governments of Member States about the handling and presentation of information from studies such as that undertaken by Eurocare into cancer survival rates. A united effort against Europe's major health scourges cannot be guaranteed to lead to increased harmony amongst Member States, and may well raise politically inconvenient questions and issues.

Europe Against AIDS

Experience with the Europe against Cancer programme en-couraged the Commission and European health ministers to support another Community public health campaign known as Europe against AIDS. The key Council Decision to launch the programme was taken in June 1991. The initial AIDS programme (which ran from 1991 to 1993) was aimed at promoting preventive actions and emphasised information and education. In March and September 1993 the Commis-sion extolled the strengths of the work on AIDS and ob-tained the support of health ministers to continue the Europe against AIDS programme on into 1994.

AIDS and some other communicable diseases were said to have 'been identified as a priority for Community ac-tion' because they resulted in high levels of mortality and morbidity and because they had a profound impact on the quality of life as well as major socio-economic effects, such as high health care and treatment costs, and considerable absenteeism and unfitness for work (CEC 1994b). It was also the Commission's view that there were actions which could be taken that would limit their spread and, most im-portantly, that there 'would be added value from the Com-munity undertaking actions, particularly through economies of scale' (CECs 1994b). Once again, it is noteworthy that the priority given to AIDS has reflected consensus amongst elected representatives and national leaders about the ap-propriateness of a European health policy dimension (CECs 1994b).

Information published as part of the Commission's 1994 proposal for an AIDS and communicable diseases programme underlines the community of fear that exists about the spread of AIDS and the links between AIDS and other communi-cable diseases. Just 86 people were recorded as suffering from AIDS in 1982 – a number that had increased to over 13 500 by 1990. The increase continues, but at a slower rate, and by June 1993 nearly 89 000 EC citizens were officially recorded as suffering from AIDS. Whilst the Commission had no precise figures on those people in the EC who were HIV positive, it drew on World Health Organisation estimates that put the number at 500 000, and drew attention to the 'recent resurgence of tuberculosis, often associated with AIDS' (CECs 1993: paras 63 and 64).

The Europe against AIDS programme has been designed to give special emphasis to health education initiatives aimed at those who have only recently reached sexual maturity: 'activities targeted at young people in the field of culture, communication and information' (CECs 1994b). But Europe against AIDS represents only a part of the common European AIDS effort. Other EC policies highlight the role that research into disease can play. At the heart of the EC's research efforts into disease has been the BIOMED programme, which had a total budget of over ECU 130 million between 1990 and 1994 (EHMA 1994a) and included work on AIDS and other infectious diseases (CECs 1994b).

Few would disagree with the conclusion of a recent appraisal of priorities and directions for EU health policy:

> Aids is of particular importance at a Union level because of its increasing incidence, the absence of a vaccine or a cure, the potential impact of increasing mobility on future incidence and the scope for prevention.
>
> (Abel-Smith *et al.* 1995: 15)

European Policy and Drugs Dependency

If ever there were a field in which the advantages of European co-operation seem to be undeniable, then it is substance abuse and drug control. The community of interest that exists among Member States relates not only to control of the spread of AIDS amongst injecting substance abusers and their sexual partners, but also to the interaction of different drug control regimes, operating within a Union which champions a single market and the free movement of its citizens.

European documents are filled with statements about the need to promote integrated approaches to combating the use of illicit drugs. The Commission's activities on the public health front address one of three key elements identified in the three *European Plans to Combat Drugs* (1990 1992 and 1994), namely, *Action on Demand Reduction* (CECs 1994c). The other two key elements illustrate how far it is thought

European policy-makers will have to reach in order to combat substance abuse: *Action to Combat Illicit Trafficking* and *Action at the International Level.*

So far as measures to reduce substance abuse are concerned, the emphasis on combating drug dependence mirrors those in other public health programmes supported by the Commission – specifically, emphases on health education and information activities (CECs 1993a).

Other aspects of the European policy objective to reduce demand are aimed at supporting the social and occupational reintegration of drug addicts and actions which target high-risk groups of substance abusers, such as intravenous drug users.

One of the principal problems faced by policy-makers, including those who are directly charged with promoting European collaboration, is the poor quality and limited comparability of much of the data that exist on morbidity from substance abuse. Because the trade in illicit drugs is illegal, obtaining accurate information presents substantial difficulties. The desire to improve the arrangements for sharing information and co-ordinating policy led to the establishment of the European Committee to Combat Drugs (CELAD) in 1989. A European Monitoring Centre for Drugs and Drug Addiction (EMCDDA) was established in 1994 on the recommendation of CELAD. EMCDDA, which is based in Lisbon, has the task of providing European governments and institutions with comparable data on substance abuse and of developing networks embracing national drug information centres, specialised agencies and international bodies (Bainbridge 1995: 195). Once again the role of Europe's political leaders in shaping the European health policy agenda should not be underestimated. As the Commission's 1994 Communication on its *Action Plan to Combat Drugs* makes clear:

> The wide range of initiatives adopted by the Council and the European Parliament demonstrates the great importance that they attach to this problem and their view that action to tackle it is needed at Community level.
>
> (CECs 1994c: para. 20)

Article 129

Despite the lack of a secure legal basis for developing an EC-wide health policy EC leaders found at the end of the 1980s and the beginning of the 1990s that the EC had acquired a public health role which the European Commission was actively managing. When the Maastricht Treaty on European Union was signed in February 1992 it reflected a desire to regularise and develop that health role and included a provision detailing a public health competence. Article 129 came into force in November 1993 (see Figure 13.6). Some Member States took the view that the new public health provision was no more than a tidying up measure. The Department of Health, responding on behalf of the UK government to a House of Commons Health Committee report on *The European Community and Health Policy*, clearly took this view:

> the public health article (A. 129) . . . [avoids] references to the delivery of health care, which is the responsibility of Member States . . . [and] places Community action on health competence on a sounder legal footing.
>
> (Department of Health 1992: para 1.2)

However, Article 129 does appear to extend and enhance the role of the Commission considerably, most particularly the role of Directorate-General V (DGV). DGV deals with employment, industrial relations and social policy issues and contains the European Commission's Public Health Unit, established in the late 1980s.

What Can Be Done?

Article 129 empowers the Commission to lend its support to Member States in order to encourage co-operation between them and ensure a high level of human health protection throughout the EU. It gives a wide-ranging authority to the Commission to build health protection into all its activities and policy-making work. The fact that public health proposals from the Commission do not have to have the unanimous support of Member States also seems to enhance

Figure 13.6

ARTICLE 129

1. The Community shall contribute towards ensuring a high level of human health protection by encouraging co-operation between Member States and, if necessary, lending support to their action.

Community action shall be directed towards the prevention of diseases, in particular the major health scourges, including drug dependence, by promoting research into their causes and their transmission, as well as health information and education.

2. Member States shall, in liaison with the Commission, co-ordinate among themselves their policies and programmes in the areas referred to in paragraph 1. The Commission may, in close contact with the Member States, take any useful initiative to promote such coordination.

3. The Community and the Member States shall foster co-operation with third countries and the competent international organisations in the sphere of public health.

4. In order to contribute to the achievement of the objective referred to in this Article, the Council:

 – acting in accordance with the procedure referred to in Article 189b, after consulting the Economics and Social Committee of the Regions, shall adopt incentive measures, excluding any harmonisation of the laws and regulations of the Member States.

 – acting by a qualified majority on a proposal from the Commission, shall adopt recommendations.

---

the prospects for European health policy-making. But this apparent empowerment of the Commission is very carefully qualified. The Commission is expressly forbidden, in accordance with the principle of subsidiarity, from straying beyond public health issues into the health care/health service territory reserved for individual governments. It is required to steer clear of the management, funding and organisation of health services in Member States (see Sheldon 1993). Harmonisation of national policies, the target of so much of the adverse commentary on the work of the Commission in the British press, is specifically ruled out.

The limitation of European health policy-making to measures of primary and secondary prevention – in other words, to measures which 'make the onset of disease less likely' and to actions which are directed at the early detection of disease – is also generally thought likely to hamper the Commission's work in future years, because 'it is difficult to plan a coherent prevention programme ... without there being any implications for treatment programmes' (EHMA 1994a; see also EMHA 1994b).

Perhaps the most significant restraint on the exercise of the Commission's health competence is that it has only a small budget and limited staff resources to deploy in order to develop and implement public health policies. The Commission has fewer than 130 full-time equivalent staff committed for the major part of their time to health work (Public Health Unit 1995). Also, the annual budgets for each of the principal European public health programmes (drug dependency, AIDS and cancer) are set to remain below ECU 15 million between 1995 and 1999 (CECs 1994d; 1994b; 1994a). By way of comparison it should be noted that the Health Education Authority, based in London (a Special Health Authority which has just part of the responsibility for public health work in the United Kingdom) spends over £37 million (or ECU 48.8 million) a year on its health education work (Health Education Authority, 1995).

Given the potential for developing the work of the Commission's Public Health Unit and the Commission's other health-related responsibilities, a good deal of attention has been focused on the fact that, despite the adoption of Article 129, public health makes up only a part of the activities of DGV, whilst other health-related work is dispersed throughout the Commission. There does seem to be a good case for establishing a new Directorate-General which could devote all its energy to health issues, including the continuous review of the health impact of EU legislation and policy.

The Annual Report

One solid achievement, flowing directly from the adoption of Article 129, was the production of the first annual report *On the State of Health in the European Community* (CECs 1995).

The report has been produced in conjunction with the World
Health Organisation's Regional Office for Europe and deals
with health in just 12 EU states (i.e. excluding the three
new members, Sweden, Finland and Austria, which became
full members of the EU in January 1995). The logic of producing a health report is, in the words of its authors, that
'health problems are tending to become more and more
international in character... [and] similar across countries
as well' and because it is important and worthwhile to lay
the foundations for 'common solutions and to increase the
exchange of experience and expertise' (CECs 1995: 1).

The prescription offered for improving the health of
Europe's citizens is one that focuses on the role of health
educators in changing behaviour, on social and economic
policies which tackle social exclusion and on improvements
in health data which can underpin prevention. The Commission's first European health status report also promises
further reports which will be targeted at 'important developments in health status... [and] take account of the concerns of the Community population' (CECs 1995: i). It is a
formula for advancing the European health agenda which
reflects a decade of Commission activity in the health field,
which has set out to work with the grain of Community politics
rather than against it. That is why the full range of proposals contained in a research report presented to Padraig
Flynn, the Commissioner responsible for Employment and
Social Affairs, whose brief includes public health, about the
future role of the European Community may have given rise
to some anxieties within the Commission (cited in Abel-Smith
et al. 1995).

Amongst the recommendations on health put before the
Commissioner was one calling on the EU to 'coordinate the
output of doctors in Member States' (Abel-Smith *et al.* 1995:
129). The relevance of the recommendation to health care
cost containment, a common European concern, is unques-
tionable – the political difficulties likely to be encountered
by the Commission in securing greater co-operation are easy
to imagine. Another recommendation, which calls upon the
EU to co-ordinate technology assessments, reflects the research team's view that 'technology is increasingly regarded
as the main cause of health care cost escalation' (Abel-Smith

et al. 1995: xx). The risks of becoming embroiled in commercially sensitive issues, linked to health care costs, are likely to influence the Commission to proceed slowly and with great caution.

The research team's work and recommendations quite rightly reflect a definition of health which associates good health with the opportunity to enjoy full membership of society. Its concern with social exclusion led the team's members to recommend that the 'Community should press ahead with its initiative to establish a minimum income in each Member State for health as well as other reasons' (Abel-Smith *et al.* 1995) – a recommendation that requires a much more expansive role for European health policy-makers in future, and one that is unlikely to be endorsed by recent British health ministers.

The issue of social exclusion and health status is one from which political leaders may run, but from which they are unlikely to be able to hide. It has been coupled by the Commission with the question of cost containment. The strength of the Commission's motivation to become an important player in the European debate about limiting growth in health service spending is in fact closely allied to its concern about social exclusion. The Commission (1993a) argues that 'lower service spending has disproportionate effects on the poor, sick and old. Hence the need for well-balanced responses to the inevitable pressures to adjust health spending . . .' (Commission of the European Communities 1993a: para. 6).

CONCLUSION

Social policy, including health policy, in the EU has attracted considerable attention since the signing of the Maastricht Treaty. Some observers (e.g. Weale 1994) have offered a variety of typologies which can help to sustain and elaborate different views about how the social and political dimensions of the EU might develop. Of Weale's three typologies, the 'market liberal position' is closest to the EU's past and current role in the health field. It seems extremely unlikely that the Commission will be permitted by Member States to acquire either the resources or the powers that are necessary for it to become much more than a clearing house for ideas and information and a manager of demonstration projects. That should not be read as support for the view that the elaboration of the Commission's public health competence under Article 129 has little significance. If Europe's social partners are prepared to play a constructive and active part, then the co-ordinating role that the Commission is well placed to undertake could make a valuable contribution to shaping European health care systems: thus enabling and assisting the health care systems of Member States to devote more effort to promoting health and preventing illness and to make more effective use of resources that are devoted to clinical work.

REFERENCES

Abel-Smith, B., Figueras, J., Holland, W., McKee, M. and Mossialos, E. (1995), *Choices in Health Policy: An Agenda for the European Union*, Office for Official Publication of the European Communities and Dartmouth, Luxembourg.

Bainbridge, T. with A. Teasdale (1995), *The Penguin Companion to European Union*, Penguin Books, London.

Brearly, S. (1992), 'Medical Education', in T. Richards (ed.), *Medicine in Europe*, British Medical Journal, London.

Burstall, M.L. (1990), *1992 and the Regulation of the Pharmaceutical Industry*, IEA Health Series No. 9, The IEA Health & Welfare Unit, London.

Commission of the European Communities (1990), *Europe against Cancer*, European File 11–12/90, CECs, Brussels.

Commission of the European Communities (1993a), *Commission Communication on the Framework for Action in the Field of Public Health*, Com(93) 559 final, CECs, Brussels.

Commission of the European Communities (1993b), *General Framework for Action by the Commission of the European Communities in the Field of Safety, Hygiene and Health Protection at Work 1994–2000]*, Com(93) 560 final, CECs, Brussels.

Commission of the European Communities (1994a), *Communication from the Commission Concerning the Fight against Cancer in the Context of the Framework for Action in the Field of Public Health and Proposal for a European Parliament and Council Decision Adopting an Action Plan 1995–1999 to Combat Cancer within the Framework of Action in the Field of Public Health*, Com(94) 83 final, CECs, Brussels.

Commission of the European Communities (1994b), *Communication from the Commission concerning a Community Action Programme on the Prevention of AIDS and Certain Other Communicable Diseases in the Context of the Framework for Action in the Field of Public Health* and *Proposal for a European Parliament and Council Decision Adopting a Programme of Community Action on the Prevention of AIDS and Certain Other Communicable Diseases within the Framework for Action in the Field of Public Health*, Com(94) 413 final, CECs, Brussels.

Commission of the European Communities (1994c), *Communication from the Commission to the Council and the European Parliament on a European Union Action Plan to Combat drugs (1995–1999)*, Com(94) 234 final, CECs, Brussels.

Commission of the European Communities (1994d), *Communication from the Commission Community Action in the Field of Drug Dependence* and *Proposal for a European Parliament and Council Decision Adopting a Programme of Community Action on the Prevention of Drug Dependence within the Framework for Action in the Field of Public Health (1995– 2000)*, Com(94) 223 final, CECs, Brussels.

Commission of the European Communities (1995), *Report from the Commission to the Council, the European Parliament, the Economic and Social Committee and the Committee or the Regions on the State of Health in the European Community*, CEC/V/F/1/LUX/13/95, CECs, Brussels.

Department of Health (1992), *European Community and Health Policy: Response by the Government to the Third Report from the Health Committee, Session 1991–92*, Cm 2014, July, HMSO, London.

Economic and Social Committee (1994), *Opinion of the Economic and Social Committee on the Proposal for a European Parliament and Council Decision Adopting an Action Plan 1995–1999 to Combat Cancer within the Framework for Action in the Field of Public Health* (Com(94) 83 final), CECs, Brussels.

European Healthcare Management Association (1994a), *European Union and Health*, European Healthcare Management Association, Brussels.

European Healthcare Management Association (1994b), *Healthcare and European Integration*, Second Conference, EHMA, Toledo.

Ham, C. (1992), 'The European Community and UK, Health and Health Services', in A. Harrison and S. Bruscini (eds.), *Health Care UK 1991*, King's Fund Institute, London.

Hall, C. (1995), 'UK "failing in diagnosis of cancer patients"', *Independent*, 17 May.

Hantrais, L. (1995), *Social Policy in the European Union*, Macmillan, London.

Health Education Authority (1995), *Investing in Health*, Annual Report 1994/95, HEA, London.

House of Commons Health Committee (1992), Third Report 1991–92, *The European Community and Health Policy (Report together with an Appendix, the Proceedings of the Committee, Minutes of Evidence and Appendices)*, HC. 180, HMSO, London.

ter Kuile, B.H. (1992), 'Introduction', in H.E.G.M. Hermans, A.F. Casparie and J.H.P. Paelinck (eds.), *Health Care in Europe after 1992*, Dartmouth, Aldershot.

Public Health Unit – Directorate General V (1995), personal communication with Commission staff about numbers of civil servants and Community public health policy resources.

Sauer, F. (1992), 'The European Community's Pharmaceutical Policy', in H.E.G.M. Hermans, A.F. Casparie and J.H.P. Paelinck (eds.), *Health Care in Europe after 1992*, Dartmouth, Aldershot.

Sheldon, T. (1993), 'Vive la difference?', *Health Service Journal*, 15 July.

Smith, T. (1992), 'European Health Challenges', in T. Richards (ed.), *Medicine in Europe*, British Medical Journal, London.

Stallknect, K. (1992), 'Nursing in Europe' in T. Richards (ed.), *Medicine in Europe*, British Medical Journal, London.

Taylor, D. (1992), 'Prescribing in Europe – Forces for Change', in T. Richards (ed.), *Medicine in Europe*, British Medical Journal, London.

Turner, J. (1995), 'What Ken Collins Has to Say', *Eurohealth*, Vol. 1, No. 1, June.

Weale, A. (1994), 'Social Policy and the European Union', *Social Policy and Administration*, Vol. 28, No. 1, March, pp. 5–19.

14 The Emergent European Union: Democratic Legitimacy and the 1996 Inter-governmental Conference

Juliet Lodge

INTRODUCTION

The obsession in the European Union (EU) with the issue of whether or not it conforms to some ideal type of a liberal-democratic, representative polity believed to typify contemporary West European regimes is honorable and symptomatic of the extent to which the concept of the EU and working within it has become entrenched in the minds of government and non-government actors as well as the public in the Member States. That efforts should be undertaken to make the emergent EU polity conform to liberal, democratic practice based on open, transparent, accountable and representative (if not altogether efficient) government is laudable. It is also a response to two forces: prospective enlargement to states with totalitarian traditions; and the growth of cynicism and disaffection from political processes among the populace of the EU's Member States.

Public distrust of government has increased. Public suspicion that government is less than open and evades an assumed obligation to act 'in the common good' of the majority has led to a sense of alienation from political processes and a disinclination to see government as being based on the rule of law. The notion of 'citizenship' introduced through the Maastricht Treaty has not yet countered this. The view that

government operates in ways that are less than fair and open
– whether at local, regional, national or supranational level
– has spurred the decline in the perceived legitimacy of the
systems of governance across the EU. Consequently, it is
not accurate to surmise that issues of democratic legitimacy
and democratic deficits are unique and intrinsic features of
a flawed emergent polity at the supranational level only.
They are not. But the democratic deficits at other levels are
accentuated by probing the extent and nature of, as well as
possible remedies to, the democratic deficit at EU level.

It is possible to argue that modern government is so complex as to elude the checks and balances characteristic of
liberal-democratic norms and practices. However, few subscribe to the view that the EU should develop as a Eurocracy.
European integration is a function and a product of political processes. Decisions and financial redistributive mechanisms impinge directly on the lives of those who live within
the boundaries of the Member States. The founding treaties
entrench commitments which imply the existence of checks
and balances on the unlawful exercise of power and which
guarantee redress against the infringement of rights inherent
in EU decisions. In short, there is a link between the concept of the governed and the EC/EU's bodies that collec-
tively might loosely be termed the EU's putative 'government'.

However, it is not simply the fact of the direct effect EC/
EU law takes in the Member States, or of the supremacy of
EC/EU law, which inclines observers to advocate the development of institutions, practices, norms and decision rules
in line with liberal-democratic and parliamentary parameters.
The evolution of the EU polity cannot be separated from
the wider Euro-geopolitical environment. The political legacies
of fascism and totalitarianism commended liberal-democratic
practice. That is right and proper. The question is not, therefore, whether Eurocracy should be promoted as the most
efficient, cheap and effective means of meeting the wealth
of goals advanced today, but how technocratic procedures
and political processes operating within the EU at all levels
might be effectively scrutinised and rendered open, effective, legitimate, democratic and accountable. It is, therefore,
not altogether helpful to draw parallels between national
and supranational practices in the hope of revealing the

EU polity as inherently and irretrievably flawed compared to national polities.

However, maximising open, democratic government and reconciling it with the often contradictory requirements of effective and efficient government is especially difficult at the EU level. This is partly because of the complexity, diversity, heterogeneity and number of systems operating within the EU's component states and across them. Can new technologies be put to the service of contemporary democracy as devotees of the Internet suggest? Or are the problems of modern government and the difficulties associated with the imperfect implementation of EU legislation by national and sub-national authorities with differing briefs, traditions, practices, constituents and interests so vast as to preclude the EU from evolving into a liberal, democratic polity at all?

The answer to this rhetorical question must be 'no'. It is not that the EU lacks the institutional and structural attributes associated with democratic polities. Rather, the processes for ensuring openness, transparency, democracy and responsiveness are imperfectly operated. Such imperfections are the product both of deliberate evasion (notably by member governments via the Council of Ministers and the imperfect power-sharing with the elected arm of the EU's legislature – the European Parliament) and the rudimentary nature of the EU's incipient civil society. It is true that compared to national polities, the EU appears weaker in terms of its democratic credentials. But appearances can be deceptive and some of the EU's Member States' systems of government leave much to be desired in terms of openness and the opportunities for participatory democracy as the furore over 'transparency' in the EU revealed. Moreover, it is misleading to suppose that the EU should or could evolve in a linear fashion from, for example, liberalism to liberal democracy. The former is not a necessary transition stage. However, there is some agreement on the essentials of any organisation purporting to uphold liberal democratic values, norms and practices. What are they?

First, it is broadly agreed that the organisation – in this case, the EU – must be limited in scope and checked in practice. A constitution by itself will not guarantee freedom for individuals unless there is an appropriate Bill of Rights and modes of participation. Second, liberal values embrace the idea that state interference in the private sphere of the citizen must be limited to what is essential: arbitrary state power must be curtailed. Third, liberal democratic values underline the notion of elected representatives of the community governing within the rule of law. Hence, constitutional control must be entrenched. There must be opportunities for 'the people' to exercise choice through constitutional, legal mechanisms to facilitate the election and removal from office of governing officals. There must be provision for universal suffrage; the right to run for government office; and freedom of association and expression. Liberal democracy is widely held to entrench democratic accountability through open elections. Accountability in other areas – economic, social, cultural, etc. – may be practised differently. But the principles of accountability and participation are firmly rooted in the institutions that give expression to the political ideals held for the society. They are, of course, meaningless if they cannot be operationalised. That is clearly not the case in the EU.

Democratic legitimacy in the EU has traditionally been seen in limited terms as a problem of securing the election of the European Parliament by direct, universal suffrage. The issue is more complex and multifaceted. Legitimacy is contested. It is conditional and evolutionary. It is expressed through the dispute over the appropriate balance of power and exercise of authority among the key supranational decision-making institutions and the argument over the issue of decision-making appropriateness, efficiency, transparency and accountability. The continuing problem of democratic legitimacy inheres in the EU's crisis of political authority and identity. The new provisions introduced through the Maastricht process may delegitimise rather than reinforce legitimacy: they are essential but not sufficient preconditions to remedying the democratic deficit and democratic legitimacy.

IGC 1996

The deliberations over the holding of an Intergovernmental Conference (IGC) in 1996 highlighted the diffuse nature of the EU's democratic deficit. Informed discussion of Maastricht having neither taken place across the EU nor within the Member States led domestic political forces to continue using the EU and European integration broadly conceived as a scapegoat and evade their own political responsibilities vis-à-vis their electorates and citizens. The unintentional effect, however, was a questioning on the latter's part of the degree to which politicians could be trusted and the degree to which the national, let alone EU-level, political systems were 'democratic'.

While governments glibly deployed the rhetoric of insisting on openness and transparency on the part of the EU Commission, they simultaneously endorsed and insisted on measures to do precisely the opposite. The openness of decisions were accompanied by a series of restrictions on public (and even civil service) access to EU information, which seriously compromised openness and which showed the extent to which certain governments were loathe to promote transparency. The discrepancies in the positions of governments regarding access to documentation and information were such that the very principle of the quintessential equality of EU citizens was undermined by governments which, in the past, had adopted legislation to prevent discrimination on the basis of nationality, but which now restricted the access of their own nationals to information in the EU open and available to other EU nationals.

What this skirmishing showed was that the alleged democratic deficit in the EU was both more complex and less supranational than had fondly been believed. It was more complex in that it had horizontal and vertical dimensions. It was less supranational in that national constraints rather than supranational practice exacerbated the democratic deficit and compounded the information deficit. The information deficit had been identified as but one reason in explaining the public's lack of enthusiasm for the EU. Rectifying it was part of a Commission strategy designed to heighten citizens' awareness of (1) how easily and freely EU information could be attained; (2) the EU and its relevance to their daily lives; (3) their rights, obligations and entitlements; and (4) the local impact of the EU.

Many of these issues inform much of the debate about

precise policy areas that have been identified for discussion within the context of the 1996 IGC. There is clearly a feeling that openness must be addressed in all its ramifications. However, it is also apparent that the notion of the democratic deficit is associated with particular institutions, their inter-relationship, the EU's policy-making and legislative procedures and the highly delicate matter of the pillar structure of the Maastricht Treaty (the TEU). It is not surprising, therefore, that in some government quarters (notably in the United Kingdom) the need for an IGC was somewhat disingenuously contested.

The Maastricht Treaty contains numerous references to the 1996 Intergovernmental Conference (IGC). Consolidation and intensification of existing mechanisms engage the EU in a dynamic process of change. Neither the institutions' nor the enlarged EU's capacity to act and have credibility can be enhanced unless practices which impair the institutions' capacity to interact effectively and efficiently are eliminated. Sophistry over a federal Europe versus a Europe of nation-states or a variable geometry, multi-speed Europe needs to give way to mutual acceptance of the reality of the EU. The consent of the people to further reform is desirable, but it is questionable that the holding of a series of contemporaneous referendums in the Member States upon the completion of the next IGC reforms will cement legitimacy. The EU will seek to avoid a repetition of the 'Maastricht' ratification fiascos and referendums, which evaded the real issue of the kind of Europe that was being developed.

The EU faces one of the greatest challenges in its history. Not only is it confronted by states seeking rapid accession to it, but its own internal policy-making procedures and legitimacy are contested. The acrimonious political confrontations occasioned in some Member States during the ratification process to approve the TEU agreed at Maastricht revived a debate about the EU's *raison d'être* and orientation. The spectre of a monolithic, bureaucratic, overcentralised, intrusive, closed and undemocratic federal system was raised, and not quite eclipsed, as the TEU reforms were implemented. However, whereas in the past it had often been argued – not least by British politicians – that reforms should be gradual, modest and relatively cost-free, the political imperatives in the aftermath of 1989 encouraged a bolder approach These factors, combined with continued economic problems within the Member States, highlighted the fact that useful as the reforms introduced to facilitate the completion of the Single Market had been, they were insufficient to meet the challenges and opportunities confronting the Member States in the 1990s.

Change was then as now ineluctable. Reform in the scope of the EU's competence is necessary if the EU is to meet domestic and outside expectations that it can both act as a unitary actor and is willing and financially and politically able to shoulder greater responsibilities commensurate with its pretensions to being a major international player. In addition, while the EU still clings to the notion of itself as a civilian power devoid of military intention or capacity, political rhetoric suggests that it should assume responsibility for preserving and promoting peaceful resolution of conflicts and socioeconomic and political stability inside the EU and on its immediate eastern flanks. This still sits most uneasily with its far more limited preferred role and competences, defined first by the Rome Treaty and then by the amendments introduced through the Single European Act (SEA). In the 1980s, external pressures meant that it had to contemplate expanding its competences, and hence its financial operational capabilities, into areas once regarded as taboo. Above all, the SEA's tentative incursion into the 'economic and political aspects of security' had to be reinterpreted: a defence – that is, a military component – to security had to be recognised; relations with the WEU and NATO had to be reappraised; and security itself examined from the external and the domestic, internal perspectives of a border-free single market. Consequently, a far greater number of domestic agencies were to become directly involved in implementing and trying to influence and shape EU policy. A far greater number, too, were therefore to be concerned with practices that restricted access to information or deprived local representatives of the ability to influence, let alone approve, policy proposals they would ultimately have to implement. The broad issues of accountability, combined with pressure for greater openness at all levels of government, meant that a more refined appreciation of the nature of the democratic deficit and democratic legitimacy was necessary. It also meant that the realities of the changing parameters of EU governance had to be confronted.

The issue of whether this meant the demise of the nation-state and the creation of a Euro-superstate had been partly dealt with through the semantic nuances of subsidiarity. But this could not obscure the qualitative change in European integration that had occurred on the eve of the 1990s. This change is encapsulated in the TEU: an expedient response to myriad pressures surrounding the EC Member States at the time. As such, and as the various annexes to the TEU reveal, it was recognised that, just as with the Single Act, further reforms would have to be introduced within the short to medium term. However, it should also be recalled that during the deliberations on modifying the Rome Treaty to incorporate amendments collected together in the shape of the Single European Act, further major treaty reform was not anticipated. Indeed, the SEA merely required the Member States to consider whether any revision of Title III (on political co-operation in foreign affairs) was necessary five years after the SEA came into force, that is, in 1992 (Corbett 1993: 7).

THE MAASTRICHT TREATY

The TEU expanded the scope of European integration significantly. The TEU was divided into three pillars (known as the temple approach). This separated supranational (EC) decision-making rules and competences from two inter-governmental pillars: one on foreign policy and the other on judicial co-operation. Both were subject to intergovernmental decision-making: government autonomy was respected and national governmental supremacy remained unchallenged. Neither could function without significant inputs from supra-national institutions, notably the Commission. Both pillars were candidates for subsequent incorporation into the *acquis communautaire* (a process sometimes called communitisation) and are likely to become supranational competences in future.

The TEU widened the area of the EC institutions' competence and entrenched intergovernmentalism in a supranational treaty. This was a major break with past practice. The SEA had paved the way for this development by incorporating a special Title (Title III) on Political Co-operation in a single document that primarily encompassed reforms to existing articles of the Rome Treaty. Title III was especially significant, however, because it broached the taboo subject of security. Whereas the SEA referred to the economic and political aspects of security, the TEU referred specifically to defence and the development of a common foreign and security policy and to the possibility of developing a common defence in future. Moreover, it explicitly granted the supranational institutions a role in decision-making in this area. (For example, the Commission is to be fully associated with common foreign and security policy (CFSP) work (Article J9) and recognised the potential of the WEU as the EU's operational defence arm.

SECURITY AND THE DEMOCRATIC DEFICIT

The internal and external facets of security are inextricably linked. The problems, for example, created by immigration in the wake of regional conflicts (both refugees and asylum-seekers) raise questions that cannot neatly be addressed in one pillar as opposed to the other. Moreover, they directly encroach on areas of EU competence. Since such sensitive matters are also affected by decisions in these areas, over which co-operation among EU states has been developing in a piecemeal fashion, national divisions are more pronounced and, consequently, national governments are much more anxious about declaring their hand: in other words, openness and transparency conflict with their desire to bargain and negotiate behind closed doors. Whilst a case for greater transparency can be made, it is obvious that the demands of international diplomacy frequently require secrecy. How are these conflicting positions to be reconciled? Should, for example, all issues under the justice and home affairs pillar of the TEU be made justiciable and open to effective parliamentary scrutiny and influence at the EU level? Or would that compromise effectiveness and efficiency? What should be the priority? Does experience in respect of the common foreign and security policy pillar – the CFSP – offer any clues?

Openness and the CFSP

In theory, the European Parliament has a limited role in respect of the CFSP. In practice, it has developed its assent rights in such a way as to enhance its ability to influence both foreign policy decisions and related spending. Formally, it has the right to be kept *informed regularly* by the Council Presidency and Commission and may be *consulted* by the Presidency on the *main aspects and basic choices of the CFSP*. It may question the Council, make recommendations to it, hold an annual debate on the CFSP and exercise all its existing (and potentially far more important) rights in the external relations field. These include the right to approve measures with financial implications (e.g. financial protocols attached to trade agreements) and enlargement and association agree-ments. Used imaginatively, of course, these rights amount to a veto power, as the European Parliament demonstrated when it insisted on an agreement with Israel being amended to the benefit of Palestinian exporters. Similarly, it stated that it would not approve EU enlargement to Turkey until that country respected human rights. It also insisted that any enlargement would be suspended pending institutional reform in general.

The TEU expanded its powers in this delicate foreign affairs area where parliaments in Europe tend to have negligible roles. The European Parliament can discuss any foreign affairs issue it chooses, since it alone has the right to set its agenda. This is a potent means of publicising matters, but it must be remembered that the new TEU powers are discretionary and relatively untried. In the past, neither the Council nor the Commission has yielded much to the European Parliament without a fight. For real progress to be made, it has always been essential for the European Parliament to have allies within both institutions. There has been a good deal of confrontation between them as the European Parliament has tried to assert the principle of open government, usually by seeking reforms in legislative procedures and to the voting practices of the Council of Ministers. More recently, it has also tried to ensure that as the scope of EU policy competences has grown, there has not been a commensurate growth in the democratic deficit. In this, it has not been altogether successful. The foreign affairs and justice pillars of the TEU elude effective scrutiny let alone co-decision by MEPs, who have sought and still seek rectification of these omissions.

Moreover, it was clear that the functioning of the Single Market itself imposed new demands for supranational action on specific areas which had hitherto been seen as the preserve of national governments. The section on judicial and home affairs co-operation was a case in point. Labour mobility rules under the SEA's provisions on the 'Four Freedoms' (of movement of goods, persons, capital and services to realise the single market) meant that if internal frontiers were removed and the external frontier around the EU strengthened, there would be consequences for internal and external border controls of legal and illegal movement of persons and goods as well as customs formalities. This had implications for issues that had not formally been considered either at all within an EU context or only on an ad hoc intergovernmental basis through European Political Co-operation (EPC). Among such issues were immigration, refugee, asylum, police and anti-crime activities (Council Secretariat 1994).

The realisation of the single market impelled a need for, at a minimum, co-operation and later on a degree of co-ordination and harmonisation or approximation of national provisions in order to prevent the proliferation of discriminatory practices based on national rules which could be unfairly invoked or exploited, for example, by outsiders. There had been a marked reluctance on the part of some states (the United Kingdom again included) to advance supranational co-operation in these areas, with the result that five of the original six founded the Schengen group to take measures more quickly. This inner core not only drove progress forward but ensured that any measures they agreed conformed to EC provisions. Indeed, the Commission was fully consulted over these provisions, many of which then formed the basis for subsequent EC level action both through EPC (and the TREVI group, and later the K4 committee) and through the EC proper (Lodge 1992).

DEMOCRATIC BEHAVIOUR AND SUPRANATIONAL
ACTION IN INTERGOVERNMENTAL FIELDS:
THE EXAMPLE OF THE JHA

Racism, xenophobia, child prostitution, pornography, eco-
terrorism, Euro-wide telephone tapping, immigration, drug
trafficking, organised crime and nuclear plutonium smuggling are a test for both national governments and EU authorities. While all agree that action must be taken to combat
their growth, the mechanisms best suited to attaining this
are open to dispute. How the 15 respond affects the long-
term viability of the JHA.

That judicial co-operation among the 15 is desirable is
not doubted. What remains open to debate, however, is the
issue of how judicial co-operation can best be developed in
order to enable the Member States, within the context of
the EU, to safeguard internal security and to combat cross-
frontier crime. The 1996 IGC will have to confront some
extremely sensitive and delicate matters. Although it was
originally thought that the JHA pillar would develop only
very slowly, events have outpaced political endorsement. The
issues raised relating to judicial co-operation and internal
security cannot be evaded nor can they be dealt with solely
on the basis of bilateral intergovernment bargains. The re-
sultant serious implications for the exercise of judicial and
political authority in the EU are only just beginning to be
appreciated by several member governments.

At the heart of the matter is how judicial co-operation
should be accomplished: what should its scope be? What
institutional arrangements should exist? What should the
relationship be between policy and enforcement? What safeguards might be necessary in policing such sensitive areas
in order to prevent an abuse of power?

Operationally, what can be realistically accomplished? The
EU has limited personnel and minuscule budgets for these
activities compared to Member States' budgets. Confusion
persists over the precise meaning and interpretation of the
term 'security'. Some member governments' anxiety that the
current promotion of 'transparency' in EU decision-making
will lead to greater pressure domestically for more openness and public scrutiny of their own policies and national

and regional and local government-level action has deterred some governments from accepting the logic of transparency at the EU level. Consequently, some governments have been determined to limit severely public access to information. Some have been fearful of the consequences of appointing a Euro-Ombudsman. All this adds up to a lack of clarity about the proper scope and role of the instruments set up under Maastricht to develop EU competence in respect of the obligations under the justice and home affairs pillar of the treaty. Contradictions abound. Governments state their commitment to combating trans-frontier crime, but recoil from the operational implications of facilitating a co-ordinated response to enhance successful crime detection. The rudimentary nature of EU-wide let alone broader Euro-wide training of law enforcement agencies, for instance, illustrates this. Judicial co-operation may be highly desirable, but the absence of safeguards – such as a Euro-Bill of Rights – and effective parliamentary scrutiny and control powers is a matter of increasing public concern.

The notion of an EC citizen must be clarified. The European Parliament was quick to link the idea of *political* rights and obligations (such as the right to contest and vote in direct elections) to the far more limited concept of citizenship (Closa 1992), which derives solely from a concept of economic – that is, labour mobility – rights customarily inferred from the Rome Treaty and later the SEA and Single Market. Issues formerly chiefly regarded as technical have become politicised. As earlier problems over differing national practices in respect of the selection and vetting of officials in EU institutions covering sensitive (security) issues had shown, reconciling divergent practices uncovered the potential for discrimination on the basis of nationality – something the Rome Treaty proscribes. With politicisation has come a recognition of the need to ensure that decisions that are taken are seen as rightful and legitimate. As they impinge more directly on people's lives and as decisions taken within the EU setting are not subject to adequate parliamentary supervision at either the national or supranational level, the actual extent of the European Parliament's position in EU legislative processes has become a matter of wider political importance. The extent to which the European

Parliament has a power of co-decision over policies has come to symbolise the degree to which the EU system can be said to be open and democratic. This remains an important issue for the next IGC, as does, increasingly, the future of the JHA.

In the absence of an overarching accountable EU political authority, some would argue that it is neither proper nor feasible to tackle through a supranational arrangement questions that directly impinge on national sovereignty. At the same time, it is difficult to support the alternative view that co-operation in the absence of adequate oversight has been sufficient to attain the increasingly ambitious expectations and goal set for it. In some Member States, there was clearly disappointment that more had not been achieved. Why? The External Frontiers Convention was not adopted. The new instruments provided by Maastricht (joint actions, joint positions and conventions) have hardly been used. The one joint action adopted concerned visa requirements for school trips within the EU. It was decided that a child from a third country resident in a Member State would not need a visa for such trips. There was some debate as to whether or not this decision could have been taken under Pillar I. Reporting to the European Parliament in December, the German Council President Kanther outlined problems faced in devising satisfactory procedures to deal with drug smuggling, immigration and crime in the context of freedom of movement. He noted that of 800 criminal cases before the German courts in 1993, 60 per cent involved international criminal syndicates comprising people from 91 countries.

Difficulties are compounded by the fact that decisions have to be adopted in accordance with the Member States' respective constitutional requirements. This protracts decision-making. If Pillar III continues its separate existence, greater efforts will have to be made to co-ordinate policy with developments in Commission departments (such as DGV and those dealing with freedom of movement) to prevent overlaps and contradictory measures. The IGC will have to confront this regardless of general disappointment with Pillar III, which might otherwise induce some to favour its abolition. Instead, for a variety of reasons associated with the actual operation of the JHA and the commitment to redress

the democratic deficit at all levels, the IGC will have, at a
minimum, to ensure that any Pillar III actions are subject
to judicial review, even though such a reform of judicial co-
operation in matters of internal security goes to the core of
national sovereignty.

A QUESTION OF NATIONAL SOVEREIGNTY?

The Member States retain responsibility for maintaining law
and order and internal security, but the removal of internal
borders within the Single Market has repercussions for the
way in which civil and criminal matters are addressed. In
the Single Market devoid of internal frontiers, internal and
external security issues are no longer readily separable. Military
and defence issues also interface with internal security. The
enlarged EU has borders with Russia and Slovenia. There is
an increased burden on Member States in managing judicial co-operation in civil and criminal matters, and in safe-
guarding internal security. The two terms are easily but
erroneously conflated. Judicial and home affairs are dealt
with differently in the 15 Member States. This is exempli-
fied by the existence of ministers of justice and ministers of
home affairs. Their briefs vary. So, crucially, do their priorities. The administrative and operational demands on the
forces that have to forge and develop new co-operative mechanisms and cultures are heavy. The organisation of an EU-
wide system for exchanging information within a European
Police Office (Europol) is far from simple. A common interest in promoting co-operation exists, but a Euro-police
culture, for example, does not. Nor do common penalties.
Does the EU need them?

The principle behind advocacy of a system of common
penalities derives from those endorsed in practice by the
Council of Europe, for instance, in respect of the European
Convention on the Suppression of Terrorism where the basic
principle rests on the idea of apprehended suspects being
tried or extradited as appropriate. However, while the notion of common penalities for specific offences may have
the advantage of being transparent and clear, invoking them
could pose innumerable problems for individual states whose

judicial and political cultures differ substantially from those from whom a certain penalty is derived. The extradite or try principle alone proved extraordinarily problematic because for some states terrorism was seen as a political rather than a criminal offence and prosecuted accordingly.

Beyond this, of course, any system of common penalties would require substantial investment in cross-frontier training and information exchange from magistrate level upwards. This is desirable in itself.

The Treaty on European Union simply notes that EU action under Pillar III

> shall be in compliance with the European Convention for the Protection of Human Rights and Fundamental Freedoms of 4 November 1950 and the Convention relating to the Status of Refugees of 28 July 1951 and having regard to the protection afforded by Member States to persons persecuted on political grounds.

Again, the Member States diverge. There has been pressure in some quarters to develop an EU Bill of Rights.

Crime – A Proper Concern of the European Union?

It is no longer a matter of arguing that in the EU criminal matters should remain more or less the exclusive preserve of the Member States. It is true that national legal systems differ widely. It is equally true that much trans-frontier crime can only be tackled through trans-frontier co-operation. Facilitating that co-operation in order to combat crime would seem a logical response. Indeed, the Commission has shown through the operation of its small but effective agricultural fraud office that co-operation works. Over the years, the experience of co-operation first under European Political co-operation and the TREVI networks (now transformed into the K4 committee system) has yielded positive results.

However, piecemeal successes highlight both the operational limitations of ad hocery and reliance on tactical responses and the need for a strategic, long-term view of EU security needs and concerns. The concept of the EU judicial area may need to be bolstered by the creation of a

European criminal justice system. There is a need to create EU-wide, enforceable conventions to guide action on common problems such as abuses of information technology, computer crime, data protection, eco-terrorism, immigration, asylum-seeking, drugs and internal crime.

Closed or Open Government?

It must also be admitted that it is very easy for any advances in this area to be misrepresented to the public. In the United Kingdom, for example, politicians have advocated the adoption of identity smart cards, but have been extraordinarily reluctant to offer a counterweight: a Bill of Rights. The idea that British EU citizens are subjects and not participants in a polity is still surprisingly widespread. Too many have agonised over the transparency debate and the question of who should have access to the Euro-Ombudsman and what information s/he might be entitled to see; maintaining secrecy has seemed to have supremacy over the goal of open government. This is myopic. If the public is to accept the need for EU judicial co-operation and all that that entails in terms of police co-operation, training and budgets, then the Bill of Rights question should not be eschewed. Political gains could be made here.

A QUESTION OF CIVIL LIBERTIES?

Individual liberties imply different things across the 15: there is no common accord, for example, on a basic outline of a Charter of Fundamental Human Rights, the right to silence, the use of ID cards, privacy of personal data, etc. How, when, where and through what mechanisms in the EU should these issues be addressed? Or should practice, judicial expediency and the need for pragmatic steps, for example in respect of combating fraud – notably in the agricultural sector – precede political and constitutionally validated agreement? But before one falls into the trap of believing conspiracy theories, it must be remembered that the public are not alone in their concerns about EU-wide police co-operation, transparency and secrecy. During the summer of 1994, officials employed by the Council and Commission grew increasingly concerned about the operationalisation of transparency as differences became apparent over the Member States' different systems and practices regarding positive-vetting. Some politicians have argued that there may be a case for an EU Charter for Intelligence services.

All these concerns point to the inescapable fact that transfrontier co-operation to combat crime, including terrorism, is a minefield. It not only raises the issue of a Bill of Rights, but goes to the heart of national sovereignty. States can no longer be considered the only appropriate vehicles for action to combat trans-frontier problems that have criminal overtones. The creation of a single market in which internal frontiers have been largely removed, if not entirely eradicated, means that trans-frontier responses must be the norm not the exception.

National interests cannot, however, be seen as a reason to prevaricate over an issue that clearly has an EU dimension. The creation of a common external frontier around the EU as a result of the single market inevitably Europeanises a whole raft of policy issues that formerly could be considered in relative isolation by national authorities. This is no longer the case. That being so, it is high time that the operational requirements and consequences are tackled. This means not only co-operation with countries and authorities outside the EU in the international system, but above all that the Member States devise appropriate mechanisms within the EU and agree on the appropriate scope and competences for EU agencies in these areas and also agree on the appropriate role, liaison procedures and political oversight mechanisms for national authorities engaging in judicial co-operation.

All agree that trafficking should be an offence, but many reject penalising the use and possession of drugs for personal consumption. Indeed, many believe that decriminalisation across the EU would help to stem the crimes attendant upon raising cash to service the habit, including prostitution, burglary, extortion, and so on. These are valid issues that should be discussed and regulated at the EU level. But how is any regulation to be conducted? Should existing EU-level agencies and those of the Member States be asked to Europeanise their operations?

For example, what role – if any – might intelligence agencies have in combating drug trafficking at the EU level? The EU has already set up a European Drugs Monitoring Unit for collating data. The SIS (Schengen Information System) covering seven Member States holds some 10 million[1] records and will become the European Information System (EIS) following the ratification of the Europol Convention (see below) covering the 15 Member States. Europol is to deal with 'organised crime' as foreseen by the TEU (and will work with the EIS, as well as with non-EU intelligence bodies such as the FBI and US Drug Enforcement agency; the EIS with 'low-level'crime, public order, security threats and migrants – all potentially highly delicate and politically sensitive areas.

It is also necessary to confront micro-level matters relating to combating crime at the EU-level. The police cultures, for example, of the Member States differ. Euro-level action would not depend upon a Euro-police culture, but it would be desirable to promote one and to instil basic values to which all Member States subscribe. The need for effective, political – and that implies parliamentary – oversight is self-evident. Ensuring that it happens is a far more difficult proposition.

The Example of the Europol Convention

The Europol Convention signed in 26 June 1995 is a case in point. When it was first suggested, the expectation was created that Europol would primarily be an information collection and dissemination operation covering 'organised crime', especially drug trafficking and money laundering – areas of particular interest to the relatively recently established European Drugs Monitoring Units. It quickly became clear that its brief would be far broader. There is no need to infer or invoke a conspiracy theory to explain the widening of its brief. There may be very good operational reasons why Europol should have wider competences and obligations. The problem is, however, that it is generally felt that the Convention is insufficiently transparent and that it will escape effective public scrutiny, both now and in its operation. The attendant risk is that individual rights and liberties (taken for granted in the older members of the EU) could be inadvertently eroded and that newer members might not feel obliged to honour, let alone advance, the kind of civil liberties and democratic practices that many feel should become the norm throughout the EU if it wishes to retain its democratic credibility and advance a civil society based on respect for the rule of law and commited to upholding liberal, democratic values, norms and practices.

Moreover, single conventions should not be seen in isolation from other developments which directly relate to them. In this case, other conventions – for example, on simplified extradition, the customs information system and the EU's financial interests – are all relevant to the work that may be undertaken by Europol. Similarly, because of different administrative and cultural traditions, the various Member States have different provisions on data protection: how easy or hard is it, for instance, for a citizen to find out what information is held on police systems and to change it if it is incorrect? The provisions on data protection in the Europol convention are accordingly highly complex and it is far from clear that inaccurate data, which may have been acquired from a non-EU source, can be rectified. Europol has to take into account the Council of Europe Convention (1981) but it is not required to comply with it. It is obvious that serious issues about access, accountability, openness and democratic legitimacy are raised and that they have not yet been adequately addressed. There is nothing to be gained from, on the one hand, promoting the notion of EU citizenship and, on the other hand, undermining the very civil liberties which the same governments have proudly championed over the years.

Clearly, there are good reasons for insisting that Europol be accountable politically and to the European Court of Justice. All but the United Kingdom's government endorsed that position. This underlined anxiety among MPs that the Convention in particular and the JHA pillar in general are liable to abuse by governments unwilling to disclose information and determined to proceed in secrecy and with the minimum amount of public accountability.

Such concern has been mirrored in the European Parliament, which was not consulted (as required under Article

K6 of the Maastricht Treaty) at any point during the nego-
tiation of the Convention. Its views have not been 'duly taken
into consideration' as required. The European Parliament
will only receive an annual report on the Convention. Clearly,
this situation is intolerable to MEPs who have pressed, therefore, for the JHA to be given an overhaul through the IGC.
The alternative – persistent ad hocery – would compromise
the EU's ability to be transparent, open, accountable and
responsive to its citizens. It would also compromise its efficiency, effectiveness and democratic legitimacy.

THE IGC BEYOND 1996: CIVIL LIBERTIES AND THE CREATION OF A CIVIL SOCIETY

The practical need for cross-frontier co-operation, notably
in combating organised trans-frontier crime, could impel
local enforcement agencies to develop ad hoc responses. Is
this in their best interest? How would such developments
actually expand the scope of EU competence in advance of
political decisions being taken to endorse such developments?
How would the public or civil rights groups react to the
expansion, for example, of police activity in the absence of
'public safeguards' for issues loosely defined in terms of civil
rights? Is a Bill of Rights needed to safeguard civil liberties
as well as to entrench and legitimise the inevitable expansion of law enforcement agencies' authority? Will it become
necessary to re-examine, for example, the category of people who might legitimately be the subject of positive vetting
if the concept of security is 'domesticated'?

How might local authorities react to gypsies seeking to
enforce their right to freedom of movement? To whom might
law enforcement agencies be accountable? What role, if any,
should national parliaments and the European Parliament
have? Once the civil issues are more closely examined,
a whole range of new potential questions enters into consideration. If the JHA is to be relevant to ordinary citizens,
its preoccupations must, in part, reflect theirs. The experience of the Council of Europe shows what kinds of issue
have an emotive impact. Already in the EU a number of Member States approve of closer co-operation, for example, in

respect issues of family law: adoption, child abduction, marriage, divorce, etc.

The common foreign and security policy and justice and home affairs pillars do not provide for adequate parliamentary input or scrutiny. Justice and home affairs raise serious sensitive matters concerning data protection, civil liberties, co-operation over drug trafficking, asylum and police affairs and the proper role of and scrutiny over Europol (which progressed very slowly).[2] They also interface with concerns over human rights and the pressure among some governments for a charter of Fundamental Human Rights and Freedoms to be accepted by the EU (either by accession to the Council of Europe's Convention or in a separate Bill of Rights).[3] These issues will have to be addressed.

There can be little doubt that security issues highlight the need to inject some clarity of thinking into how the democratic deficit and the problems of democratic legitimacy might be addressed appropriately in the expanding EU. Equally, there can be little doubt that the Commission in general and the European Parliament in particular remain the guardians of the EU's legitimacy and conscience and, with the ECJ, have a special responsibility for ensuring the rule of law and the prevention of the abuse of power.

The European Parliament is not satisfied with the range or scope of its powers and will continue to seek a greater role for itself, as it must, in respect of new areas of competence and responsibility bestowed by the member governments on the EU. Continued pressure for a parliamentary role is the inevitable consequence of member governments' reluctance to deal with the central issue of what kind of polity the EU is and what kind of institutions it should have given its repeated stated commitment to the principles of liberal, representative, open, accountable, responsible government.

The European Parliament has become more than a symbol of these values, but its members continue to press for greater authority to entrench open, liberal, representative government. For over a decade and throughout the IGC reform processes, the European Parliament has acted as the EU's conscience in trying to give concrete expression to these ideals. More recently, its Institutional Affairs Committee, which has been entrusted with this since the early 1980s, secured

MEPs' support for a further series of very modest reforms designed to encourage the IGC to introduce treaty reforms to: improve the EU's ability to deliver on key policy objectives; regain citizens' support by addressing the legitimacy gap between the EU and the people; and prepare for future enlargement.

The kinds of arrangement it now seeks are also likely to inform the institutional changes accepted by member governments at the next and subsequent IGCs. That is why a number of measures sought by the European Parliament – including the introduction of a single legislative procedure (to avoid the complexities and confusion produced by the co-existence of over eight different legislative procedures coupled with comitology) – are potentially so important to the evolution and shape of the future EU. In particular, the European Parliament favours a reduction of legislative procedures to three: co-decision for all normal legislation; assent for third country agreements and enlargement; and consultation for foreign policy issues. Apart from the importance it attaches to measures to ensure the effective functioning of the TEU commitments in new policy areas as well as the imperative of addressing unemployment and promoting social integration, its representatives to the IGC *Groupe de Réflexion* have a list of issues that the European Parliament wishes to see confronted. The European Parliament also wants the IGC to reform EU decision-making; examine working methods and promote co-decision as the norm in place of other legislative procedures.[4]

Further provisions attest to the Parliament's right to hold other institutions accountable.[5] The following now have to report to or inform the European Parliament: the European Council, the Council of Ministers,[6] the Council President, the Commission,[7] the Court of Auditors, the Ombudsman[8] and the European Monetary Institute/European Central Bank.[9] In practice, close liaison between the Commission and the European Parliament is the precondition of effective action. The two are mutually dependent: the European Parliament requires the Commission's technical know-how and the Commission needs MEPs to legitimise and lend democratic support to it. The European Parliament retains its interest in preserving a strong Commission able to act independently of national governments. Any weakening in the Commission's authority (as the SEA and TEU seemed to presage) would undermine further integration. The European Parliament is, therefore, mindful of the need to ensure a balanced distribution of power between the legislative institutions in order to promote legitimacy, reveal the distribution of authority to be just and open, and to insert appropriate checks and balances which are not open to arbitrary interpretation and abuse. Subsidiarity does not meet this test.

Openness and Transparency

In 1993 Denmark (the country largely responsible for delaying implementation of the TEU after its electorate voted against the treaty in a referendum in May 1992) took over the Council Presidency. One of the first measures that it introduced played straight into the European Parliament's hands. Condemning excessive secrecy and a lack of transparency, the Danish Council President made history in opening up the hitherto secret Council sessions to the public. This was supposed to assuage Danish fears of an over-centralised and bureaucratic rather than a democratic EU, but it also bolstered the legitimacy of the European Parliament's quest for generalised improvements in democratic practice and greater openness in decision-making. The problem was, however, that the newly built Council accommodation in Brussels lacked a public gallery, even though the Council has a primary legislative function and the governments were not generally prepared to relinquish Council secrecy. Instead, they passed the buck on to the Commission and thereby exploited public antipathy towards it without appreciably augmenting openness where it was most needed: in the Council.

A declaration annexed to the TEU affirmed member governments' acceptance of transparency as a condition of democracy, but they were loathe to translate this into greater openness in the Council. On 25 October 1993, the Council, Commission and European Parliament concluded an interinstitutional agreement on democracy, transparency and subsidiarity designed to enhance openness. In practice, however, the impression was left of a democratic deficit residing primarily within the ranks of a Commission that was wrongly portrayed as aloof and closed. Although one of the most open of all bureaucracies in Europe, the Commission nevertheless took steps to increase the transparency of its procedures (Lodge 1994). One of the paradoxical effects of the openness measures was to render decision-making arguably less rather than more open because rules and procedures were prescribed curtailing or delineating access to information and documentation. But the restrictions on the availability of documents meant that lobbyists and those 'in the know' and familiar with Brussels procedures retained a privileged position. In short, the form but not necessarily the substance of openness had been enhanced. The institutions may refuse access to documents according to rules set out in the code of practice adopted in December 1993, which sets out exceptions based on public and private interests or the need to ensure the effective functioning of the institutions. The Commission had, by March 1995, agreed to almost 54 per cent of requests for documents, rejecting 18 per cent under the terms of the code of conduct. Twenty-eight per cent of requests fell outside the terms of reference and some 15 per cent of these related to documents that had already been published and 11 per cent to documents which were not Commission documents (Lodge 1994).

Increasing Transparency

The Commission improved a number of existing practices to increase general awareness of its proposals and decisions. These included steps to seek wider-ranging advice from interested parties at the pre-decision stages of proposal drafting. Access to databases is also to be improved. The coherence of proposals was ameliorated by steps to simplify legislation, to improve its drafting and by regrouping various proposed EU measures in one legislative text when they dealt with the same policy area or when several measures could be regrouped in a single, new legislative act without affecting the basic content of those measures. This should help not only the private and public sectors, interest groups and the public to become more familiar with Commission proposals, but also encourage national parliaments (otherwise largely irrelevant to the progress of EU legislation) to be better informed. This, too, is something that the European Parliament has pressed hard for.

Institutional Prerequisites of Effective Action

It is one thing for the European Parliament to have won more powers, whether of the legislative, scrutiny and control or budgetary nature. It is quite another to make those powers effective. The necessary preconditions for effective European Parliament action remain improved party discipline inside the European Parliament and effective co-operation and co-ordination with the Commission and the Council. A further area for improvement concerns the role of national parliaments in the EU. Their role has traditionally been negligible. However, the European Parliament's tactics for promoting the EU along maximalist lines have rested on the establishment and maintenance of parliamentary consensus both inside the European Parliament and inside the national parliaments. Closer liaison between the two would be mutually beneficial (Commission Européene 1995). The IGC is likely to reaffirm the importance of national parliaments in a system from which they have largely been eclipsed by decisions of their own national governments.

Democratic legitimacy is not just about Euro-elections, reforming the current electoral provisions to bring national provisions broadly into line under a system of proportional representation. Nor is it only a matter of improving the transparency, efficiency, accountability and democratic nature of EU institutions (Millar 1995; Lodge 1995a). Inadequate parliamentary control over the Commission and more especially the Council, coupled with the absence of direct elections, originally lay at the heart of the democratic deficit. The residual weaknesses on both counts contribute to today's deficit. Ideas of representativeness, accountability and democratic practice remained intertwined. However, the democratic deficit is not just a problem of horizontal distribution of power among EU institutions. The vertical dimension is important, both as it affects relations internal to EU institutions and as it affects relations between supranational, national, regional and local levels of government and administration.

A Crisis of Authority and Legitimacy?

The EU suffers from both an authority crisis and a legitimacy crisis. The suspicion persists that EU institutions are unable to act authoritatively and are not entirely appropriate for the exercise of functions and tasks bestowed on them by the treaties. The authority of EU institutions is open to challenge, notably by jealous national political elites who can manipulate dissent and blame the supranational institutions for their own failings. Moreover, the paradoxical effect of the TEU revisions to the European Parliament's powers is to make its actions more visible, but not necessarily more tangible or intelligible. Further confusion as to the locus of popular authority may also arise given the introduction of a Committee of Regions (with negligible powers). This compounds the problem of national parliaments having a small role and even less influence in the EU. As a result, the problem of the EU's democratic legitimacy and the alleged persistence of the democratic deficit has not been fully rectified by the Maastricht Treaty. Its revision clauses are therefore important and the next IGC must address these gaps.

The democratic legitimacy crisis can only be remedied through further treaty revisions to clarify the relative positions and powers of the institutions in line with an agreed view of what elements make up a functioning democratic polity, since this is clearly what is being built at the EU level. There is a pressing need for the EU to be clarified. The European Parliament's role in it remains contested but it has perhaps the greatest responsibility – as the legatee of the Spinelli draft treaty establishing the EU – to ensure that appropriate practices are enshrined in a representative, pluralist, liberal democratic, parliamentary system at the EU level. Beyond that, there can be little doubt that coherence needs to be re-established by abolishing the existing pillar structure of the TEU and reasserting '*unicité*'. This means that the intergovernmental pillars covering foreign affairs, and justice and home affairs, need to be properly integrated into the EU decision-making structure in order to render their work open, subject to effective, supranational level democratic scrutiny and to ensure coherence between their objectives and those of related policy areas subject to the normal decision-making procedures.

NOTES

1. Data supplied by *Statewatch*, London, 1995.
2. See Nassauer Report for The European Parliament (1995).
3. See The Newman Report on Human Rights in the EU, which was rejected by MEPs by 210:176 with six abstentions on 18 May 1995, *European Parliament Working Document* A4–76/95; Conseil européen (1978); Conseil européen (1990); Conseil européen (1991a); Conseil européen (1991b); Conseil et Etats membres (1991); Parlement Européen (1994); Parlement Européen (1989); Parlement Européen, Conseil et Commission (1977); Schermers (1990).
4. For fuller details, see Lodge (1995).
5. See the arguments presented during the SEA deliberations by the EP Committee on Institutional Affairs, Working Document on the EP proposals submitted to the IGC on the appointment and powers of the Commission (Fanti Report) PE 101.517/1, 28 October 1985.
6. See Fanti Report, op. cit.
7. Ibid.
8. Ibid.
9. See Commission of the EP, *The Commission's Programme 1993–4*, SEC(93) 58 final, 26 January 1993; and the reply on the investiture debate by Commission President Delors.

REFERENCES

Closa (1992), 'The Concept of Citizenship in the Treaty on European Union', *Common Market Law Review*, No. 29, pp. 1147–69.

Commission Européene (1995), *Rapport sur le functionnement du traité sur l'Union Européenne*, 10 May, Brussels.

Conseil et Etats membre réunis au sein du Conseil (1991), 'Résolution sur les Droits de l'Homme, la Démocraties et le Développement', *Bulletin of the European Communities*, 28 November, 11.

Conseil européen de Copenhague (1978), 'Déclaration sur le Democratie', *Bulletin of the European Communities*, 8 April, 4.

Conseil européen de Dublin (1990), 'Déclaration sur l'Antisémitisme, le Racisme et la Xénophobie, *Bulletin of the European Communities*, 25–26 June, 6.

Conseil européen de Luxembourg (1991a), 'Déclaration sue les Droits de l'Homme', *Bulletin of the European Communities*, 28–29 June, 6.

Conseil européen de Maastricht (1991b), 'Déclaration sur le Racisme et la Xenophobie', *Bulletin of the European Communities*, 9–10 December, 12.

Corbett, R. (1993), *The Treaty of Maastricht*, Longman, London.

Council Secretariat (1994), *Berlin Declaration of Increased co-operation in Combating Drug Crime and Organised Crime in Europe*, Berlin 8 September, Brussels.

European Parliament (1995), *European Parliament Working Document*, B4–348/95.

Lodge, J. (1992), *Internal Security and Judicial co-operation Beyond Maastricht*, ECRU, Hull University.

Lodge, J. (1994), 'Transparency and Democratic Legitimacy', *Journal of Common Market Studies*, September pp. 343–68.

Lodge, J. (1995), *Institutional Affairs*, Discussion Paper No. 3 by the Jean Monnet Group of Experts in the series, *The European Union and the 1996 IGC – Crisis or Opportunity?*, May, Centre for European Union Studies and the Representation of the European Commission in the UK, London.

Lodge, J. (1995a forthcoming), 'Democratic Legitimacy and the EC: Crossing the Rubicon', *International Journal of Public Administration*.

Millar, D. (1995), *Constitutional Issues: The European Parliament and National Parliaments*, Discussion Paper No. 2 by the Jean Monnet Group of Experts in the series, *The European Union and the 1996 IGC: Crisis or Opportunity?*, May, Centre for European Union Studies and the Representation of the European Commission in the UK, London.

Parlement Européen (1989), 'Déclaration sur les Droits et Libertés Fondamentaux', 12 April. *Journal Officiel*, C120, 16 May.

Parlement Européen (1994), *Le Parlement Européen et Les Droits de l'Homme*, Brussels.

Parliament Européen, Conseil et Commission (1977), 'Déclaration Commune sur les Droits Fondamentaux', *Journal Officiel*, C103, 27 April.

Schermers, H.G. (1990), 'The European Communities Bound by Fundamental Human Rights', *Common Market Law Review*, No. 27, pp. 249–58.

Index